MNCs in Global Politics

ELGAR POLITICS AND BUSINESS

Series Editors: Aynsley Kellow, *School of Social Sciences, University of Tasmania, Australia*, Tony Porter, *Department of Politics, McMaster University, Canada* and Karsten Ronit, *Department of Political Science, University of Copenhagen, Denmark*

Business is intrinsically woven into our societies, affecting in crucial ways how wealth is produced and distributed, the way our societies are governed and how power is exercised.

Recognising this fact, the Elgar Politics and Business series is an innovative new arena for original research across the breadth of this dynamic and important area of study. Covering a broad range of topics, the series examines issues such as: the politics of business taxation, business as an 'active force' in politics, the political power of corporations, business and regulation, and the politics of global value chains. Drawing key inspiration from political science, the series is interdisciplinary in nature, and will attract submissions from across the social sciences and law. Both international and comparative in its approach, this exciting series encompasses theoretical and empirical work from both well-established researchers and emerging scholars.

Titles in this series include:

Business, Civil Society and the 'New' Politics of Corporate Tax Justice
Paying a Fair Share?
Edited by Richard Eccleston and Ainsley Elbra

MNCs in Global Politics
Pathways of Influence
Edited by John Mikler and Karsten Ronit

MNCs in Global Politics

Pathways of Influence

Edited by

John Mikler

Associate Professor, Department of Government and International Relations, University of Sydney, Australia

Karsten Ronit

Associate Professor, Department of Political Science, University of Copenhagen, Denmark

ELGAR POLITICS AND BUSINESS

 Edward Elgar
PUBLISHING

Cheltenham, UK • Northampton, MA, USA

Published by
Edward Elgar Publishing Limited
The Lypiatts
15 Lansdown Road
Cheltenham
Glos GL50 2JA
UK

Edward Elgar Publishing, Inc.
William Pratt House
9 Dewey Court
Northampton
Massachusetts 01060
USA

A catalogue record for this book
is available from the British Library

Library of Congress Control Number: 2020948092

This book is available electronically in the **Elgar**online
Social and Political Science subject collection
http://dx.doi.org/10.4337/9781789903232

MIX
Paper from
responsible sources
FSC° C013604

ISBN 978 1 78990 322 5 (cased)
ISBN 978 1 78990 323 2 (eBook)

Printed and bound by CPI Group (UK) Ltd, Croydon, CR0 4YY

For our families

Contents

Figures

Tables

Contributors

Ainsley Elbra is a Lecturer in the Department of Government and International Relations in the School of Social and Political Sciences at the University of Sydney. Her research examines globalization, private governance and business–state relations, with a particular focus on the Global South. Her research has been published in journals such as *Business and Politics*, *Global Policy*, *The Australian Journal of Political Science* and *Resources Policy*, and two books: *Governing African Gold Mining: Private Governance and the Resource Curse* (Palgrave Macmillan, 2017), and *Business, Civil Society and the 'New' Politics of Corporate Tax Justice: Paying a Fair Share?* (co-edited with Richard Eccleston, Edward Elgar Publishing, 2018).

Christian Hendriksen is an Assistant Professor in the Department of Operations Management at the Copenhagen Business School. His research interests are the mechanisms of political influence of private actors, the role of firms in sustainable regulation, and lobbying from an organizational institutionalist perspective. His recently published doctoral dissertation is built on several years of participant observation of the International Maritime Organization as an observing delegate.

Kate Macdonald is a Senior Lecturer at the University of Melbourne, having held previous positions at the London School of Economics and Political Science, the Australian National University and Oxford University. Her research focuses on transnational governance and accountability, with a particular focus on social, labour and human rights regulation of global business. She has published three books and over 40 journal articles and book chapters. Her recent articles have appeared in *Regulation & Governance*, *European Journal of International Relations*, *Governance*, *Philosophy & Public Affairs*, *International Theory* and *Ecological Economics*.

Christian May is a Research Associate at Goethe University. His research focuses on comparative and international political economy, emerging economies and firms in the global economy. He has recently published *State-Permeated Capitalism in Large Emerging Economies* (with Andreas Nölke, Tobias ten Brink and Simone Claar, Routledge, 2020), *Handbook of the International Political Economy of the Corporation* (co-edited with Andreas Nölke, Edward Elgar Publishing, 2018) and *New Directions in*

Comparative Capitalisms Research (co-edited with Matthias Ebenau and Ian Bruff, Palgrave Macmillan, 2015), as well as articles in *European Journal of International Relations*, *Journal of Economic Policy Reform*, *Contemporary Politics* and *Revue de la Régulation*.

John Mikler is an Associate Professor in the Department of Government and International Relations in the School of Social and Political Sciences at the University of Sydney, Australia. His research interests revolve around global corporate power, institutional variations in capitalism, and globalization. He has edited two journal special issues, and published over 30 journal articles and book chapters. He has also published four books, including *The Handbook of Global Companies* (Wiley-Blackwell, 2013) and *The Political Power of Global Corporations* (Polity Press, 2018).

Hannah Murphy-Gregory is a Lecturer in the Politics and International Relations Program of the School of Social Sciences at the University of Tasmania, Australia. Her research focuses on civil society campaigning in Australia and globally in the areas of marine governance, tax justice, and labour standards. Her research has been published in a range of international journals including *Environmental Politics*, *Global Policy*, and *Review of International Political Economy*. She is a co-editor with Aynsley Kellow of the *Handbook of Research on NGOs* (Edward Elgar Publishing, 2018).

Karsten Ronit is an Associate Professor in the Department of Political Science at the University of Copenhagen. His research interests are in the areas of business associations and various kinds of private actors in politics at domestic and international levels. He has published numerous articles and book chapters, and 20 books on different aspects of private organizations and their relations with public authority, especially in the economic sphere. His most recent book is *Global Business Associations* (Routledge, 2018).

Lian Sinclair is a Postdoctoral Associate at the Asia Research Centre, Murdoch University, Australia. Her research focuses on the political economy and governance of social conflict in extractive industries. Lian's PhD, *Undermining Conflict: Multinational Miners, Conflict and Participation in Indonesia* at Murdoch University was conferred in August 2020. In 2017, she was an Endeavour Postgraduate Scholar and visiting scholar at the Centre for Security and Peace Studies, Gadjah Mada University.

Elizabeth Thurbon is a Scientia Fellow and Associate Professor in the School of Social Sciences at the University of New South Wales, Australia. She is interested in the role of the state in techno-industrial development, upgrading and adaptation, especially under conditions of 'globalization' and climate change. She writes widely on these topics for academic and popular audiences.

Her most recent book *Developmental Mindset: The Revival of Financial Activism in South Korea* (Cornell University Press, 2016) offers a new way of conceptualizing East Asia's developmental states and of analyzing their emergence and evolution, with a focus on South Korea.

Linda Weiss is a Fellow of the Academy of the Social Sciences in Australia, Professor Emeritus in Government and International Relations at the University of Sydney, and Honorary Professor of Political Science at Aarhus University. She specializes in the comparative and international politics of innovation and economic development in industrialized countries, with a focus on state capacity and public–private sector relations in a globalized environment. Several of her books on these topics have appeared in Korean, Chinese, Turkish, and Romanian editions. Her latest book, *America Inc.? Innovation and Enterprise in the National Security State* (Cornell University Press, 2014), integrates political economy with security scholarship.

Preface and acknowledgments

There is nothing new about big economic entities acting on the global stage, or economic interests being pursued beyond the borders of individual states in an organized way. Still, we can say that there is growing interest in the way in which economic interests are pursued today via multinational corporations (MNCs), and not just for economic reasons. MNCs play a key role in global politics, which of course is a result of the processes of globalization we have experienced in recent decades, many foundations of which were laid in the years after World War II. This globalization has unfolded to such a degree that the academic study of MNCs has not kept pace with economic, social and political developments, and the many and diverse roles performed by these large corporations. The central purpose of this book is to address this analytical 'lag'.

We started work on pulling together this collection in Baltimore in February 2017 during the Annual Convention of the International Studies Association. Over lunch, we discussed the role of global business as a political actor and agreed that despite many years of academic attention, the subject was unfortunately still side-lined in the field of politics and international relations. We also agreed that the focus remains far too much on states and their governments. MNCs figure as executers, modifiers, or underminers of state power, as key players in markets, as entities that serve elite interests and so on, but where was the literature on them as political actors in their own right? It exists, to be sure, and there are some quite wonderful studies done by other authors. Yet, it is hardly voluminous. So, we wanted to make a contribution to the existing literature in order to shed more light on the political behavior of MNCs.

The question was how best to do so. As the then Chair of Research Committee 38 (RC38) on Politics and Business of the International Political Science Association (IPSA), Karsten Ronit suggested to John Mikler that this forum could be used as one of the relevant vehicles for the identification and dissemination of research on the topic. The initial conversation leading to this joint project went something like this:

Karsten: You know John, IPSA runs several panels on politics and business at its biannual World Congress, and since you are an expert on MNCs, it would be great

if you could organize some panels. There is, in fact, a tradition starting in the 1980s of bringing out edited volumes as a result of these panels.
John: Sure, but you know it takes time and I have many other things on my plate. I'm finishing a whole book on *The Political Power of Global Corporations*, and I need to do this before thinking about what comes next! Plus, I would prefer not doing it alone. It's always great to bring others together with similar interests, to collaborate on such projects, and that includes you. So, why don't we do it together?

Despite also having quite a full research agenda, Karsten found it hard to decline the kind invitation, just as John found it hard to resist Karsten's challenge, and our partnership for the project was born.

We started thinking about bringing others on board, and IPSA was actually the ideal vehicle for doing so. As John stepped up into the role of Chair of RC38 when Karsten stepped down to Deputy Chair later in 2017, we started to think about panels we could organize with the theme of this book in mind. The result was that several of the papers leading to chapters in this book were presented on RC38 panels at IPSA's 25th World Congress in Brisbane in July 2018. Also around this time, Karsten was a Visiting Fellow with the Department of Government and International Relations at the University of Sydney, so this was a wonderful opportunity to move the project forward.

As we did so, one of our main ambitions has been to combine different perspectives on MNCs. We both have different perspectives as well as specializations in politics and business, but a key premise we agreed on was that business, not least manifested by MNCs, is not just another group in society. Today, business is a key *force* in market economies and important roles are attributed to private enterprises as vital drivers in development and welfare. These are factors that offer particular opportunities for business influence on governments and regulations, sometimes to such a degree that action is not even necessary. Because of the roles played by business, its most visible actors can also be targeted for having excessive influence and for not serving the public interest. The result is that the practices of MNCs are often particularly in the public spotlight.

Another ambition of this book is to analyze and theorize the role of MNCs from a holistic perspective. The political dimension of MNCs' behavior cannot be analyzed in isolation from their place in the market, but more than that, their political actions need to be studied in relation to many other actors in their environment. In other words, as a series of interrelated pathways of potential influence. Because MNCs have different properties, face different conditions, and operate in different environments, each of these pathways are not always equally important and equally activated. Therefore, MNCs cannot just 'strategize' and behave in a manner defined simply by their interests and resources. Their behavior is also shaped by these environments and pathways.

As with many other book projects, the completion of this volume has taken a little longer than expected. But the process has been made more enjoyable with the support and advice of the wonderful contributors to this collection, as well as many more friends and colleagues than we can name here. We would like to thank all those who attended the IPSA panels in Brisbane where some of the initial ideas that led to this work were first presented, and the incredible team at Edward Elgar Publishing, particularly Alex Pettifer and Rachel Downie. Also, members of the Australian International Political Economy Network who have offered constructive criticism as well as advice. Our thanks go to people with whom we have discussed the different ideas behind the project and whose feedback and suggestions were invaluable, particularly Madison Cartwright, Tom Chodor, Lindy Edwards, Susan Engel, Shahar Hameiri, Kelly Gerard, Neil Harrison, Stewart Jackson, Aynsley Kellow, Marieke Louis, Diarmuid Maguire, Adam Morton, Susan Park, Nicola Phillips, Volker Schneider, Rodney Smith and Amos Owen Thomas.

Finally, it must be noted that as the book's manuscript was delivered in early 2020, the world was being severely hit by the COVID-19 pandemic that paralyzed our societies. The result was that the last stages of writing and editing were strangely expedited by unfortunate circumstances that enabled us to spend more time with the manuscript, while engaged in various kinds of online teaching. We hope and trust that by the time this book is published, durable solutions have been found to stop or counter its effects.

John Mikler and Karsten Ronit
Sydney and Copenhagen
April 2020

Abbreviations

ABAC	APEC Business Advisory Council
ACFOA	Australian Council for Overseas Aid
AGED	A Department of Defense Advisory Group on Electronic Devices
ALRI	Australian Legal Resources International
APEC	Asia Pacific Economic Community
ASEF	Active Shipbuilding Experts' Federation
BBC	BRICS Business Council
BEPS	Base erosion and profit shifting
BIAC	Business at OECD, Business and Industry Advisory Committee to the OECD
BIMCO	Baltic and International Maritime Council
BIT	Bilateral investment treaty
BNDES	Banco Nacional de Desenvolvimento Econômico e Social
CAA	Community Aid Abroad
CCP	Chinese Communist Party
CFIA	Cooperation and Facilitation Investment Agreement
CFMEU	Construction, Forestry, Mining and Energy Union
CoW	Contract of work
CRA	Conzinc Riotinto of Australia
CSO	Civil society organization
CSR	Corporate social responsibility

EME	Emerging market economy
ETI	Ethical Trading Initiative
FDI	Foreign direct investment
FET	Fair and Equitable Treatment
FICCI	Federation of Indian Chambers of Commerce and Industry
GAR	Golden Agri-Resources
GBC	Global Business Coalition
GDP	Gross domestic product
GFC	Global Financial Crisis
GMI	Global Mining Initiative
GVC	Global value chain
GWC	Global wealth chain
ICAF	Industrial College of the Armed Forces
ICAO	International Civil Aviation Organization
ICC	International Chamber of Commerce
ICEM	International Federation of Chemical, Energy, Mine and General Workers' Union
ICMM	International Council on Mining and Metals
ICS	International Chamber of Shipping
IGO	Intergovernmental organization
ILO	International Labour Organization
IMO	International Maritime Organization
IOE	International Organization of Employers
IP	Intellectual property
IPC	Intellectual Property Committee
IPRs	Intellectual property rights
ISO	International Organization for Standardization
ISPO	Indonesian Sustainable Palm Oil

ITIF	Information Technology and Innovation Foundation
JATAM	The Mining Advocacy Network
KEM	PT Kelian Equatorial Mining
LKMTL	Lembaga Kesejahteraan Masyarakat Tambang dan Lingkungan (Council for Mining Communities' Prosperity and the Environment)
M&A	Merger and acquisition
MARPOL	The International Convention for the Prevention of Pollution from Ships
MEPC	Marine Environment Protection Committee
MFT	Most Favored Party Treatment
MMSD	Mining, Minerals and Sustainable Development
MNC	Multinational corporation
MNE	Multinational enterprise
MSPO	Malaysian Sustainable Palm Oil
NGO	Non-governmental organization
NSTC	National Science and Technology Council
OECD	Organisation for Economic Co-operation and Development
OFDI	Outward foreign direct investment
PCAST	President's Council of Advisors on Science and Technology
POIG	Palm Oil Innovation Group
PPR	Pollution Prevention and Response
RSPO	Roundtable on Sustainable Palm Oil
RTZ	Rio Tinto – Zinc Corporation
SOE	State-owned enterprise
TABC	Trans-Atlantic Business Council
TNC	Transnational corporation

TRIPS	Trade Relates Aspects of Intellectual Property Rights agreement
UNCTAD	United Nations Conference on Trade and Development
UNDP	United Nations Development Programme
UNESCO	United Nations Educational, Scientific and Cultural Organization
USCIB	United States Council for International Business
WALHI	Friends of the Earth Indonesia
WBCSD	World Business Council for Sustainable Development
WCF	World Chambers Federation
WEF	World Economic Forum
WIPO	World Intellectual Property Organization
WSC	World Shipping Council
WTO	World Trade Organization

1. Introduction: MNCs and their pathways of influence in global politics

John Mikler and Karsten Ronit

Multinational corporations (MNCs) have been active for a very long time in global markets and they also play a leading role in global politics, although the latter side of their activity has been far more contentious and often difficult to map. The traditional and dominant focus on states and their interests and strategies has generally marginalized the role of corporations, or at least the study of them. The result is that while some might be tempted to declare that what is and is not possible in global politics is an answer along the lines of 'it's the economy, stupid',[1] it could be more accurate to say 'it's the MNCs, stupid!' The role of MNCs needs to be considered when analyzing key issues in contemporary global politics.

Of course, many alternative approaches exist, bringing the operations and interests of MNCs closer to our attention and informing research. However, scholarly work on MNCs tends largely to pull in two different directions. On the one hand, there is an economics and management literature concerned with analyzing the behavior of MNCs in terms of economic statistics and organizational forms. On the other hand, there is a politics and international relations literature that views their activities through the prisms of grand power politics. In the process, they go somewhat 'missing' between studies that detail a variety of economic and industrial properties of MNCs, versus those that discuss different dimensions of corporate power in terms of market forces, class relations, ideologies, national interests, international relations and so on. When it comes to political studies of MNCs the result is that 'instead of mountains of scholarly achievement, we have a few oases in an arid landscape' (Wilks, 2013, p. 2).

While acknowledging that the various analyses of MNCs' operations are enormously helpful and reveal important aspects of corporate conduct, the contributors to this collection aim to further bridge the extant scholarly cleavages to examine the many and intricate ways MNCs influence politics in the global realm. They combine firm-centered and institutional approaches and, as

such, are concerned with identifying and evaluating the shifting roles of different pathways of influence employed by MNCs, highlighting major procedural
patterns, rather than determining the ultimate power of business *per se*.

As a starting point, in this introductory chapter we note that MNCs have
various established home bases, in addition to operations that are globally
dispersed. They should therefore not be narrowly conceived as actors operating amorphously in markets, but as entities that exist in particular places and
spaces and exercising political strategies in diverse institutional contexts. They
also do not constitute a homogeneous category, with great variation possible
between the economic and political profiles of different MNCs. Furthermore,
there are a wide range of options available to them for seeking influence. At
a very basic level, it is possible for single MNCs to administer their control of
markets and, using this market authority, in some cases build specific relations
with other key actors in their environment. In general, a range of relational
arrangements with other MNCs in business associations, with the organized
aspects of civil society, and intergovernmental organizations (IGOs) are also
possible and pursued. The political options available to MNCs may also align
with other small and large corporations, through which they form networks
and associations and build other entities to coordinate interests in the business
community and enhance their influence.

So, MNCs cannot be conceived as simply unitary actors. The networked
attributes of their operations are central to their pathways of influence, as they
manage supply chains and coordinate with subcontractors across multiple
national jurisdictions. It is important to recognize this in research, and not perceive large MNCs as sufficiently strong to render collective action redundant.
As their operations are spread globally, they must engage with various public
authorities, including states and IGOs, to support regulation and encourage
agendas that benefit their interests. If they find it necessary, they attempt
to prevent public initiatives that threaten these interests. Their activities to
influence global politics also include relations with the organized elements of
civil society in multiple scenarios, which in many areas exercise what may be
thought of as 'moral' authority. MNCs therefore take steps to address pertinent
social and environmental issues, ward off various criticisms and build more
solid relations. Sometimes they even establish joint institutions with civil
society organizations (CSOs)[2] if they believe this to be required.

So, global politics is not a simple matter of states versus states, states
versus private 'actors', or simply the pressures of particular individual MNCs.
Instead, a range of actions and initiatives occur simultaneously and in a range
of combinations that are hard to predict *a priori*. This implies that in the analysis of MNCs, we should conceive global politics in a fundamentally holistic
way, rather than reducing our analysis to traditional policy processes organized

around states and IGOs, with contending private actors nebulously exerting influence at the margins.

In the following sections of this chapter, we develop our framework for analysis. After seeking insights in existing research and highlighting how this book contributes to the literature, we show how MNCs are positioned in a greater and more complex system and how different contexts of influence must be considered. We then discuss the role of MNCs in relation to the political institutions of states, as well as to the business community and civil society, to formulate a framework for analysis that underpins the chapters to follow, prior to a brief outline of these.

UNDERSTANDING THE ROLE OF MNCS IN AND BEYOND MARKETS

MNCs are labeled as such because they invest, produce, and sell their products and services in more than one national jurisdiction. This is increasingly the 'normal' form that business takes. In 1970, there were around 7000 corporations that had foreign affiliates (Clapp, 2005), but by 2011 there were over 100 000, with nearly 900 000 foreign affiliates (United Nations Conference on Trade and Development [UNCTAD], 2011). The geographical extensity of their operations has led some to label them transnational corporations (TNCs), placing them in a wider group of transnational organizations or non-state actors. This goes beyond conceiving them as operating in several jurisdictions to seeing them as passing across borders as if these were irrelevant. In other words, they rival nation states, potentially operating 'as if the entire world (or major regions of it) were a single entity' (Levitt, 1983, p. 92). The term multinational enterprise (MNE), most often used in the international business literature, also suggests transnationality, as it recognizes that corporations that operate across borders are not unitary actors but oversee and are embedded in networks. This is because modern business involves corporations that manage the operations of multiple other firms in supply chains, across multiple national territories. Yet, care must be taken to acknowledge all corporations' national anchoring, as well as their international and sometimes global presence. This is not some mere hair-splitting exercise, because it matters politically and may influence their various pathways of influence, particularly the ways in which they combine national and global actions. Therefore, it is analytically important to see corporations as first MNCs, before they potentially exhibit aspects of TNCs or are involved in MNEs. While a multinational dimension to almost all major corporations is now taken for granted, where and how MNCs express and pursue their interests is still ill-defined and underexamined. And this is what the contributors to this collection examine.

These issues are important to examine because, according to commentators like Korten (2015; see also see Harrod, 2006; Kollman, 2008; Zadek, 2013), MNCs are among the most, if not *the* most, important political, economic and social actors in the world. Given their command over resources, and relations with not just their employees but stakeholders in society more broadly, they may be more important for addressing the challenges faced by the world than a range of nation states. Others think that they may actually be taking over the role played by states, to the point that studies of state sovereignty should be accompanied by a focus on corporate sovereignty (e.g., Barkan, 2013). Their importance, the role they play, and their pathways of influence are questions worth considering, and yet up to now it still seems reasonable to say that they significantly go 'missing' in studies of domestic and global politics.

What is usually done is that their motivations are assumed in material terms, and therefore their actions are determined on the basis of the assumptions made about their interests. Underdrawn as primarily 'market actors', they are ascribed economic motivations (e.g., see Broome, 2014). This view represents a reductionist approach, and one that is not particularly accurate when groups of firms come to dominate rather than compete in markets. A major reason for this individualized, economic, market-focused understanding of MNCs is no doubt that major theoretical inspiration is taken from the economics tradition, where 'the firm' takes center stage and is assumed as the unit of analysis. This atomistic view is carried over into other social sciences, resulting in an under-institutionalized approach to corporate behavior. Of course, it is not that this is necessarily wrong, but the political motivations of MNCs and the political influence they exercise in the various contexts in which they operate are underplayed in much analysis as a result. Sometimes they are even absent.

Related management and business administration studies have also colored approaches to research on MNCs. These traditions are concerned with the organization and diverse strategies of single corporations with, again, a key emphasis on their behavior in markets. Indeed, the strong focus on corporate social responsibility (CSR) since the 1990s, and a quite vast literature that now surrounds it, is part of these different management traditions that today also spill over into MNC research in different areas of sociology and political science. But this interest in corporate behavior rarely addresses the potential *power* of corporations in society, or the relations of business with political institutions. As Wilks (2013, p. 210) puts it, CSR is 'not just a struggle over practices, but one over the locus of governance authority', and yet it remains rarely discussed in these terms. It *should* be because, due to their size and territorial reach, they are not the simple servants of markets and market forces but controllers of them.

The result of these one-sided views on MNCs is that broader questions about their pathways of influence are sometimes not asked at all. Or if they are, then questions about the nature of MNCs' actions, as well as the motivations for them, are answered *before* they are asked. This is more or less done along the following lines. We live in a globalized world in which policies of privatization and deregulation have undermined the role of the state to the point where all forms of political and social interaction have become marketized. States must don neoliberal 'golden straightjackets' (Friedman, 2000), because MNCs are unconstrained by borders, while the governments of nations are. If the interests of MNCs are not served, they will go somewhere else, and therefore states tend to become 'competition states' with the policy objectives of 'the promotion of free enterprise, innovation and profitability in both the private and public sectors' (Cerny, 2000, p. 302; see also Cerny, 2010). Taken to the extreme, all states will inevitably come to perform in such a manner over time, and MNCs are seen as slipping their territorial bonds to such an extent that they are 'no longer dependent clients of their home states and the new global partnerships between states and corporations are more likely to be manifest in collaborations in transnational networks and sharing in regulation and economic governance' (Wilks, 2013, p. 166). Accordingly, the result is that we live in a world of a neoliberal order that benefits market actors like MNCs, and neoliberal disorder that impacts the efficacy of national, democratically representative government and governance (e.g., see Cahill, 2014; Teeple and McBride, 2011).

Now, all this may be true to one degree or another, and depending on what the issue is that is being considered. But rather than stressing the power of market 'forces' that must be obeyed in a globalized world, and for which MNCs are merely the conduits, it is important to look at the politically motivated actions of MNCs with regard to other actors. Corporations are not zombies responding to market imperatives, or eating states and their societies' 'brains', but an organizational form employed to act on the demands of shareholders and various key actors in their environment. Therefore, there are a range of factors that necessitate an analysis of their more subtle pathways of influence. They should not be underdrawn as purely economic actors any more than states should be seen as purely political, or citizens and civic groups as purely social. The reality is rather this: there are enormous and powerful MNCs, there are states that contrary to the early globalization literature are not 'dying', and there are societies comprising citizens who are organized, and who demand governance in their interests rather than disembodied forces that are 'out there' and impacting on them like meteors on the face of the Earth.

The world has come a long way from the scenario Adam Smith imagined of entrepreneurial individuals and their firms competing on the basis of the market's 'invisible hand' rather than the visible hand of the state.[3] According to Nolan, Sutherland and Zhang (2002), by the end of the twentieth century, no more than five global corporations controlled each of the world's major industries, with around a third of these having one corporation accounting for more than 40 percent of global sales. According to Tepper and Hearn (2019), this concentration of oligopolistic to monopolistic power has increased in the years since then. As Crouch (2011, p. 49) observes, there has been a 'corporate takeover of the market' by these enormous entities. The situation we have today is not the invisible hand of the market that attacks or modifies the visible hand of the state, but instead a visible handful of global corporations.

With the dominance of *their* markets comes immense potential for corporate engagement in politics. MNCs' size alone shows this to be the case. In 2018, the Fortune Global 500 companies together had sales totaling US$32.7 trillion (*Fortune*, 2019). Given that the size of the global economy was estimated to be US$85.9 trillion in the same year (World Bank, 2019), this means that they effectively accounted for 38 percent of it. In fact, the sales of the world's 20 most global MNCs are greater than the combined gross domestic product (GDP) of the bottom 138 states, and greater than the combined expenditure of the bottom 166 states (see Mikler, 2018, p. 8; based on UNCTAD, 2014 and International Monetary Fund, 2015). And their sales versus the GDP or expenditures of states are a good measure, rather than that of value added that economists would use, because these corporations are best seen as networks. For example, Walmart does not own any manufacturing operations but contracts over 100 000 suppliers that produce the products it sells (LeBaron, 2014; Walmart, 2013, 2017). Other MNCs like Apple, Gap, and Nike also produce no goods themselves. Instead, as a result of the intellectual property they own for the products they design, their core function in the production process is the contracting and logistical management of their global supply chains. They sit atop these chains, coordinate them, and therefore embody the value added of the firms that they contract within them.

This a large part of the reason trade data does not reflect exports and imports between states, but the strategic decisions of the management of MNCs coordinating their supply chains. Of course, trade data has long been dominated by firms, but the point is that it is now dominated by MNCs. This means that the trade data for manufactured goods does not represent finished products, but movement within MNCs' global supply chains. Even by the 1990s, up to 70 percent of trade in manufactured goods between Organisation for Economic Co-operation and Development (OECD) countries was intra-firm, rather than inter-state, in nature (Bonturi and Fukasaku, 1993; see also Karliner, 1997). The data on financial MNCs tells a similar story of concentration and control. Seventy percent of the banking market in OECD countries is accounted for by their largest three banks (OECD, 2014; see also Beck, Kunt and Levine, 2005), while globally 14 banks dominate foreign exchange rate markets and ten dominate global options markets (OECD, 2011). In 2017, the world's top ten banks had combined assets of over US$28.3 trillion (Banks Around the World, 2018). These insights are helpful in guiding us when analyzing the role of MNCs in global politics. We know the MNCs' names, we know their size relative to states, and we therefore need to study their dominance of the global economy and their political pathways of influence in respect of it. They do this in many ways: in their own right and in relation to states, IGOs, the business community at large and civil society (see Figure 1.1).

INFLUENCE IN THEIR OWN RIGHT

Influence in their own right is the first pathway of MNCs' influence. The potential for this is the starting point from which the other pathways flow, and it comes from the key authority that MNCs hold in markets. This is a private authority that is both won and defended by MNCs themselves, but also granted and solidified by public authority. It does not come out of thin air, as, most basically, MNCs' influence 'in their own right' rests on the authority to hire and fire, and the authority to set prices and to invest. But this is not a completely unalterable state of affairs, and corporations must proactively work to keep this authority. Political considerations are therefore involved, but the political place and space occupied by corporations, and for our purposes MNCs in particular, are not straightforward. They operate at and above the level of nation states, yet they obviously have relationships with states and their societies, as well as IGOs and CSOs, rather than operating in a vacuum.

Given the emergence of new forms of cooperation as a result of such relationships, what has been labeled the 'three faces of power' framework can be useful for understanding the pathways employed by MNCs in their own right with regard to these other actors and in their institutional environments. Such a framework was originally employed in the theoretical politics literature to states and political actors in general. However, attempts have been made to employ it specifically to understand global business power (Fuchs, 2007; Mikler, 2018). As such, it can provide inspiration to analyze how MNCs work to influence agendas through employing instrumental power, and potentially set agendas through their possession and exercise of structural and discursive power.

In a simplified version, instrumental power focuses on the direct influence of one actor on another to achieve a desired outcome (Dahl, 1957, p. 201). This is done through inducements in the form of rewards or threats, and so instrumental power is about leverage exercised to achieve a desired end (i.e., it is instrumentally motivated). In terms of MNCs' pathways of influence, it is most clearly seen in efforts to directly influence policy-makers to produce desired outcomes. There are many examples of the extensive political efforts of corporations, and the associations to which they belong, leveraging political institutions at the national and international levels. Some have likened the relationship as akin to a *revolving door*, in the sense that the interactions are so pervasive and extensive that the barrier between what is public and private seems to no longer apply (e.g., see Davies, 2015).

The explicitly relational aspect of the first face of power suggests that there are fundamentally territorial aspects to it. This is because although corporate interests and operations may be increasingly multinational, instrumental power must be exercised somewhere, and often at multiple territorial levels. Such territoriality is potentially less the case for the second structural face of power, and this is therefore where MNCs can really exert influence in their own right. This is because structural power emphasizes the way issues are organized 'in' and 'out' of politics due to political actors' capacity for agenda-setting. As Bachrach and Baratz (1962, p. 948) explain, it means 'A devotes his energies to creating or reinforcing social and political values and institutional practices that limit the scope of the political process to public consideration of only those issues which are comparatively innocuous to A' (see also Strange, 1988). In respect of business, this suggests the possession of underlying control of processes and resources. MNCs certainly possess such control. As noted above, their size and dominance of global markets that are overwhelmingly oligopolistic to monopolistic means that they are in a position to punish or reward states for the provision of (un-)favorable conditions. This is true both within, as well as between, their territories. This further means that in addition to enjoying a revolving door relationship with policy-makers, they are in what has been termed a *privileged position* by comparison to other private actors in society (Lindblom, 1977; see also Cox, 1987; Culpepper, 2011; Frank, 1978; Tienhaara, 2014). Their voice is not just one in a range of competing interests. Instead, MNCs' indispensability to the economic bases of states and the global economy, and the control they can exert across levels from the local to national to international, means that sometimes they can get what they want without even asking for it. Their business interests are inevitably considered.

If this is indeed what happens, then the strongest position they can hope to be in is one in which their concerns do not just have to be taken into account but also *deserve* to be so. This brings us to the third face of discursive power, which focuses on the role played by ideas. It is the hardest to observe, because it relates to the creation of one political actor's interests in another. As Lukes (1974, p. 23) once explained, 'A may exercise power over B by getting him to do what he does not want to do, but he also exercises power over him by influencing, shaping or determining his very wants'. It is therefore not just about getting desired outcomes, but about the *right* to get them. If power is 'the production, in and through social relations, of effects that shape the capacities of actors to determine their own circumstances and fate' (Barnett and Duvall,

2005, p. 39), then this is surely the most powerful face of it. It is about ideas that become valid at the domestic and global level and penetrate society, essentially creating 'truths' about policy. This allows MNCs to promote the 'projection of a particular set of interests as the general interest' (Levy and Newell, 2002, p. 87). Discursive power may even underpin perceptions of legitimacy. Not legitimacy *per se*, but legitimacy in the sense of *discursive legitimacy* (Mikler, 2018), as it creates 'a generalized perception or assumption that the actions of an entity are desirable, proper, or appropriate within some socially constructed system' (Suchman, 1995, p. 574).

Of course, in reality, political power is not so easily divided up as discussed here. The different faces of power have many and intricate relations, and because they are often so integrated, they can be difficult to entangle, map and analyze. Yet, the division has heuristic value because it serves to suggest the nature of the pathways of influence produced. Indeed, discursive power that leads to legitimacy reinforces instrumental and structural power by institutionalizing widely accepted norms of behavior on the basis of it. It may even shape widely accepted beliefs as self-evident about the nature of globalization and the operation of the global economy, such as the widely believed 'truth' of the desirability of free and deregulated markets that underpins corporate power. What is considered legitimate at the national level may potentially also be transferred to the global level. This can benefit MNCs as they can increase their economic, political, and social control not just in the states where they are headquartered, but wherever they operate and have interests. To understand these processes, we therefore have to examine in further detail how MNCs interact with governments and other public institutions at the level of the state, and beyond it, in support of their interests.

INFLUENCE PATHWAYS AND STATES

Corporate influence and states is the second pathway of MNCs' influence in global politics examined in the book. This relationship addresses the question of whether MNCs just rely on their home states to have their interests represented in international contexts, or whether MNCs must be active themselves at international levels and take a relatively independent role. No doubt the answer is both, and therefore a matter of degree contingent on a range of factors, but even so, territory still matters to MNCs as it does to the governments of nations. Therefore, the exercise of their power at this level must be studied as a distinct pathway.

There is a wealth of prima facie evidence for this, such as the research of Rugman and Verbeke (2009), who demonstrate that only nine of the Fortune Global 500 MNCs have sales in so many regions of the world that they may be regarded as truly global. Three hundred and twenty of them still derive 80 percent of their sales from their home region, while for the others, 25 are more accurately defined as bi-national or bi-regional on the basis of their sales. The same may often be said of where their productive assets are located. For example, authors like Voss (2013) have noted that corporations headquartered in Taiwan and Hong Kong are often MNCs on the basis that their manufacturing capacity is located in mainland China, but nowhere else. In reality, they are therefore more accurately regionally Chinese corporations as opposed to MNCs.

Similar observations have been made in respect of ownership and control. For example, an analysis by Staples (2007) of the world's 80 largest MNCs demonstrates that no more than 25 percent of their board members comprised those of another nationality to the corporation's headquarters. Only for 10 percent of them were the majority of board members from another nationality. This study is supported by others done on a regional basis, such as van Veen and Marsman (2008) for European MNCs specifically. These studies were done around a decade ago, and it could be claimed that there is a tendency over time towards greater multinationality on the part of board members as there are in corporations' operations. Yet, these studies also demonstrate that the main way corporate boards become more globalized is through mergers and acquisitions, *not* always as a result of the geographical spread of their activities.

It should therefore not be as surprising as some may find it that economically powerful states still account for 80 percent of world output, 70 percent of international trade, and up to 90 percent of foreign direct investment (FDI) (Chang, 2008, p. 32). This is because it is the MNCs from these states that do so. This is likely to have a bearing on their pathways of influence. In addition, the proliferation of MNCs also enables them, and potentially their home states' governments, to move beyond domestic boundaries in an attempt to influence foreign governments. This is because they are not placeless entities. Just ten states are the headquarters for 84 percent of them. The US alone accounts for 42 percent (*Financial Times*, 2016). With the emergence of Brazil, Russia, India, and China (collectively known as the BRICs) as economic powers it may no longer be as true as it once was that 'a statistical profile for the current corporation indicates that it is predominantly Anglo-American' (Harrod, 2006, pp. 27–8) – although lately, it is looking a lot more Chinese – but it remains the case that the home bases of the world's largest corporations are like a map of global economic power (e.g., see Mikler, 2018). As the global economy is said to be geographically triadic, so are the main headquarters of the world's major MNCs. Hence, the close correlation between the national economic and corporate data: the FT Global 500 are responsible for at least 80 percent of the world's stock of FDI, around 70 percent of world trade, and 30 percent of the world's GDP (Rugman, 2000; see also Bryant and Bailey, 1997).

The relationship between MNCs and states has important implications for global politics. It is not just that there is a relationship between national economic and corporate data but also that, as noted above, trade statistics reflect intra-firm, rather than inter-state patterns of economic interconnectedness. This gives MNCs a key role in relation to states, because rather than trade occurring on the basis of Ricardian comparative advantage, and on the basis of merchants 'preferring the support of domestic to that of foreign industry' (Smith, 1776 [2003], p. xvii), it instead occurs on the basis of competition between the suppliers of intermediate goods and services to MNCs. And these MNCs *govern* through contractual, and indirectly subcontractual, arrangements and rules how the global economy and trade relations are structured. In many ways, they are engaged in shaping government strategy and impacting the sovereignty of the states where these suppliers are based, as well as those where they are headquartered, and they are able to confer the benefits of employment and economic growth on these states, or remove them.

The result is that they are in a position to influence the rules of commerce and social and political relations across, as well as within, national territorial boundaries. Of course, influencing governments is crucial for MNCs when active in national markets, but strong relations are also important when following up on rules adopted at the global level, or when governments are formulating positions to be prosecuted in international fora. Therefore, the pathways of influence between MNCs and states are not solely confined to the national level and national institutional contexts. MNCs are also important players in global politics, including in the deliberations and agreements made in IGOs.

INFLUENCE PATHWAYS AND INTERGOVERNMENTAL ORGANIZATIONS

Corporate influence with IGOs is the third pathway of MNC influence and, like relations at the national level, how we conceptualize this is not straightforward. Capitalism is global and MNCs are some of the key actors that help make it so, but, as suggested above, the sources of their power are located at different levels, varying from country to country. They also may vary from industry to industry and from issue to issue. It would therefore be erroneous to radically re- or de-territorialize the political pathways employed by MNCs. Any analysis must necessarily be complex as a result, yet there is a simple point that may be made in respect of it – that is, if MNCs express their political power, they must do so in multiple places and relationally with multiple actors at different levels, from the local to national and international levels.

This is a contested area of study though. On the one hand, there are claims that, increasingly, corporate influence is seen at the highest of these levels to move downwards to lower levels, rather than produced at lower levels to be manifested at the highest level. This is essentially Büthe and Mattli's point, who observe that 'the view that most regulatory issues start out as domestic problems before globalization makes them international issues underplays the fact that a good deal of transnational regulation is motivated by uniquely transnational problems; and that transnational institutional structures may offer privileged access to some actors, biasing global regulatory outcomes in ways difficult to comprehend from a purely domestic perspective' (2011, p. 9). On the other hand, there is the view that corporate influence essentially flows more the other way. For example, Harrod (2006, p. 34) stresses that 'the international or global power of the corporation is more a function of the power it has achieved within powerful headquarter states'. Therefore, 'to focus on the study of the global activities of the corporation means to study the point of entry rather than the source of its power and activity'.

An emblematic and much cited example of the debates around this in practice is the negotiation of the Trade Related Aspects of Intellectual Property Rights (TRIPs) agreement in the World Trade Organization (WTO). Approximately a dozen US MNCs formed the Intellectual Property Committee (IPC), a cross-sectoral business alliance, with the purpose of extending the rights that they enjoyed in the US to the world. However, they did not just work at the national level in leveraging the US government and its representatives in the WTO. Executives from these MNCs also engaged their European and Japanese counterparts to influence their governments for a strong TRIPs agreement. The result is that by working with each other internationally, as well as at their respective national and regional levels (in the case of the EU), these MNCs presented both a powerful united front in their own right, and were assisted by negotiators who pushed for 'globalizing enforceable intellectual property standards' (Braithwaite and Drahos, 2000, p. 71). In her analysis of this process, Susan Sell (2003, p. 96) concludes that the result is that they ultimately 'made public law for the world'. But did they make it in the WTO through various states to affect the rules adhered to by others? Or did they take arrangements existing at various national levels and through their relations with their home states shift them upwards to the global level? Perhaps they did both, and we can simply say that the CEOs of these MNCs acted together and with their home states' representatives in an IGO to achieve the goal they desired.

As a general rule though, MNCs and their executives do not enjoy consultative status with IGOs. Some IGOs do not formally engage with non-governmental organizations of any kind, but those that do prefer formal relations with representative organizations, such as business associations. This practice is related to the original UN Charter and is used in many intergovernmental organizations within or beyond the UN family. It states that: 'The Economic and Social Council may make suitable arrangements for consultation with non-governmental organizations which are concerned with matters within its competence. Such arrangements may be made with international organizations and, where appropriate, with national organizations after consultation with the Member of the United Nations concerned' (United Nations, 1945). This suggests that MNCs' relations with UN agencies either go through states as members of these bodies, or through associations or similar entities in business. For MNCs this is a strong incentive to work through these pathways of influence.

In some cases, exceptions are made to this rule. The best-known example is the UN Global Compact where single corporations are members, giving them a unique opportunity to shape global policy. This design clearly broke with established traditions for consultations, much to the dismay of many other IGOs that see strong value in building relations with private organizations that can speak for broader interests, and not those of individual corporations. An example of this practice is the International Organization for Standardization (ISO). Individual MNCs cannot be members of the ISO, but nor can states. Instead, the ISO's membership comprises 163 national standards associations, the membership of which includes industry associations, government organizations, standard-setting and conformity assessment bodies, trade associations, labor unions, professional societies, consumer groups, and academia (ISO, 2016a, 2016b).

As there are subnational, national, regional, and global aspects to the dissemination of the ISO's standards via its membership, so too are there political implications in the sense of its operations and whose interests it represents. As such, the pathways of influence of MNCs figures in understanding this, even if they are not individually directly members of it. As the ISO increases the scope of its activities beyond technical production standards, to standards in management (ISO 9000 series), the environment (ISO 14000 series), and social responsibility (ISO 26000 series), MNCs have seen an opportunity to reduce the potential proliferation of multiple national standards in these areas (Clapp, 1998). They have used their influence at multiple levels to create standards across borders that 'become *de facto* requirements for doing business around the world' (Haufler, 2000, p. 128), and that are in their interests.

When MNCs succeed in ensuring their interests are not just considered but pursued by IGOs, they are potentially in a position not just to influence but also to set global agendas. The growing role of corporate interests in the United Nations illustrates the point. A study by Seitz and Martens (2017) considers the role of corporate funding for UN initiatives. These include funding projects to improve access to water, water quality and water management for the United Nations Development Programme (UNDP); HIV AIDS education for the United Nations Educational, Scientific and Cultural Organization (UNESCO); and support for the UN Women Private Sector Leadership Advisory Council, which is chaired by the CEO of Coca-Cola. In addition, philanthropic organizations, like the Bill and Melinda Gates Foundation, are responsible for around 10 percent of all aid flows under the OECD's Development Assistance Committee. In fact, in 2014 the Bill and Melinda Gates Foundation was the second highest funder of the World Health Organization after the United States of America. This may be desirable if funding is available for important international programs in respect of a range of economic, environmental, and social concerns. However, it does raise concerns in respect of transparency and accountability related to the motivations for MNC involvement in these programs – for example, if they are not motivated by strategically addressing the issues as opposed to enhancing corporate reputation. The problem, therefore, is that there is 'a growing reliance on corporate-led solutions to global problems' (Seitz and Martens, 2017, p. 46) as MNCs are increasingly not just influencing the agendas of IGOs but defining and funding them. This shows that in addition to many traditional contacts and pathways, new and hitherto less explored avenues need to be examined. This includes those within the business community itself.

INFLUENCE PATHWAYS AND THE BUSINESS COMMUNITY

The fourth pathway in our study embraces the business community in its widest sense, as this is institutionally remarkably diverse, and is organized at both national and international levels, creating multiple linkages across territories. If MNCs are not isolated actors standing alone in the market, nor exerting political power in isolation, then it must be the case that they interact with many other entities in the business community. By drawing on existing literatures on MNCs – including management, economics and international political economy – we can improve our understanding of corporate influence (Greif, 2005; Hollingsworth and Boyer, 1997; Lawton and Rajwani, 2015), but it is not only a matter of assembling already known parts to form a more coherent whole. In the business community, a large universe of organizations in the form of, for instance, cartels, clubs, associations, and other networks, are available to MNCs and need to be mapped and understood to analyze the pathways of MNCs' influence. Through these entities, MNCs are able to coordinate with each other as well as with other firms.

These different forms of coordination are shaped in national as well as in international and global contexts. The varieties of capitalism literature is helpful in identifying national institutional variations (Hall and Soskice, 2001). For example, some states rely more on non-market modes of economic coordination, including between firms, organized labor (i.e., unions), and government, while others stress an arm's-length relationship between government and business, and promote the role of unfettered market forces. We accept that this is the case, while recognizing that it can also be argued that there is generally much more similarity between the 'capitalisms' than is often stressed (e.g., see Streeck, 2011). In this sense, there are varieties or variations *in*, as well as *of*, capitalism (Hay, 2019). But more fundamentally, there is a tension between stressing the different national institutional contexts for business, versus the idea that with the rise of MNCs, a specific and relatively independent global business community has been created that is not necessarily as nourished by a multiplicity of national institutional traditions, nor as defined by national borders, as was once the case.

One result of this is that collective action through national business associations is not needed in all areas of business for MNCs to coordinate their activities. In some cases, it is possible for large MNCs to act together in specific 'clubs' for business leaders, or to coordinate with other elites outside the business world. A well-known example is the World Economic Forum (WEF), which has no national chapters but has a long list of MNCs as members on a direct basis (Ronit, 2016). Yet, it remains the case that at both the domestic and international levels MNCs, owing to their role in the market, are in a position to wield strong influence on organizations in the business community. When competition leads to economic concentration, MNCs become dominant in many sectors of the economy and in many parts of the value and production chain. Thus, as noted above, many industries are today dominated by a relatively small number of firms. This concentration enables very large corporations to act on their own, as national 'champions' at home but also at the global level. Furthermore, such patterns of market hierarchy are likely to have an effect on the character of cooperation with other firms and can have an important impact on the resources employed to influence politics. These different individual and collective options, however, do not exclude each other but can be combined in many ways. For example, the development of single MNCs with significant resources can facilitate the formation of individual strategies and encourage independent action, of which the tech giants are prominent examples. And firm-centered studies in economics and management, being focused as they often are on the organizational strategies of individual firms, are inclined to emphasize the opportunities for them to do so (e.g., Funk and Hirschman, 2015; Hillman, Keim and Schuler, 2004; Lawton, McGuire and Rajwani, 2013; Windsor, 2007). However, we cannot extrapolate and conclude that MNCs will, with increasing size, necessarily act alone, shunning alliances with other firms. In some cases where few corporations come to dominate a global industry, cooperation between otherwise strong competitors may seem a more logical choice, and they benefit from the advantages of small group size in doing so (Olson, 1965).

It is difficult to predict the concrete consequences of dynamics in the market for cooperation in the business community, but, as already mentioned, we anticipate that various asymmetries will spill over into social and political forms of exchanges. Therefore, a more detailed analysis is necessary to reveal the quite extensive concerns managed by organizations in the global business community, and the opportunities they offer MNCs. To fully appreciate how these mechanisms work, however, we must differentiate between a variety of organizations in the global business community (Ronit, 2018). Some organizations seek to formulate strategies to influence traditional public policy adopted by IGOs, with the International Chamber of Commerce as a prominent example (Kelly, 2005), while others define and implement regulation without the involvement of public authority at all. For example, beyond the ISO there are many other standard-setting organizations that are completely private in their membership (Hale and Held, 2011). Some work to represent the general business voice, maybe even with the ambitious goal to speak for the 'capitalist class' as such (van der Pijl, 1998), while others are concerned about the organization and representation of specific industries with specific interests. Some are focused on delivering various services to enhance the competitiveness of corporations but also assist with strategy building, as demonstrated by the role played by the Big Four consulting firms (Morgan, Sturdy and Frenkel, 2019), while others are interested in setting agendas and improving the reputation of companies, as we have seen in the all-encompassing CSR movement. It is beyond the scope of this chapter to identify all the different subsets of actors and organizations active in the business community, but it suffices to say there is immense variety in their forms and purpose. It is also important to note that, in addition to working with states, they often work directly with CSOs.

INFLUENCE PATHWAYS AND CIVIL SOCIETY

This is the fifth and last path of influence considered in the book, because to develop an approach spanning the diverse paths of MNC influence in global politics we must consider not just the way that MNCs organize and influence each other and states, but also the relations MNCs have with organized civil society. Just as firms have become MNCs, so too has civil society experienced a significant degree of globalization (e.g., see Scholte, 2005). Therefore, MNCs increasingly encounter CSOs at both the national and international levels. When civil society is organized at different territorial levels there are ample opportunities for them to coordinate and link domestic and international activities. Although it is not the case that all CSOs exist to confront and challenge business behavior, when they do, patterns in the challenges they mount may be observed. On the one hand, civil society can pose a serious challenge to MNCs and question their strategies and practices. Indeed, CSOs can develop into serious countervailing powers, and through various forms of activism ultimately address the power of corporate influence in global politics (Dauvergne and LeBaron, 2014). On the other hand, civil society may in some cases become partners with business in the solving of specific problems, sometimes with the risk of CSOs losing their identity and independence (Roberts, Jones and Fröhling, 2005), as they build alliances and partnerships that may enhance the influence of business (Ronit, 2007). In relation to civil society, various pathways of influence are available for MNCs, but much depends on the strategies of CSOs and the willingness of MNCs to either work with, respond to, or oppose them. In general, however, it seems that MNCs must learn how to deal with critical voices in civil society and adjust their strategies. The whole development of the CSR movement in business can be seen in this light, but then this raises the question of whether or not the resulting initiatives are mere acts of 'window dressing', or in the case of the environment 'greenwashing', as opposed to real changes in behavior (Bowen and Aragon-Correa, 2014; Ramus and Montiel, 2005).

The CSOs themselves are located in different positions, not just geographically, but with regard to MNCs specifically. Some are closely linked to MNCs' production and value chains and represent interests that corporations can enter into direct contractual relationships with, such as unions or consumer groups, but this does not always lead to arrangements *with* business in a partnership sense (Cumbers, Nativel and Routledge, 2008; Stevis and Felli, 2015). Furthermore, other groups such as environment and human rights movements, which do not formally represent actors in the market with whom MNCs conclude contracts, nevertheless may influence the nature and terms of these contracts. For example, environmental standards or regulations in respect of labor rights are often promoted by CSOs, sometimes aligned with or represented by consumer organizations or labor unions, and therefore these CSOs may achieve a stronger position in relation to corporations (Ruggie, 2013). In turn, these dynamics in the civil society community are important in (re-)defining the strategic thinking of MNCs. The result is that we must be careful not to see possible interactions between MNCs and civil society exclusively as a set of bilateral relations, as the different pathways of influence are intertwined. In many cases, CSOs pose a challenge to corporations when they influence governments and IGOs to encourage the global regulation of business in many policy fields (Braithwaite and Drahos, 2000; Stone and Maloney, 2019). Influencing political parties and government agencies at domestic levels also become crucial in this context. This is, for instance, the case in areas where principal authority is nested in national public institutions, such as tax policy (Eccleston and Elbra, 2018; Palan, Murphy and Chavagneux, 2010; Rixen, 2011).

We must also be careful not to narrow down the analysis of CSOs and business to exchanges in, or close to, the market. Although markets are a key focus of corporations, as noted above MNCs are in a position to control markets, and they are political actors that can be influenced by many other processes in their environment. Therefore, as CSOs strive to set agendas and change public perceptions, they can build moral authority that gives them certain advantages in relation to MNCs' interests. As argued by Vogel (2005), CSOs have the ability to provide MNCs with what can be regarded as a 'social license' to operate. They can also withdraw it. Mining is a key case in this regard, as the operations of MNCs in this industry are geographically fixed and therefore vulnerable to the displeasure or criticism of CSOs. Conflicts are therefore frequent (Moffat and Zhang, 2014), and organized civil society has in some cases been influential in changing corporate practices (Bloomfield, 2017).

CSOs launch various campaigns that are sometimes targeted at an industry, or sometimes at individual MNCs whose behavior is deemed immoral, and they urge them to change their practices (Yaziji and Doh, 2009). Sometimes MNCs can ignore such campaigns, but not always. As a major environmental organization, Greenpeace managed to influence the toy company Lego to terminate its contract with Shell (Vaughan, 2014), considered an irresponsible company in respect of environmental and climate change issues. In many ways, various CSR initiatives can be seen as a response, or a pre-emptive measure to forestall influential civil society. MNCs, thus, have many ways to maintain or extend their influence adapting to dynamic changes in or beyond the economy.

In a number of cases, however, the active presence of civil society can be an important opportunity as well. Many initiatives in civil society have an integrative character, in the sense that they seek to involve business in joint rule-making. For example, various CSOs appeal to business to join standard-setting schemes on a voluntary basis in areas where no proper public regulation exists (Abbott and Snidal, 2009; Lambin and Thorlakson, 2018; Porter and Ronit, 2015; Toffel, Short and Ouellet, 2015). The significant rise of such schemes has received strong attention in the study of business and politics, and they are studied under different concepts, but the perspective of MNCs and their pathways of influence are always involved. In fact, these schemes may bring some benefits to those MNCs that are more efficient and more willing to comply with rules, as this will sharpen their profiles in competition and as a result leaders will tend to outcompete laggards, an issue that has been much discussed in relation to the development of climate-friendly technologies (e.g., Gunningham and Sinclair, 2002). Initiating or joining such schemes, even pioneering them, may improve the overall reputation of the MNCs involved.

Such arrangements therefore often have a multi-stakeholder character and are neither exclusively civic, nor corporate. They also offer opportunities for participating MNCs to influence the rules they adopt. Although some schemes are very close to self-regulation adopted in the context of business associations and specialized clubs, where MNCs have a significant input, they have often emerged under the impact of civil society, as is, for instance, shown in the case of the Global Apparel Coalition, an initiative embracing a range of MNCs in the apparel industry (Kozlowski, Searcy and Bardecki, 2015).

From the perspective of MNCs, it is crucial that they manage to respond effectively to different challenges from civil society, and if necessary, thwart or join civil society initiatives, one of the many pathways to influence. However, we need to emphasize that there is a range of areas where there is no real struggle over agendas between business and civil society. Given the private authority of business, there are simply areas and decisions that corporations control and that are taken for granted and are very hard to wrest from the hands of corporations. In addition, MNCs usually dispose of significant resources and expertise that makes it comparatively harder for CSOs to mobilize interests and formulate alternatives in the global realm.

A FRAMEWORK FOR ANALYSIS AND THE CONTRIBUTIONS TO THIS VOLUME

We have identified five different pathways of corporate political influence based on the foregoing discussion, and these are indicated in Figure 1.1. It shows that MNCs may act on their own or together (hence the double vertical arrows) and in different institutional contexts (hence the boxes). First, individual MNCs, and for that matter groups of MNCs, can be seen as political actors in their own right. They wield authority as well as compete in markets, and make key decisions to hire and fire workers, invest in productive capacity, and contract other firms. They are also in a position to deliberately employ significant economic and political resources to influence other private and public actors in their environment. Second, MNCs are in a position to influence governments in their home states that make regulations and in various ways that shape the overall conditions for business. Their home states may further the interests of these same corporations in international settings when assistance is needed, especially when these interests are shared between states and MNCs. The same potentially goes for the states in which they invest and operate abroad. Third, and relatedly, MNCs need to closely follow and influence many different international agendas that may have an impact on the conditions under which they operate. Therefore, they provide input to agreements negotiated in IGOs that will affect their work at the international level. This implies building expert knowledge and solid relations with the relevant IGOs.

Fourth, MNCs have an important place in the business community. While MNCs can act on their own, they are also involved in setting norms and rules through various contracts and coordinating mechanisms, including business associations and self-regulatory bodies that govern behavior in the business community and represent interests before other actors in, and beyond, markets. Finally, MNCs engage with both critical and supportive voices in civil society that challenge and modify their behavior. In some cases, agreements and rules are produced through cooperation that eventually may grant corporations stronger legitimacy and enhance their social license to operate. It is important to note that these different pathways for political action can be employed separately. However, depending on the preferences and opportunities available at a particular time, in a particular situation, or in respect of a particular issue, they often tend to be combined (hence the horizontal arrow).

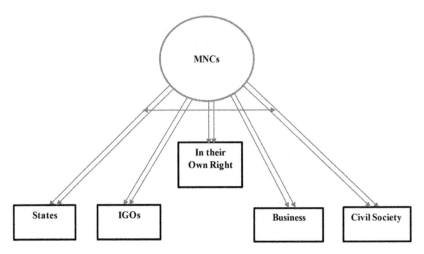

Figure 1.1   Potential pathways of political influence

Using this framework, we contend that MNCs are not simply one out of several actors equally positioned to exert influence in global politics. Instead, they enjoy certain basic privileges in the economy, in society, and in politics that stem from the preponderant position of business in different types of market economies, and from the special role of large corporations in the processes of globalization. This does not suggest that business can expect that other actors will necessarily yield to, or 'obey', corporate demands in respect of interests though. As such, a continuous effort is required to leverage states, IGOs, other sections of business and civil society groups to secure beneficial outcomes. The results of MNCs' political strategies cannot be assumed, and that their interests will be served is never guaranteed, as there are many obstacles to the power of MNCs that must be considered as well. Therefore, a careful analysis of the various pathways is required to understand these finer mechanisms.

The contributors to this book help to unpack the complexity of the pathways, and their interactions, to argue that corporations, and MNCs specifically, seek political influence in different stages of decision-making, in different scenarios, at different territorial levels, and through different mechanisms, with variation across policy fields. Hence, different pathways of influence are possible: sometimes a single pathway is preferred, or at least given priority, while sometimes a combination of pathways are taken. The contributors theorize these different pathways and give examples of how they are pursued. Only a few examples from the enormous variation and immense material that is available are considered but based on these cases it is possible to illustrate the key pathways of influence in global politics employed by MNCs. Furthermore, an embedded firm-centered approach is taken. MNCs are examined as general political actors involved in economic and political exchanges in complex institutional environments. Embeddedness, therefore, implies that although we can elucidate some general patterns of MNC behavior, these features must be established on the basis of the variable territorial, sectoral and cultural contexts in which corporations find themselves and that enable or constrain the pathways of influence.

In Chapter 2, 'Globalizing State Capitalism? Selective Internationalization of MNCs from Emerging Economies', Christian May argues that the ability of MNCs to shape global operations can be used as an indicator of their power. Indeed, they are able to use this structural power to influence global politics. In this sense, large firms from emerging economies might not appear as global as their Western peers. This is due to their limited capital base and different insertion into global value chains. However, on closer inspection, it is the particular relationship between MNCs and their home states that shapes the internationalizing efforts by emerging economies' MNCs. This political aspect is often overlooked and, hence, understated. The chapter looks at the corporate sector in Brazil and India to shed light on the connections.

In Chapter 3, 'MNCs and State Infrastructural Power', Linda Weiss and Elizabeth Thurbon examine the extraordinary capacity of the modern state with regard to its pre-industrial predecessor. They consider why and how some states are able to execute their decisions and pursue their ambitions. Focusing on the US, they show that its economic power may seem stronger than ever, ostensibly bolstered by being home to the world's most globalized companies. However, the strength of US MNCs may have contradictory consequences. By internationalizing its infrastructural power, the US has achieved significant benefits for its MNCs by extending national intellectual property rules into foreign jurisdictions. Yet, by the same actions, the US has fostered the conditions that have been steadily diminishing the state's infrastructural power at home.

In Chapter 4, 'Corporate Influence and Environmental Regulation in Shipping: Navigating Norms and Influence Pathways in the International Maritime Organization', Christian Hendriksen examines the role of MNCs in the regulation of international shipping. First, the chapter explains how the structure of the maritime industry and the regulatory framework provides the basis for MNCs as political actors. Second, the chapter shows how this translates into MNCs' influence in the International Maritime Organization (IMO), which is the designated UN agency tasked with regulating the industry. Third, the chapter explores how the role of MNCs in the IMO relates to the relationship between MNCs and individual states and what lessons we can draw from MNCs' political activities in international shipping.

As analyzed by Kate Macdonald in Chapter 5, 'Private Sustainability Governance and Global Corporate Power', the social and environmental impacts of global business are regulated by an array of schemes. These include labels such as Fairtrade, Rainforest Alliance and the Forest Stewardship Council, alongside multi-stakeholder roundtables and working groups. While these schemes are lauded as innovative tools for promoting global sustainability norms, others perceive them as tools that reproduce global corporate power and insulate companies from societal pressure. Studying schemes in the agribusiness and forestry sectors, the chapter theorizes and illustrates sources and pathways of global corporate influence, and the contested political processes through which the legitimacy of corporate power is asserted and resisted.

Business is often portrayed as consisting of individual firms without a capacity to develop relevant collective action, but in Chapter 6, 'MNCs and their Role in Global Business Associations', Karsten Ronit shows that MNCs acting through national associations can participate in a range of leading business associations at the global level. In general, global peak associations are concerned with representing the broad interests of business and draw on national associations as members. However, in different contexts, peak associations admit single corporations as members. Direct membership offers stronger opportunities for MNC influence in some organizations, a practice that has grown stronger, but still these changes do not alter the big picture.

In Chapter 7, 'The Power of Mining MNCs: Global Governance and Social Conflict', Lian Sinclair analyzes how mining MNCs pursue their interests through social and political strategies across political scales, and how they respond to social conflict and challenges to their legitimacy from people affected by mining and their civil society allies. Using data from Rio Tinto's Kelian mine in Indonesia, she shows how local concerns 'jumped scales' when activists created alliances with national and international civil society groups. In response, mining MNCs established a network of global business associations and governance standards that emphasize consultation and participation. Mechanisms based on these standards seek to contain and re-localize conflict through participation.

In Chapter 8, 'Knowledge and Power: The Role of the Big Four in in the Competitive Disharmonization of Global Corporate Tax Avoidance Regulations', Ainsley Elbra, John Mikler and Hannah Murphy-Gregory scrutinize how the Big Four professional services firms (PwC, Deloitte, KPMG and EY) promote, sanction, and regularize the behavior of other MNCs as well as governments. Their services are neither purely technical nor neutral because they construct and enhance the legitimacy and discursive power of MNCs. This chapter looks at their role in facilitating and discursively defending global corporate tax avoidance, and it shows that MNCs use their ability to operate across multiple jurisdictions to take advantage of opportunities to reduce or eliminate their taxation obligations.

Finally, in Chapter 9, we bring together the different findings and explain the general pathways through which MNCs seek influence in global politics. We show that this influence is not restricted to traditional arenas of policy-making but also encompasses multiple actors and relations that are intrinsically entangled. Arguing for a much-needed synthesis in the study of MNC engagement in politics, we demonstrate how different approaches in the social sciences can be improved via a more holistic approach.

MNCs and their pathways of political influence in global politics is a huge theme. We have consulted different literatures that can guide our study and many insights can be helpful. Various disciplines and subdisciplines, however, have tended to identify particular modes of corporate action and sidestepped others, but it is important that we recognize the complexity of MNCs and synthesize these into a general framework for analysis. This is an ambitious endeavor, but we are attempting it because we believe that a holistic approach is necessary to capture the diverse actions of corporations in general, and MNCs specifically, and the different mechanisms of influence they employ. The traditional focus on single and separate pathways can yield important insights but cannot fully grasp their complex role in global politics. A substantial number of cases and issues must be examined to distill some general patterns of MNC behavior, and we cannot complete such a project here. But we can begin this venture by devising some principal elements for an analytical framework applied by the contributors to this volume.

NOTES

1. As per President Clinton's campaign in the 1990s.
2. We deliberately use this term because the term 'non-governmental organization', which is often used, explicitly refers only to those that are non-government, and,

in principle, includes organizations representing interests in both the market and civil society.
3.   More specifically, Smith's invisible hand was not the basis for competition but the concept of a mechanism where the pursuit of enlightened self-interest led to the unwitting advancement of the common good.

REFERENCES

Abbott, K.W. and D. Snidal (2009), 'The governance triangle: regulatory standards institutions and the shadow of the state', in W. Mattli and N. Woods (eds), *The Politics of Global Regulation*, Princeton, NJ: Princeton University Press, pp. 44–88.
Bachrach, P. and M. Baratz (1962), 'Two faces of power', *American Political Science Review*, **56**(4), 947–52.
Banks Around the World (2018), 'Top 100 banks in the world', accessed 30 August 2019 at http://www.relbanks.com/worlds-top-banks/assets.
Barkan, J. (2013), *Corporate Sovereignty: Law and Government Under Capitalism*, Minneapolis, MN: University of Minnesota Press.
Barnett, M. and R. Duvall (2005), 'Power in international politics', *International Organization*, **59**(1), 39–75.
Beck, T., D. Kunt and R. Levine (2005), 'Bank concentration and fragility: impact and mechanics', *NBER Working Papers*, No. 11500, accessed 10 June 2014 at http://www.nber.org/papers/w11500.
Bloomfield, M.J. (2017), *Dirty Gold: How Activism Transformed the Jewelry Industry*, Boston, MA: MIT Press.
Bonturi, M. and K. Fukasaku (1993), 'Globalisation and intra-firm trade: an empirical note', *OECD Economic Studies*, No. 20, 145–59.
Bowen, F. and J.A. Aragon-Correa (2014), 'Greenwashing in corporate environmentalism research and practice: the importance of what we say and do', *Organization & Environment*, **27**(2), 107–12.
Braithwaite, J. and P. Drahos (2000), *Global Business Regulation*, Cambridge, UK: Cambridge University Press.
Broome, A. (2014), *Issues and Actors in the Global Political Economy*, Basingstoke: Palgrave Macmillan.
Bryant, R.L. and S. Bailey (1997), *Third World Political Ecology*, Abingdon/New York: Routledge.
Büthe, T. and W. Mattli (2011), *The New Global Rulers: The Privatization of Regulation in the World Economy*, Princeton, NJ: Princeton University Press.
Cahill, D. (2014), *The End of Laissez Faire? On the Durability of Embedded Neoliberalism*, Cheltenham, UK and Northampton, MA, USA: Edward Elgar Publishing.
Cerny, P. (2000), 'Political globalization and the competition state', in R. Stubbs and G. Underhill (eds), *Political Economy and the Changing Global Order*, Oxford: Oxford University Press.
Cerny, P. (2010), 'The competition state today: from raison d'État to raison du Monde', *Policy Studies*, **31**(1), 5–21.
Chang, H. (2008), *Bad Samaritans: The Myth of Free Trade and the Secret History of Capitalism*, New York: Bloomsbury Press.
Clapp, J. (1998), 'The privatization of global environmental governance: ISO 14000 and the developing world', *Global Governance*, **4**(3), 295–316.

Clapp, J. (2005), 'Transnational corporations and global environmental governance', in P. Dauvergne (ed.), *Handbook of Global Environmental Politics*, Cheltenham, UK and Northampton, MA, USA: Edward Elgar Publishing, pp. 284–97.

Cox, R.W. (1987), *Production, Power and World Order: Social Forces in the Making of History*, New York: Columbia University Press.

Crouch, C. (2011), *The Strange Non-Death of Neoliberalism*, Cambridge, UK: Polity Press.

Culpepper, P.D. (2011), *Quiet Politics and Business Power: Corporate Control in Europe and Japan*, Cambridge, UK: Cambridge University Press.

Cumbers, A., C. Nativel and P. Routledge (2008), 'Labour agency and union positionalities in global production networks', *Journal of Economic Geography*, **8**, 369–87.

Dahl, R. (1957), 'The concept of power', *Behavioral Science*, **2**, 201–15.

Dauvergne, P. and G. LeBaron (2014), *Protest Inc.: The Corporatization of Activism*, Cambridge, UK: Polity Press.

Davies, A. (2015), 'CSG industry hires well-connected staffers', *Sydney Morning Herald*, 25 May, accessed 22 July 2015 at http://www.smh.com.au/nsw/csg-industry -hires-wellconnected-staffers-20150524-gh2rg3.html.

Eccleston, R. and A. Elbra (2018), *Business, Civil Society and the New Politics of Corporate Tax Justice: Paying a Fair Share?*, Cheltenham, UK and Northampton, MA, USA: Edward Elgar Publishing.

Financial Times (2016), 'FT Global 500 2015', accessed 5 June 2016 at www.ft.com/ ft500.

Fortune (2019), *Fortune Global 500*, accessed 3 September 2020 at http://fortune.com/ global500/2019/

Frank, A.G. (1978), *Dependent Accumulation and Underdevelopment*, London: Macmillan.

Friedman, T. (2000), *The Lexus and the Olive Tree*, revised edition, London: HarperCollins.

Fuchs, D. (2007), *Business Power in Global Governance*, Boulder, CO: Lynne Rienner Publishers.

Funk, R.J. and D. Hirschman (2015), 'Beyond nonmarket strategy: market actions as corporate political activity', *Academy of Management Review*, **42**(1), 32–52.

Greif, A. (2005), 'Commitment, coercion and markets: the nature and dynamics of institutions supporting exchange', in C. Ménard and M.M. Shirley (eds), *Handbook of New Institutional Economics*, Dordrecht: Springer, pp. 727–888.

Gunningham, N. and D. Sinclair (2002), *Leaders and Laggards: Next Generation Environmental Regulation*, Sheffield: Greenleaf Publishing.

Hale, T. and D. Held (eds) (2011), *The Handbook of Transnational Governance: Institutions and Innovations*, Cambridge, UK: Polity.

Hall, P.A. and D. Soskice (eds) (2001), *Varieties of Capitalism: The Institutional Foundations of Comparative Advantage*, Oxford: Oxford University Press.

Harrod, J. (2006), 'The century of the corporation', in C. May (ed.), *Global Corporate Power*, Boulder, CO: Lynne Rienner Publishers, pp. 23–46.

Haufler, V. (2000), 'Private sector international regimes', in R. Higgott, G. Underhill and A. Bieler (eds), *Non-state Actors and Authority in the Global System*, Abingdon/ New York: Routledge, pp. 121–37.

Hay, C. (2019), 'Does capitalism (still) come in varieties?', *Review of International Political Economy*, **27**(2), 302–19.

Hillman, A.J., G.D. Keim and D. Schuler (2004), 'Corporate political activity: a review and research agenda', *Journal of Management*, **30**(6), 837–57.

Hollingsworth, J.R. and R. Boyer (1997), 'Coordination of economic actors and social systems of production', in J.R. Hollingsworth and R. Boyer (eds), *Contemporary Capitalism: The Embeddedness of Institutions*, Cambridge, UK: Cambridge University Press, pp. 1–48.

International Monetary Fund (2015), 'April 2015 edition', World Economic Outlook Database, accessed 12 January 2016 at http://www.imf.org/external/pubs/ft/weo/2015/01/weodata/index.aspx.

International Organization for Standardization [ISO] (2016a), 'Members', accessed 4 August 2020 at http://www.iso.org/iso/home/about/iso_members.htm?membertype=membertype_MB.

International Organization for Standardization [ISO] (2016b), 'ANSI, United States', accessed 4 August 2020 at http://www.iso.org/iso/home/about/iso_members/iso_member_body.htm?member_id=2188.

Karliner, J. (1997), *The Corporate Planet: Ecology and Politics in the Age of Globalization*, San Francisco, CA: Sierra Club.

Kelly, D. (2005), 'The International Chamber of Commerce', *New Political Economy*, **10**(2), 259–71.

Kollman, K. (2008), 'The regulatory power of business norms: a call for a new research agenda', *International Studies Review*, **10**(3), 397–419.

Korten, D. (2015), *When Corporations Rule the World*, 3rd edition, Oakland, CA: Berrett-Koehler Publishers.

Kozlowski, A., C. Searcy and M. Bardecki (2015), 'Corporate sustainability reporting in the apparel industry', *International Journal of Productivity and Performance Management*, **64**(3), 377–97.

Lambin, E.F. and T. Thorlakson (2018), 'Sustainability standards: interactions between private actors, civil society, and governments', *Annual Review of Environment and Resources*, **43**(1), 369–93.

Lawton, T., S. McGuire and T. Rajwani (2013), 'Corporate political activity: a literature review and research agenda', *International Journal of Management Reviews*, **15**(1), 86–105.

Lawton, T. and T.S. Rajwani (2015), *The Routledge Companion to Non-Market Strategy*, Abingdon/New York: Routledge.

LeBaron, G. (2014), 'Subcontracting is not illegal, but is it unethical? Business ethics, forced labor, and economic success', *Brown Journal of World Affairs*, **20**(2), 237–49.

Levitt, T. (1983), 'The globalization of markets', *Harvard Business Review*, **61**(3), 92–102.

Levy, D.L. and P.J. Newell (2002), 'Business strategy and international environmental governance: towards a neo-Gramscian synthesis', *Global Environmental Politics*, **2**(4), 84–101.

Lindblom, C. (1977), *Politics and Markets*, New York: Basic Books.

Lukes, S. (1974), *Power: A Radical View*, London: Palgrave Macmillan.

Mikler, J. (2018), *The Political Power of Global Corporations*, Cambridge, UK: Polity Press.

Moffat, K. and A. Zhang (2014), 'The paths to social license to operate: an integrative model explaining community acceptance of mining', *Resources Policy*, **39**, 61–70.

Morgan, G., A. Sturdy and M. Frenkel (2019), 'The role of large management consultancy firms in global public policy', in D. Stone and K. Moloney (eds), *The Oxford Handbook of Global Policy and Transnational Administration,* Oxford: Oxford University Press.

Nolan, P., D. Sutherland and J. Zhang (2002), 'The challenge of the global business revolution', *Contributions to Political Economy*, **21**(1), 91–110.

Olson, M. (1965), *The Logic of Collective Action: Public Goods and the Theory of Groups*, Cambridge, MA: Harvard University Press.

Organisation for Economic Co-operation and Development [OECD] (2011), *Bank Competition and Financial Stability*, accessed 4 August 2020 at http://www.oecd.org/finance/financial-markets/48501035.pdf.

Organisation for Economic Co-operation and Development [OECD] (2014), 'Concentration of the banking sector: assets of three largest banks as a share of assets of all commercial banks, percent, 2011', *OECD Economic Surveys: Netherlands 2014*, accessed 4 August 2020 at https://read.oecd-ilibrary.org/economics/oecd-economic-surveys-netherlands-2014/concentration-of-the-banking-sector_eco_surveys-nld-2014-graph31-en#page1.

Palan, R., R. Murphy and C. Chavagneux (2010), *Tax Havens: How Globalization Really Works*, Ithaca, NY: Cornell University Press.

Porter, T. and K. Ronit (2015), 'Implementation in international business self-regulation: the importance of sequences and their linkages', *Journal of Law and Society*, **42**(3), 413–33.

Ramus, C.A. and I. Montiel (2005), 'When are corporate environmental policies a form of greenwashing?', *Business and Society*, **44**(4), 377–414.

Rixen, T. (2011), 'From double tax avoidance to tax competition: explaining the institutional trajectory of international tax governance', *Review of International Political Economy*, **18**(2), 197–227.

Roberts, S., J.P. Jones III and O. Fröhling (2005), 'NGOs and the globalization of managerialism: a research framework', *World Development*, **33**(11), 1845–64.

Ronit, K. (2007), 'Introduction: the new policy arrangements of business and countervailing groups', in K. Ronit (ed.), *Global Public Policy: Business and the Countervailing Powers of Civil Society*, Abingdon/New York: Routledge, pp. 1–14.

Ronit, K. (2016), 'Global employer and business associations: their relations with members in the development of mutual capacities', *European Review of International Studies*, **3**(1), 53–77.

Ronit, K. (2018), *Global Business Associations*, Abingdon/New York: Routledge.

Ruggie, J.G. (2013), *Just Business: Multinational Corporations and Human Rights*, New York: W.W. Norton & Company.

Rugman, A. (2000), *The End of Globalization*, London: Random House Business Books.

Rugman, A. and A. Verbeke (2009), 'Location, competitiveness, and the multinational enterprise', in A. Rugman (ed.), *The Oxford Handbook of International Business*, 2nd edition, Oxford: Oxford University Press.

Scholte, J. (2005), *Globalisation: A Critical Introduction*, 2nd edition, Basingstoke: Palgrave Macmillan.

Schwartz, H. (2000), *States versus Markets*, 2nd edition, Basingstoke: Palgrave Macmillan.

Seitz, K. and J. Martens (2017), 'Philanthrolateralism: private funding and corporate influence in the United Nations', *Global Policy*, **8**(5), 46–50.

Sell, S. (2003), *Private Power, Public Law: The Globalization of Intellectual Property Rights*, Cambridge, UK: Cambridge University Press.

Smith, A. (1776 [2003]), *The Wealth of Nations*, New York: Bantam Classic.

Staples, C.L. (2007), 'Board globalisation in the world's largest TNCs 1993–2005', *Corporate Governance*, **15**(2), 311–21.

Stevis, D. and R. Felli (2015), 'Global labour unions and just transition to a green economy', *International Environmental Agreements: Politics, Law and Economics*, **15**(1), 29–43.
Stone, D. and K. Moloney (eds) (2019), *The Oxford Handbook of Global Policy and Transnational Administration*, Oxford: Oxford University Press.
Strange, S. (1988), *States and Markets*, London/New York: Continuum.
Streeck, W. (2011), 'Taking capitalism seriously: towards an institutionalist approach to contemporary political economy', *Socio-Economic Review*, **9**(1), 137–67.
Suchman, M.C. (1995), 'Managing legitimacy: strategic and institutional approaches', *Academy of Management Review*, **20**(3), 571–610.
Teeple, G. and S. McBride (eds) (2011), *Relations of Global Power: Neoliberal Order and Disorder*, Toronto: University of Toronto Press.
Tepper, J. and D. Hearn (2019), *The Myth of Capitalism: Monopolies and the Death of Competition*, Hoboken, NJ: Wiley.
Tienhaara, K. (2014), 'Corporations: business and industrial influence', in P.G. Harris (ed.), *Routledge Handbook of Global Environmental Politics*, Abingdon/New York: Routledge.
Toffel, M.W., J.L. Short and M. Ouellet (2015), 'Codes in context: how states, markets, and civil society shape adherence to global labor standards', *Regulation and Governance*, **9**(3), 205–23.
United Nations (1945), *Charter of the United Nations and Statute of the International Court of Justice*, San Francisco, CA: United Nations.
United Nations Conference on Trade and Development [UNCTAD] (2011), 'Web table 34: number of parent corporations and foreign affiliates, by region and economy 2010' in UNCTAD (ed.), *World Investment Report 2011*, accessed 20 July 2015 at https://unctad.org/Sections/dite_dir/docs/WIR11_web%20tab%2034.pdf.
United Nations Conference on Trade and Development [UNCTAD] (2014), 'Web table 28: the world's top 100 non-financial TNCs, ranked by foreign assets 2013' in UNCTAD (ed.), *World Investment Report 2014*, accessed 20 October 2015 at http://unctad.org/Sections/dite_dir/docs/WIR2014/WIR14_tab28.xls.
van der Pijl, K. (1998), *Transnational Classes and International Relations*, Abingdon/New York: Routledge.
van Veen, K. and I. Marsman (2008), 'How international are executive boards of European MNCs? National diversity in 15 European countries', *European Management Journal*, **26**(3), 188–98.
Vaughan, A. (2014), 'Lego ends Shell partnership following Greenpeace campaign', *The Guardian*, accessed 25 August 2020 at https://www.theguardian.com/environment/2014/oct/09/lego-ends-shell-partnership-following-greenpeace-campaign.
Vogel, D. (2005), *The Market for Virtue: The Potential and Limits of Corporate Social Responsibility*, Washington, DC: Brookings Institution Press.
Voss, H. (2013), 'The global company', in J. Mikler (ed.), *The Handbook of Global Companies*, Oxford: Wiley-Blackwell, pp. 19–34.
Walmart (2013), *One Mission: Save Money. Live Better. Walmart 2103 Annual Report*, accessed 18 April 2017 at https://s2.q4cdn.com/056532643/files/doc_financials/2013/Annual/2013-annual-report-for-walmart-stores-inc_130221024708579502.pdf.
Walmart (2017), 'Apply to be a supplier', accessed 18 April 2017 at http://corporate.walmart.com/suppliers/apply-to-be-a-supplier.
Wilks, S. (2013), *The Political Power of the Business Corporation*, Cheltenham, UK and Northampton, MA, USA: Edward Elgar Publishing.

Windsor, D. (2007), 'Toward a global theory of cross-border and multilevel corporate political activity', *Business and Society*, **46**(2), 253–78.

World Bank (2019), 'Gross domestic product 2018', World Development Indicator Database, 1 July, accessed 30 August 2019 http://databank.worldbank.org/data/download/GDP.pdf.

Yaziji, M. and J. Doh (eds) (2009), *NGOs and Corporations: Conflict and Collaboration*, Cambridge, UK: Cambridge University Press.

Zadek, S. (2013), 'Will business save the world?', in J. Mikler (ed.), *The Handbook of Global Companies*, Oxford: Wiley-Blackwell, pp. 474–91.

2. Globalizing state capitalism? Selective internationalization of MNCs from emerging economies

Christian May

The ascent of emerging economies – understood as developing countries characterized by higher average growth rates than developed economies and increasing participation in the global economy – has been a defining moment in the global political economy of the twenty-first century. These economies not only grow strongly but, through engaging in organizations such as the G20 or BRICs (Brazil, Russia, India, and China), also actively take part in shaping the rules of the global economy. The rising trend of outward investments by their multinational corporations (MNCs) not only matters for the business landscape but also has political implications. From the very beginnings of MNC research in international political economy, the political power of large firms has been a major issue. It follows that the international ambitions of MNCs from emerging economies likely affect the distribution of power in the global political economy. The ability to shape transnational operations serves as an indicator for the corporate power of MNCs (e.g., see Mikler, 2018). As a consequence, they are able to use this structural power to influence politics on a global scale.

However, the political importance of these MNCs cannot simply be 'read off' their scale of outward investments. Since the most successful ones are embedded in national forms of modern state capitalism, their behavior always has a political component. It is the particular relationship between corporations and home states that lends MNCs from emerging economies a particular political role: they not only heavily shape the preferences of their home governments in the domestic arena but also on the global scale.

This chapter sheds light on the political power of MNCs from state capitalist economies. It empirically looks at the cases of Brazil and India, as there is much more to infer from these two emerging economies than from the analysis of Chinese firms (which has been amply done so far). It proceeds as follows: we first look at the actual extent of the internationalization of MNCs from emerging economies and argue that these do not simply follow the example of

Western MNCs. This is, as we argue, mainly due to their special relationship with government and bureaucracies that is characteristic for contemporary state capitalism. After setting out the general lines of this relationship, we turn to the Brazilian and Indian case to highlight how the internal mechanisms of state capitalism translate into particularistic business politics that transcend respective national economies. As the behavior of emerging economies in international trade and investment politics reflects the strength and preferences of their MNCs for a good part, we end this chapter with a discussion about the rationales that arise from the connection between states and MNCs in emerging economies.

THE INTERNATIONALIZATION OF CORPORATIONS FROM EMERGING ECONOMIES

The sheer growth and dynamics of emerging economies made it attractive for researchers of MNCs to focus on countries like China, India and beyond (see, inter alia, Goldstein, 2007, Nölke, 2014; Sauvant, 2008). Empirically, there has undoubtedly been an absolute increase in the internationalization activities by MNCs from them (Marinov and Marinova, 2013, p. 7; McAllister and Sauvant, 2013, p. 15), albeit not in a universal and unidirectional fashion. Instead, internationalization by those firms has been relatively limited and even declining in recent years (United Nations Conference on Trade and Development [UNCTAD], 2018). As Figure 2.1 shows, the relative weight of outward foreign direct investment (FDI) from emerging economies remained below the level of developed countries. This means that even though emerging economies grew strongly (in terms of gross domestic product [GDP]), their outward investment position has not been strengthened to similar degrees. Broadly, this means that emerging economies spend less of their economic growth on outward investment than Western countries. Apparently, MNCs from emerging economies do internationalize, but less than one might expect if they were to imitate the trajectories of Organisation for Economic Co-operation and Development (OECD) MNCs. Thus, the question is, how different are emerging economies' MNCs and how does politics matter in this regard?

One answer to be found in the theoretical literature focuses on firm capacities. According to Rugman (2009), emerging economy MNCs do not possess significant firm-specific advantages that would enable them to internationalize. Instead, MNCs from emerging economies only have locational advantages that are available to all firms, not just domestic ones (Hennart, 2012). From a firm perspective, there would exist no difference between emerging economy and Western MNCs – limited internationalization would simply be the result of less firm-specific advantages (Buckley et al., 2007). Yet, it is still unclear

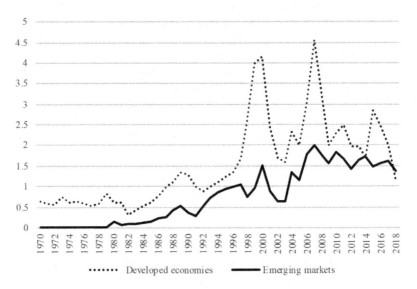

Source: UNCTAD (2019). 'Emerging markets' are those as classified by UNCTAD.

Figure 2.1   *FDI outflows by developed economies and emerging markets (as a percentage of GDP)*

how, for instance, MNCs from emerging economies would fund their foreign investments and how this differs from Western MNCs. Similarly, it has been an open question whether the choice of host countries is determined by the characteristics of the home country, that is, whether firms would choose a 'similar' investment location. Much of these questions relate to the specific characteristics of corporations from emerging economies, which include family ownership, group affiliation, pyramidal ownership systems, and associated forms of corporate finance within business networks and allied banks.

Therefore, recent studies argue that classic approaches need to be adjusted for firms from emerging economies because they do internationalize, although theory suggests otherwise. As a result, particular features of MNCs from emerging economies have been interpreted as firm-specific advantages, acknowledging the importance of the domestic institutional ecosystem (Hennart, 2012; Hernandez and Guillén, 2018; Ramamurti, 2012). This points to the discussion about firms' institutional and political context. It lends to the interpretation that firms from emerging economies would benefit less from their domestic embeddedness than their Western counterparts. This could relate either to a lack of outward foreign direct investment (OFDI) policies or a deficient institutional framework, or both (Globerman and Shapiro, 2008, p. 230; McAllister and Sauvant, 2013, pp. 32–3). However, studies rarely explicate the causal effect of such deficits – not least because the 'political factor' is often framed in general terms as 'policy support' (Bertoni, Elia and Rabbiosi, 2013) or simply as 'liberalization' (Kumar, 2007). Similarly, the institutional framework in which multinationals from emerging economies act is regularly presented as an indicator of government activity (Alcaraz and Zamilpa, 2017, p. 93; Wang et al., 2018). From an institutionalist perspective, it obviously takes much more than just government policies to create an institutional framework. In the same way, liberalization policies are not automatically OFDI policies (Pedersen, 2010). Most studies, however, fail to account for the particular institutional design of state capitalism. For instance, although the majority of studies about emerging market MNCs are actually just about Chinese MNCs, the particular nature of Chinese capitalism is missing from these analyses. This also holds for non-Chinese cases, where the characteristic relationship between state bureaucracies and firms remains obscured.

Studies that investigate the firm in state capitalism would indeed argue for the existence of a 'state-capitalist' form of internationalization. Often, this has been (and still is) discussed as instances of the state's intention to establish 'national champions' (e.g., see Musacchio and Lazzarini; 2014; Ozawa, 2014). From this perspective, states strategically intervene in the organization of domestic firms to increase their competitiveness on the global scene. Next to the creation of large corporations, states would also pursue a 'going out' strategy to penetrate foreign markets. Yet, as intuitive as this might sound, there is not enough strong evidence for the existence of such an explicit industrial strategy. For one, it is not clear why emerging economies would benefit from it. Usually, emerging economies are not swimming in capital and the merits of shifting scarce resources into going out initiatives are debatable (e.g., see Ramamurti, 2012). Furthermore, Asian catch-up examples show us that a smart developmental policy might rather include a selective *inward* FDI policy that pushes domestic firms into stronger competition, often vitalizing management and firm strategies. More specifically, there is hardly an explicit 'national champions' strategy to be found in relevant ministries. The industrial policies of countries like China, India or other developing countries usually do not contain references to a national champions strategy. There have been traces in the industrial policies of Brazil under the first and second Lula governments (see Alcaraz and Zamilpa, 2017; Balestro, 2018), but they have never seriously been met by efforts to implement them. India, as another emerging economy, had an FDI policy until 2003 that actually served as a barrier to outgoing strategies by large Indian firms. Before it embarked on the 'going global' strategy, China too followed a restrictive OFDI policy (Nölke et al., 2020; Xue and Han, 2010).

Altogether, previous research yields a somewhat divided picture: one strand focuses on firms but ignores the particular institutional configuration of contemporary state capitalism; the other strand largely portrays firms as mere 'servants' of strong states (but see Nölke, 2014). Conceptually, access to crucial state resources can be interpreted as a firm-specific, not location-specific advantage. Contrary to Rugman (2009), these resources are club goods that are only available to those firms that are part of local and regional growth alliances (Nölke et al., 2020). They allow firms to benefit from institutional advantages that are inscribed in modern state capitalism and help to explain why firms in emerging economies are less transnational than Western firms. Two implications to illustrate this point: as firms in emerging economies usually do not borrow on financial markets, their investments have less 'leverage' than those by Western MNCs, where investment banks not only devise full mergers and acquisitions (M&A) strategies but also help to organize M&A financing through global capital markets. Similarly, as corporate governance of most emerging economy corporations happens through families or networks and conglomerates, firms are strongly interested in keeping the production chain in domestic hands because any outsourcing would likely result in a decrease of corporate group control. Understanding the precise contours of state capitalism is thus required to account for the power and influence of firms in emerging economies.

THE POLITICAL INFLUENCE OF CORPORATIONS IN STATE CAPITALIST ECONOMIES

It is thus necessary to be more specific about how the outgoing activities of MNCs relate to the role of the state, politics, or government. Many studies point in the right direction when they assert 'that non-market mechanisms manifesting themselves through government involvement have a profound impact on the international trajectories of EMEs' (emerging market economies; Wang et al., 2018, p. 76). Therefore, the ways such non-market mechanisms can become effective for politically connected firms is a complicated but appropriate question. Yet, much of this research is biased in two related ways. First, much research empirically only deals with the Chinese case (e.g., see Buckley et al., 2007; Hong, Wang and Kafouros, 2015). For well-known reasons (the prominent position of the Chinese Communist Party [CCP], the absence of formal private property relations and particular historical conjuncture of China's rise, among others), this puts serious limits on the inferences for the whole state capitalist universe. Related to this, second, there is a tendency to portray the state as an omnipotent force that unilaterally directs the fates of domestic firms. Bureaucracies and agencies appear as all-powerful agents that govern the economy effectively from the top down. However, there is an abundance of cases where the state invests heavily into business-supporting policies and initiatives that do not yield the desired results in the end. Especially if we consider the establishment or support of an institutional framework decisive, as mentioned earlier, we must account for the fact that such cannot be 'implemented' by big government alone.

It is here, where the rich literature on state–business relations, especially in developing countries, becomes important (Chibber, 2003; Maxfield and Schneider, 1997; Schneider, 2004). In contrast to the widespread interpretation that such relations would compensate for weak institutional frameworks (Khanna, Palepu and Sinha, 2005), they do actually constitute a vital aspect of the institutional environment in which MNCs in emerging economies operate. It requires a balanced relationship between bureaucracies and firms to prevent capturing and predatory relations. This delicate relationship also implies that the state does not just use firms as policy instruments nor considers itself as a mere servant to business interests. Similarly, firms must not focus on their profit-maximizing strategies alone but must be receptive to the needs and interests of the state. The state would need to maintain an 'embedded autonomy' (Evans, 1995) with regard to the business sector to be a productive element in economic development, just as firms require a degree of autonomy to remain entrepreneurially active. Often, the supportive role of the state is narrowly understood as macroeconomic policies (such as liberalization or trade opening policies; see, for example, Kumar, 2007; Verma and Brennan, 2013). Such policies would affect all firms alike. The benefits of a balanced relationship between state and firms, however, would only be enjoyed by firms that play the game. Hence, there is always a degree of selectivity when it comes to state support measures.

The particular form of this balance (and the shape of political influence) depends on the internal organization of firms. The atomized stand-alone firm depends much more on a set of incentive-setting institutions than a business conglomerate that encompasses many crucial resources under its roof and in which inter-firm relations are established over a long period and grounded in personal connections. Where single firms would have to organize much of their business environment themselves, this framework is already set up within business groups, usually with clear rules. There are, for instance, no principal–agent problems in firms that are under family control (as many MNCs in emerging economies). As a consequence, emerging economy MNCs are much more autonomous than the ideal-typical firm in business research.

From this it follows that firms are less dependent on state resources but are themselves crucial for the attainment of economic policy goals. Therefore, it is not just that the state 'pushes' domestic firms to do things in the state's interest – firms also pressure the state so that it provides exclusive political support. Equally, states do not necessarily limit their supportive activities to the domestic realm. As an international political actor, the state actively shapes the global political economy in which its MNCs act. Although much focus of analysis of the state in industrial policies focuses on the domestic level, there is no reason why states would limit their influence to 'husbandry' (Evans, 1995) and exposing its firms to global competition once they are 'ready to go'. Instead, 'by virtue of its foreign policy activities, the state may provide both a kind of reputational international infrastructure and an institutional framework that is capable of supporting the country's own MNCs. The government can also assist internationally active companies through its network of diplomatic representation, its participation in international agreements (bilateral, regional, or multilateral), and its influence on those international institutions that create the international rules of FDI' (Pedersen, 2010, p. 62). Thus, we find two conditions: in emerging economies, states are much more responsive to business interests than often assumed. As they are part of growth coalitions, states are compelled to comply with their mutual obligations. Furthermore, states are able and willing to act upon these coalitions in their external relations. In conjunction, it opens up the analytical possibility that firms are not just obeying state rule but that the political influence of firms also turns states into foreign policy arms of domestic MNCs.

At first view, this suggests a pathway of influence that goes from MNCs to states, as laid out in the Chapter 1 of this book. However, this influence does not play out so much through lobbying, pressuring, or corruption – eventually leading towards state capturing. Instead, it derives from the forms of coordination within this state capitalist environment that are necessary for its persistence. Although the activity of MNCs in emerging economies does not aim at influencing global policy, it yields significant effects on global politics through the preferences of their home states. This becomes clear when we look at how the state arranges its external economic affairs in reaction to the requirements and demands of its MNCs.

STATE ASSISTANCE FOR THE EXPANSION OF BRAZILIAN AND INDIAN MNCS

The following discussion illustrates how Brazilian and Indian MNCs influence states to assist them in their OFDI activities in a selective (but exclusive) way. Both Brazil and India are examples of contemporary state capitalism, which derives their strength from large home markets. Within the developing world, MNCs from Brazil and India have been most expansive over the past two decades, with significant impact on OECD economies. They are more representative of the kind of political influence that firms have in state capitalism than would China be. As mentioned earlier, the high degree of state ownership of Chinese firms as well as the formidable bureaucratic structure that the CCP provides are but only two special conditions for Chinese capitalism, which heavily impinges upon the idea of (private) corporate power. Although we find the kind of entanglement between state and business in China as laid out earlier, it is undeniably the state that can unilaterally call the shots whenever it sees fit. Brazil and India, in turn, represent a group of emerging economies that aim to achieve growth through an increased activity of the state, which has, however, only limited capacities to steer the economy in full (see Nölke et al., 2020). At the same time, these countries usually have a 'heritage' of foreign investment and credit relations that they must deal with. In this sense, we can also obtain an informed guess about the influence of corporations in Mexico, Turkey, or Vietnam.

Unlike in former late industrializers like Japan or Korea, where firms had to orient towards the world market, firms in emerging economies do not necessarily do so. Those firms that choose to expand beyond their national borders would demand political facilitation for these operations. As 'partners', states are ready to provide it. They are not only dependent on the revenues from large firms but also have a strong interest that technological or managerial innovation would be channeled through indigenous, not foreign, firms (which the state would have less control over).

Brazil, for instance, never had a proper OFDI instrument, for obvious reasons: capital would be needed at home and foreign currency resources to fund outward investments were limited. After a decade of macroeconomic consolidation beginning in the early 1990s, the Brazilian state was able to focus not on keeping scarce resources at home but on boosting investments. Central to this strategy has been the national development bank Banco Nacional de Desenvolvimento Econômico e Social (BNDES). Instead of providing industry-wide incentives across the board, it specifically directed its funds to those firms that had good connections with the bureaucracy. From 2002 on, it also provided credit for funding outward expansion of Brazilian MNCs, although the developmental effect of OFDI is debatable (Masiero et al., 2014). The effects of this strategy are perhaps most clearly visible in the beef sector. Brazil's biggest meat-processing MNC, JBS, has been a relatively small outlet with revenues of 4 billion reals (R$; approx. 1.92 billion US$) in 2006 (de Moraes, 2017). By 2016, its revenues amounted to 170 billion R$ (42.3 billion US$). Over this period, JBS would receive almost 4 billion US$ in credit by BNDES. This has been used to acquire firms in the US and EU, making JBS the largest global meat-processing company. It has also been used, as was known by 2017, to bribe virtually all ministries and the top ranks of both government parties (Phillips, 2019). Of course, this is only one form of being 'politically connected'. Central individuals such as Marcus Vinícius Pratini de Moraes helped to maintain excellent connections to state officials: between 1970 and 2003 he served as Minister of Industry, Commerce and

Tourism, Mines and Energy and of Agriculture, and worked as an industry lobbyist (Doctor, 2017, p. 48). After these engagements, he entered JBS Investments (the holding company of JBS) until 2015, presumably to 'smooth' relations between the firm and public officials, which might explain why he is involved in a trading company in Panama (as revealed in the Panama Papers;[1] see International Consortium of Investigative Journalists [ICIJ], 2019).

These relations are crucial because the state supports its firms only selectively. JBS, together with a few other large agricultural firms stand out, but, on the whole, the agricultural sector does not receive much support from the state (da Conceição-Heldt, 2011, p. 96). As sectoral lobbying is relatively weak in the Brazilian polity, it is more efficient for firms to address political institutions directly. At the same time, it has become clear that JBS could only expand through entering foreign markets. But, as European and US markets for food products have been protected and multilateral negotiations over agricultural trade stagnated, firms would choose to acquire firms abroad as channels to their respective home markets. The Brazilian government could well negotiate in favor of its agricultural industry but whether it would be able to realize its interests in the end depended not least on the other negotiating parties. In the 2000s, this would have been a risky strategy as agriculture became a very contested issue. Unlike global trade, international investments are not regulated multilaterally, allowing much more discretion for firms to transfer capital. As a consequence, firms would ask for state support not in the realm of trade, but in investment.

This support came in many ways: primarily through direct financial assistance in the form of BNDES loans and asset ownership, but also by adhering to a selective strategy in the realm of international FDI regulation. BNDES had to take on the role as prime funder because the four big banks (mostly state-controlled) in Brazil are generally hesitant to fund large expansion projects. As domestic capital markets are too small to fund global expansion on a large scale, the Brazilian state would have to lend to large firms such as JBS directly to prevent them from leaving the country and orient towards global capital markets.

At the same time, Brazil's stance towards FDI regulation changed significantly. Until the early 2000s, its main objective has been to attract inward FDI. Brazil did negotiate a number of bilateral investment treaties (BITs), yet without ever ratifying a single one (Campello and Lemos, 2015). Following the strategic orientation towards investment-driven expansion of the domestic meat-processing industry, Brazil decided to renegotiate its BITs into the new type of Cooperation and Facilitation Investment Agreements (CFIAs) ,which should reflect the shifting interest from protection against excessive inward FDI to the promotion of outward FDI (Perrone and de Cerqueira César, 2015; Moraes and Hees, 2018). This new type of agreement 'emerged from close consultation between the Brazilian government and the private sector, which sought support in setting up shop in third countries' (Moraes and Hees, 2018, p. 198).

The influence of Brazilian MNCs changed the parameters of Brazil's negotiation position in the global political economy. By the early 2000s, multilateral trade negotiations had been stalled and it had become clear that the EU and US would not open their markets to Brazilian beef as much as expected. As JBS and other big agricultural players would not depend so much on trade facilitation, it allowed Brazil to follow a much more aggressive strategy in global trade negotiations. Big agriculture, in turn, would not demand the Brazilian government to be more accommodating in trade negotiations – to the detriment of smaller domestic producers.

A similar image emerges for Indian MNCs. Obviously, the exact configuration of the Indian case is different from the Brazilian situation: first, MNCs in India are mostly Indian MNCs, whereas we find substantial foreign MNCs in Brazil. Second, Indian MNCs are much more organized into business groups than their Brazilian peers. Third, India does not have a central development bank such as BNDES that would fund outward investment. Yet, the main thrust is similar: due to strong state–business relations, Indian MNCs are able to draw upon crucial domestic resources that allow significant outward investments. At the same time, the Indian government supports its MNCs on the international level. Naturally, this becomes visible in the politics of state-owned MNCs, particularly in the energy sector (Choudhury and Khanna, 2018). Yet, OFDI by Indian state-owned enterprises (SOEs) only account for less than 10 percent of all outward investments (Pradhan, 2017, pp. 61–2). More than two-thirds of all OFDI occurs through business group firms, while the share of capital-exporting stand-alone firms remains well below 10 percent. Interestingly, back in the 1980s, more than 20 percent of Indian OFDI was made by stand-alone firms. Hence, we observe a massive concentration of OFDI by large business conglomerates.

Again, given this structure of the corporate sector, it is misleading to portray a picture of state capitalism in which the (central) state would rule business all the way down. Instead, we have to acknowledge the structural power of large domestic businesses that manifests in at least three ways: a high institutional capacity *within* firms (the benefits of internalization, such as supplier relations and, crucially, sources for investment finance; see Nölke et al., 2020); a preferential access to large domestic markets; and excellent relations to top ranks in the bureaucracies that have been established over decades. Unlike in Brazil, MNCs in India are less dependent on financial and operational support from the state. However, since the Indian government always had stronger developmentalist objectives, Indian firms face a greater risk of the state sacrificing the success of domestic firms in favor of macroeconomic goals (which has a long tradition in independent India). Thus, it requires at least a residual macroeconomic perspective on the side of firms for the attainment of that 'embedded autonomy' necessary for state capitalism to be effective (Pedersen, 2010, p. 72).

To reiterate: unlike usual economic policies, the benefits of this 'special relationship' are only to be enjoyed by those firms that prove cooperative for joint growth projects. For instance, Pedersen lays out how the Birla conglomerate was at odds with the government's antitrust approach and, as a consequence, faced considerable hardship in their business operations (2010, p. 66). On the other side, when the Indian government set up the Investment Commission (2003–09) to formulate its investment policy, it had been staffed with, inter alia, Ratan Tata (head of Tata Industries) and Ashok Sekhar Ganguly, who served as chairman of Hindustan Unilever (and numerous board and political positions) before becoming a member of the Upper House. This ensured that any investment policy would meet the preferences of the relevant big businesses. The key element for successful state support therefore is not 'smart policies' but 'balanced state–business relations'. These are not easily implemented from above but once established, they create durable and reliable institutions. Primarily, they provide exclusive channels for the political influence of Indian multinationals.

The change in Indian investment policy has been relatively straightforward. Existing BITs, which have been negotiated in the 1990s for the most part, suffered from loopholes in Fair and Equitable Treatment (FET) as well as Most Favored Party Treatment (MFT), both of which have been used by foreign investors to sue the Indian government. The dominant interpretation puts this in the classic perspective of a developing country that sees itself under attack by foreign capital (Ranjan et al., 2018). From an analytical point of view, however, these BITs have been at odds with the model of state capitalism that came to full bloom in the 2000s. This model crucially depends on a strategic FDI policy where large domestic corporations have preferential (if not exclusive) access to domestic markets and that allows incoming FDI only as a competitive impulse for innovation or managerial modernization. Domestic markets play an even bigger role in India (compared to Brazil), therefore its protection is a much more important task for the governments to satisfy domestic firms and to uphold this particular capitalist system.

For this reason, a reform of FDI policy has been high on the Indian agenda (Dhar, Joseph and James, 2012). At the same time, OFDI by Indian companies rose tremendously. When Tata Steel acquired the Dutch steel producer Corus in 2007, it became clear that an Indian investment policy would not simply have to protect the national budget, but also the outward investments by Indian MNCs (EXIM Bank, 2014, p. 22). Consequently, all existing BITs had been terminated, to be replaced by a new bilateral investment treaty model. This new model explicitly excludes FET and MFT provisions (Department of Economic Affairs, 2016). It also does not include the local government level that protects local growth alliances between firms and municipalities from the 'shadow of litigation' that tilts the balance of state–business relations towards the firm side. At the same time, the Indian government demands a macroeconomic commitment as firms must 'recognize that corporations too have obligations towards the society' (ibid.). In return, the Indian government would acknowledge the preferences of domestic MNCs in international trade politics as it 'aims to use the revised BIT framework to negotiate future Investment Chapters in Free Trade Agreements' (Ranjan et al., 2018, p. 10). As there is more at stake in trade-related investment provisions for Indian MNCs (and therefore, for the Indian political economy) than for Western MNCs, the Indian government takes its mandate by the large domestic firms seriously and is not willing to seriously negotiate the inclusion of investor rights and competition policy into international trade agreements (May and Nölke, 2014).

Thus, although the concrete patterns differ, both Indian and Brazilian MNCs are able to influence global politics through the close and interpersonal relations they have with relevant bureaucracies. MNCs from different countries need different things: Brazilian firms want capital and market access, while Indian corporations require non-universal investment protection. Obviously, there are many firms with different preferences but, without access to crucial growth alliances, their interests are usually sidelined. The influence of MNCs from emerging economies on global politics therefore is usually selective and particularistic, with priorities given to the national level.

CONCLUSION

This chapter argues that it is crucial to look at the institutional logics of state capitalism to understand how firms influence politics – domestically as well as internationally. Previous research on MNCs from emerging economies tend to treat them not much differently than Western MNCs, thereby neglecting the difference that institutional and political embeddedness makes. Contemporary state capitalism is essentially non-liberal, but not statist. Markets play a minor role, but it is not characterized by state 'dirigisme' either. Its main elements are held together by a 'social' mode of coordination that is embodied in growth alliances or communities, supported by interpersonal relationships and a sense of reciprocity. Unlike Western capitalisms, which are often coordinated through markets principally open for everyone, contemporary state capitalism essentially divides insiders and outsiders. The political influence does not simply show up in lobbying or pressuring on particular issues in an ad hoc fashion, but also manifests in the establishment of long-standing (interpersonal) relationships.

This logic of state capitalism results in a selective stance towards investment promotion that is very much firm oriented (rather than market oriented). The examples of India and Brazil show how FDI policies become more restrictive and, therefore, particular firms can draw advantages from an FDI policy that would be tailored to them. This obviously creates winners and losers. Winners, such as JBS, greatly increase their options for outward expansion while the losers are excluded from the relevant growth coalitions. As these coalitions are at the heart of state capitalism, there is a direct connection between MNCs and governments with regard to foreign economic policy. Naturally, the perspective of these growth communities is provincial and national. Neither macroeconomic growth nor global economic relations are a top priority.

The nature of state–business relations in emerging economies implies that domestic firms have political influence in their own right. This is not because the state is captured by private interests but because this special state–business relationship is part of a functioning model of state capitalism. Yet, it translates into a particular form of influence on the international level: MNCs from emerging economies are not interested in influencing global politics as such. Speaking about pathways of influence on global politics suggests an intentional activity on the side of private actors to shape global economic governance as it is organized on the international level. However, MNCs from emerging economies only want particularistic support (also with regard to their domestic competitors), which, in turn, has global effects. It manifests rather in a lack of activity in the regulation of global economic relations because firms from emerging economies have little benefit but much to lose from global liberalization of trade and investment.

Since MNCs from emerging economies ask for particularistic benefits from their states, they immediately, albeit unintentionally, influence the position of their governments in multilateral negotiations. Putting it bluntly, the external behavior by emerging economies is shaped by domestic considerations. Hence, the political influence of MNCs from emerging economies must be theorized accordingly. As the division between the 'domestic' and the 'international' is fundamental for emerging economies, this influence on global politics is perhaps better approached as foreign economic policy (Katzenstein, 1976; Nölke et al., 2015). It is therefore necessary to shed light on the domestic arena to understand the power of large domestic MNCs for global politics. While earlier theories of this distinctive two-level game have been about the demands of national voters and how these translate into international economic policy (Moravcsik, 1997; Putnam, 1988), a political economy approach to such two-level approaches would have to include firms as relevant actors too.

Within such a theoretical framework, the political influence of MNCs in emerging economies differs from their OECD counterparts in both scope and style. First, unlike Western MNCs, who would push for universal liberalization of trade and investment, MNCs from emerging economies would have rather conservative and defensive interests. Second, their 'channels of influence' are naturally more direct and personal. Close relations to the political sphere are not suspicious; however, the terms of access are particularistic – firms cannot approach governments with any demands nor would large-scale lobbying be very effective.

This is by no means exclusive to emerging economies but highlights alternative mechanisms for business to influence global politics. In the light of an increasing sentiment that global economic relations are essentially a zero-sum game, particularistic pro-business politics are to become an option for Western economies as well (see Zingales, 2016). However, unlike in contemporary state capitalism, this form of state–business relations is not embedded in a coherent institutional arrangement, which gives rise to problems for Western capitalism in the long run.

NOTE

1. The Panama Papers are 11.5 million leaked documents that detail financial and attorney–client information for more than 214 488 offshore entities. The documents, some dating back to the 1970s, were created by, and taken from, Panamanian law firm and corporate service provider Mossack Fonseca, and were anonymously leaked in April 2016.

REFERENCES

Alcaraz, J. and J. Zamilpa (2017), 'Latin American governments in the promotion of outward FDI', *Transnational Corporations*, **24**(2), 91–108.
Balestro, M.V. (2018), 'The varying role of the state in the making of Latin American multinationals', in A. Nölke and C. May (eds), *Handbook of the International Political Economy of the Corporation*, Cheltenham, UK and Northampton, MA, USA: Edward Elgar Publishing, pp. 215–28.
Bertoni, F., S. Elia and L. Rabbiosi (2013), 'Outward FDI from the BRICs: trends and patterns of acquisitions in advanced countries', in M.A. Marinov and S.T. Marinova (eds), *Emerging Economies and Firms in the Global Crisis*, Basingstoke: Palgrave Macmillan, pp. 47–82.
Buckley, P.J., L.J. Clegg and A.R. Cross et al. (2007), 'The determinants of Chinese outward foreign direct investment', *Journal of International Business Studies*, **38**(4), 499–518.
Campello, D. and L. Lemos (2015), 'The non-ratification of bilateral investment treaties in Brazil: a story of conflict in a land of cooperation', *Review of International Political Economy*, **22**(5), 1055–86.
Chibber, V. (2003), *Locked in Place: State-Building and Late Industrialization in India*, Princeton, NJ: Princeton University Press.
Choudhury, P. and T. Khanna (2018), 'Toward resource independence – why state-owned entities become multinationals: an empirical study of India's public

R&D laboratories', in A. Cuervo-Cazurra (ed.), *State-Owned Multinationals: Governments in Global Business*, Cham: Springer, pp. 145–74.

da Conceição-Heldt, E. (2011), *Negotiating Trade Liberalization at the WTO Domestic Politics and Bargaining Dynamics*, Basingstoke: Palgrave Macmillan.

de Moraes, M. (2017), 'Saiba como a JBS sugou o BNDES para expandir seus negócios', *Estado de Minais*, 23 May, accessed 14 May 2019 at https://www.em.com.br/app/noticia/economia/2017/05/23/internas_economia,871042.

Department of Economic Affairs (2016), *Transforming the International Investment Agreement Regime: The Indian Experience*, accessed 14 August 2020 at https://worldinvestmentforum.unctad.org/wp-content/uploads/2015/03/India_side-event-Wednesday_model-agreements.pdf.

Dhar, B., R. Joseph and T.C. James (2012), 'India's bilateral investment agreements: time to review', *Economic and Political Weekly*, **47**(52), 113–22.

Doctor, M. (2017), *Business–State Relations in Brazil: Challenges of the Port Reform Lobby*, New York: Routledge.

Evans, P. (1995), *Embedded Autonomy: States and Industrial Transformation*, Princeton, NJ: Princeton University Press.

EXIM Bank (2014), 'Outward direct investment from India: trends, objectives and policy perspectives', *Occasional Papers*, No. 165.

Globerman, S. and D.M. Shapiro (2008), 'Outward FDI and the economic performance of emerging markets', in K.P. Sauvant (ed.), *The Rise of Transnational Corporations from Emerging Markets Threat or Opportunity?*, Cheltenham, UK and Northampton, MA, USA: Edward Elgar Publishing, pp. 229–71.

Goldstein, A. (2007), *Multinational Companies from Emerging Economies: Composition, Conceptualization and Direction in the Global Economy*, Basingstoke: Palgrave Macmillan.

Hennart, J.-F. (2012), 'Emerging market multinationals and the theory of the multinational enterprise', *Global Strategy Journal*, **2**(3), 168–87.

Hernandez, E. and M.F. Guillén (2018), 'What's theoretically novel about emerging-market multinationals?', *Journal of International Business Studies*, **49**(1), 24–33.

Hong, J., C. Wang and M. Kafouros (2015), 'The role of the state in explaining the internationalization of emerging market enterprises', *British Journal of Management*, **26**(1), 45–62.

International Consortium of Investigative Journalists [ICIJ] (2019), 'Offshore Leaks Database', accessed 21 June 2019 at https://www.icij.org/investigations/panama-papers/.

Katzenstein, P.J. (1976), 'International relations and domestic structures: foreign economic policies of advanced industrial states', *International Organization*, **30**(1), 1–45.

Khanna, T., K.G. Palepu and J. Sinha (2005), 'Strategies that fit emerging markets', *Harvard Business Review*, **83**(3), 6–15.

Kumar, N. (2007), 'Emerging TNCs: trends, patterns and determinants of outward FDI by Indian enterprises', *Transnational Corporations*, **16**(1), 1–26.

Marinov, M.A. and S.T. Marinova (2013), 'The global crisis and the world: the cases of emerging and developed economies', in M.A. Marinov and S.T. Marinova (eds), *Emerging Economies and Firms in the Global Crisis*, Basingstoke: Palgrave Macmillan, pp. 1–13.

Masiero, G., M.H. Ogasavara, L. Caseiro and S. Ferreira (2014), 'Financing the expansion of Brazilian multinationals into Europe: the role of the Brazilian Development

Bank (BNDES)', in A. Nölke (ed.), *Multinational Corporations from Emerging Markets: State Capitalism 3.0*, Basingstoke: Palgrave Macmillan, pp. 130–54.

Maxfield, S. and B.R. Schneider (1997), *Business and the State in Developing Countries*, Ithaca, NY: Cornell University Press.

May, C. and A. Nölke (2014), 'BRIC capitalism and the new illiberal global order', in D.A. Deese (ed.), *The International Political Economy of Trade*, Cheltenham, UK and Northampton, MA, USA: Edward Elgar Publishing, pp. 450–70.

McAllister, G. and K.P. Sauvant (2013), 'Foreign direct investment by emerging economy multinationals: coping with the global crisis', in M.A. Marinov and S.T. Marinova (eds), *Emerging Economies and Firms in the Global Crisis*, Basingstoke: Palgrave Macmillan, pp. 14–46.

Mikler, J. (2018), *The Political Power of Global Corporations*, Cambridge, UK: Polity Press.

Moraes, H.C. and F. Hees (2018), 'Breaking the BIT mold: Brazil's pioneering approach to investment agreements', *AJIL Unbound*, **112**, 197–201.

Moravcsik, A. (1997), 'Taking preferences seriously: a liberal theory of international politics', *International Organization*, **51**(4), 513–53.

Musacchio, A. and S.G. Lazzarini (2014), *Reinventing State Capitalism: Leviathan in Business, Brazil and Beyond*, Cambridge, MA: Harvard University Press.

Nölke, A. (ed.) (2014), *Multinational Corporations from Emerging Markets: Multinational Corporations from Emerging Markets: State Capitalism 3.0*, Basingstoke: Palgrave Macmillan.

Nölke, A., T. ten Brink, S. Claar and C. May (2015), 'Domestic structures, foreign economic policies and global economic order: implications from the rise of large emerging economies', *European Journal of International Relations*, **21**(3), 538–67.

Nölke, A., T. ten Brink, C. May and S. Claar (2020), *State-Permeated Capitalism in Large Emerging Economies*, London: Routledge.

Ozawa, T. (2014), 'Multinationals as an instrument of catch-up industrialization: understanding the strategic links between state and industry in emerging markets', in A. Nölke (ed.), *Multinational Corporations from Emerging Markets: State Capitalism 3.0*, Basingstoke: Palgrave Macmillan, pp. 31–73.

Pedersen, J.D. (2010), 'Political factors behind the rise of Indian multinational enterprises: an essay in political economy', in K.P. Sauvant and J.P. Pradhan (eds), *The Rise of Indian Multinationals: Perspectives on Indian Outward Foreign Direct Investment*, New York: Palgrave Macmillan, pp. 57–78.

Perrone, N.M. and G.R. de Cerqueira César (2015), 'Brazil's bilateral investment treaties: more than a new investment treaty model?', *Columbia FDI Perspectives*, No. 159.

Phillips, D. (2019), 'The swashbuckling meat tycoons who nearly brought down a government', *The Guardian*, 2 July, accessed 10 July 2019 at https://www.theguardian.com/environment/2019/jul/02/swashbuckling-meat-tycoons-nearly-brought-down-a-government-brazil.

Pradhan, J.P. (2017), 'Indian outward FDI: a review of recent developments', *Transnational Corporations*, **24**(2), 43–70.

Putnam, R.D. (1988), 'Diplomacy and domestic politics: the logic of two-level games', *International Organization*, **42**(3), 427–60.

Ramamurti, R. (2012), 'What is really different about emerging market multinationals?', *Global Strategy Journal*, **2**(1), 41–7.

Ranjan, P., H. Vardhana Singh, K. James and R. Singh (2018), 'India's model bilateral investment treaty: are we too risk averse?', *Brookings India IMPACT Series*, August 2018.

Rugman, A. (2009), 'Theoretical aspects of MNEs from emerging markets', in R. Ramamurti and J.V. Singh (eds), *Emerging Multinationals in Emerging Markets*, Cambridge, UK: Cambridge University Press, pp. 42–63.

Sauvant, K.P. (ed.) (2008), *The Rise of Transnational Corporations from Emerging Markets: Threat or Opportunity?*, Cheltenham, UK and Northampton, MA, USA: Edward Elgar Publishing, pp. 229–71.

Schneider, B.R. (2004), *Business Politics and the State in Twentieth-Century Latin America*, Cambridge, UK: Cambridge University Press.

United Nations Conference on Trade and Development [UNCTAD] (2018), *World Investment Report 2018*, Geneva: UNCTAD.

United Nations Conference on Trade and Development [UNCTAD] (2019), 'UNCTADStat Database', accessed 12 June 2019 at https://unctadstat.unctad.org/EN.

Verma, R. and L. Brennan (2013), 'An analysis of the macroeconomic determinants of Indian outward foreign direct investment', in M.A. Marinov and S.T. Marinova (eds), *Emerging Economies and Firms in the Global Crisis*, Basingstoke: Palgrave Macmillan, pp. 137–53.

Wang, C., J. Hong, M. Kafouros and M. Wright (2018), 'Exploring the role of government involvement in outward FDI from emerging economies', in A. Cuervo-Cazurra (ed.), *State-Owned Multinationals Governments in Global Business*, Cham: Springer, pp. 75–110.

Xue, Q. and B. Han (2010), 'The role of government policies in promoting outward foreign direct investment from emerging markets: China's experience', in K.P. Sauvant, G. McAllister and W.A. Maschek (eds), *Foreign Direct Investments from Emerging Markets: The Challenges Ahead*, New York: Palgrave Macmillan: pp. 305–24.

Zingales, L. (2016), 'Donald Trump, crony capitalist', *New York Times*, 23 February, accessed 20 March at https://www.nytimes.com/2016/02/23/opinion/campaign-stops/donald-trump-crony-capitalist.html.

3. MNCs and state infrastructural power[1]

Linda Weiss and Elizabeth Thurbon

Since the end of the Cold War, the subject of American power has preoccupied scholars across the globe. Carefully crafted enquiries into the nature, sources, and consequences of US power have advanced our understanding of its multidimensional features. Even so, the power of the American state still excites controversy – producing two quite different images in the literature.

On one hand, we are told that the US is as strong as ever. In this argument, the focus is on 'structural' power. Structural power is understood in this case as the capacity to project power abroad; it is manifested principally in the ability to set the rules of the game in key areas such as production, investment, knowledge, finance and trade in ways that tilt the playing field to one's own advantage (cf. Nye, 1990; Strange, 1988). Most recent arguments in this genre focus principally on US control over a disproportionate share of global production flows and resulting profits, and the unilateral ability to create credit in the global economy (Cohen, 2015; Schwartz, 2016a; Starrs, 2013). Whether we focus on finance, currency, trade or investment, many observe that US structural power has remained robust in the postwar period (for example, Cohen, 2018; Helleiner, 2014).

On the other hand, we find the mirror image that emphasizes not the external features of US power, but its decaying domestic foundations. Here, analysts highlight burgeoning debt, crumbling infrastructure, second-rate schools, industrial decline, slow growth, soaring inequality and dysfunctional politics (Fukuyama, 2014; Haas, 2013; Johnson and Kwak, 2013; Lazonick, 2014). In this genre, America's pre-eminent position in the global economy is under threat, less from external influences than from policy choices within.

Each image provides a discrete perspective on US power using data drawn from different domains – chiefly externally or internally focused. The different foci allow that both images may be true. Nevertheless, they are often presented as antithetical positions in a wider debate about the myths and reality of US decline (cf. Starrs, 2013). We take a different tack. We see these two realities as deeply interconnected. To fully grasp those interconnections, we need to bring back into discussion of American power and its foundations an aspect that is largely overlooked in this debate – one that spans both international and domestic spheres. This is the state's infrastructural power, briefly defined here as the state's spatial reach: viz. the capacity to penetrate society, to extract and deploy resources in the territory over which it rules, and thereby implement logistically its decisions throughout the realm (Mann, 1984, p. 189).

We propose that what is widely known as 'structural power' can be fruitfully understood as an outward-facing expression of the American state's infrastructural power. This is because at the most fundamental level, structural power involves the ability to extend – through negotiation and consent – the reach and writ of the American state into foreign jurisdictions. International organizations provide one obvious pathway for states to externalize their infrastructural power. As Wade observed, the US has used the World Bank 'as an instrument of its own external infrastructural power to a greater degree than any other state' (1996, p. 15).

We further contend that throughout the postwar period, a close partnership with private actors allowed the American state to pursue a 'grand strategy' centered on maintaining an open economic order to benefit US corporations (van Apeldoorn and de Graaff, 2015). To this end, it worked to shape the global rules of the economic game in America's own image, 'creating a world open to US economic penetration' (Layne, 2006, cited in van Apeldoorn and de Graff, 2015, p. 11). The vector for this was US multinational corporations (MNCs).

Since the 1980s, however, a kind of perverse relationship has emerged between these three faces of infrastructural power (depicted in Figure 3.1). US structural power remains robust – not least because of the global role of the US dollar, the 'indispensable currency' (Cohen, 2015). However, the extension of that power in specific arenas, chiefly intellectual property, is now impacting in a deleterious way on infrastructural power at home. We refer to this dynamic as a power paradox – a form of blowback. Our central argument is that by exercising its infrastructural power internationally (*qua* extending its intellectual property rights [IPRs] rules into foreign jurisdictions), the state centered on Washington has thereby strengthened its structural power and achieved significant benefits for its MNCs. Yet, as MNCs have benefited from these actions, by the same token they have diminished the American state's infrastructural power at home. While US structural power remains strong, we therefore question whether it is sufficient to offset the erosion of its extractive and (above all) its transformative capacities.

One of the benefits of the concept of infrastructural power is that it compels us to treat the organizations of the state and the organizations of society as analytically distinct, even if deeply interconnected. This allows us to study MNCs' pathways of influence by avoiding the elision of corporate and state interests, as if a unified entity. This elision occurs in arguments that assess the benefits of structural power as they flow to corporations – and then assume that what is good for US corporations is necessarily also good for the US state. As Starrs

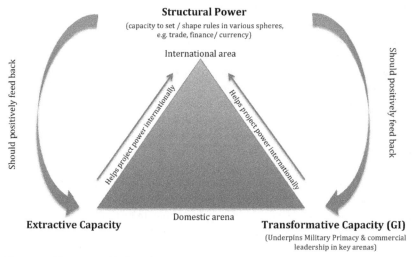

Note: GI = governed independence.

Figure 3.1   Three faces of infrastructural power

(2013, p. 828) has recently argued, since US MNCs are the most profitable in the world and indeed are racking up higher profits than ever, so the power of the US remains as great as ever. In his words, 'the American state–society complex remains the richest and most powerful in the world'. In Starr's formulation, 'society' is a proxy for US MNCs.

But is it logical to assume that what benefits its MNCs also benefits the American state? Does the state enjoy the results of its exercising structural power if the benefits flow mainly in one direction? We consider how the US state has *internationalized* its infrastructural power – which manifests as structural power – through trade agreements that globalize its intellectual property rules. We then ask the critical question: how does *the state* benefit from its ability to internationalize its rules? If the state does indeed benefit – as proponents of the structural approach tend to assume – then we would expect to find that its rule-globalizing ability, at the very least, preserves if not reinforces its infrastructural power at home. Specifically, we would expect to find that structural power equips the state with the capacity to mobilize and deploy resources in order to pursue transformative projects within its own territory. We begin by elaborating the concept of infrastructural power and bringing it into dialogue with the concept of structural power. We then introduce the three propositions that form our argument. In the remaining sections, we develop these propositions in light of the available evidence.

INFRASTRUCTURAL POWER

The concept of infrastructural power (Mann, 1984) is arguably one of the most useful in the social and political sciences. It has helped not only to illuminate the extraordinary capacity, reach, and impact of the modern state with regard to its pre-industrial predecessor, but also to cast light on why some modern states appear more able than others to execute their decisions and pursue their ambitions. It has been applied to explain failed or weak states in the developing world (for example, Centeno, 1997; Lucas, 1998), to account for developmental blockages or breakthroughs in transition economies (Stoner-Weiss, 2002; Zhu, 2003), to revise conventional explanations for the rise of the West (Hall, 1985), to explain why some states, past and present, have been more effective than others in climbing the ladder of development (Weiss and Hobson, 1995), to analyze contemporary power differences among industrial states in an era of globalization (Weiss, 2006), and most recently to better understand America's postwar rise as a high-tech hegemon (Weiss, 2014). In addition, many have explored various aspects of these issues without engaging explicitly with the concept.

Mann's concept of infrastructural power has been most fruitfully applied to explain broad historical differences in types of state, which derive from the nature of their autonomy and capacities in the domestic realm. In its original formulation, Mann distinguishes 'infrastructural power' not only from 'despotic power' (*power over* – typical of pre-industrial states), but also from the more conventional distributive (zero-sum) power that has prevailed in the social science literature. While modern states lack the ability to do whatever they wish, their autonomy derives in part from their 'unique ability to provide a territorially centralised form of organization' (Mann, 1984, p. 109): 'Only the state is inherently centralised over a delimited territory over which it has authoritative power' (p. 123). Its autonomy derives also in part from the multiplicity of essential functions (for example, internal order, military defense/ aggression, communications infrastructures, economic redistribution) that the state provides. Since these functions serve different constituents, the state is not reducible to one particular set of interests, even when a particular social group gains disproportionate influence over some functions.

In so distinguishing the power of the modern (bureaucratic-democratic) state from its absolutist predecessors, Mann also draws attention to its *relational* character: the state's infrastructural power is quintessentially collective and negotiated power acquired *through* civil society, based on consent and legitimation. Far from being a form of power 'over' society, infrastructural power is grounded in the 'organizational entwining' between state and non-state actors (Soifer and vom Hau, 2008, p. 3), and thereby best characterized as 'a two-way street'. This pioneering view of state power is a radical departure from 'statist' theories. State institutions and actors are still the analytical starting point, but power hinges on the nature of relationships forged with wider social groupings. As various scholars have observed in applying the concept, 'The relational nature of infrastructural power allows analysts to move past debates that juxtapose state and society as opponents to examine the varied forms of their interaction' (ibid.; see also Hobson, 1997; Konings, 2011; Weiss, 2003).

When specifying the mechanisms of infrastructural power in the domestic sphere, two faces of infrastructural power – extractive and transformative – have attracted most analytical attention. Extractive capacity refers to the ability to reach into society in order to mobilize and extract resources, not simply of the material kind (via taxation, for example) but also of the human variety (for example, mobilizing support for defensive and aggressive military action). Routine extractive capacity hinges on consent from civil society (Tilly, 1975; Weiss and Hobson, 1995).

The second aspect – transformative capacity – refers in this context to the state's ability to drive through its innovation projects in order to maintain the technological leadership that lies at the core of US national security strategy (Weiss, 2014). To bring their projects to life and maintain their technological advantage, agencies with national security missions (primarily defense, energy, health, and space) need access to advanced capabilities in the private sector. Thus, the state through its mission agencies regularly enjoins cooperation and support from private enterprise – notably innovative firms and start-ups. As far as the state's high-risk innovation projects are envisioned, initiated, funded (partly or wholly), and performance monitored by the mission agencies, we apply the term 'governed interdependence' to conceptualize this collaborative state–business relationship. As a dimension of infrastructural power, transformative capacity is thus grounded in collaborative arrangements between state authorities and economic actors.

Significantly, however, when discussing the foundations of America's external/global economic and military power, transformative capacity has rarely rated a mention. The focus instead rests almost exclusively on America's 'structural power'. Structural power in our account is the third face of infrastructural power. It represents the *international reach* of the American state, whereby the state is able to extend its rules – through negotiation and consent – into foreign national and international jurisdictions.

We are less concerned with how the US comes to acquire structural power, or the agents who choose to exercise it, than the *outcomes* of the exercise of that power – in particular, its impact on the state's extractive and transformative capacities. This entails treating state interests and corporate interests as analytically distinct, even when decision-making elites in both arenas have been deeply interconnected. The depth and extent of those interconnections are the subject of several studies, most lucidly examined through network analysis in the work of van Apeldoorn and de Graaff (2015).

We should not assume, however, that the *outcomes* of the joint pursuit of shared goals will be mutually beneficial. It is one thing for the state and MNCs to share the goal of market opening for corporate enrichment. It is quite another to assume enhancement of state power from corporate enrichment, as some have done (for example, Starrs, 2013). Hence, our insistence that when assessing the implications of the state's extension of its power abroad, it makes analytical sense to distinguish between its implications for corporate *actors* on one hand, and state *institutions* on the other.

According to some accounts, US economic power is now stronger than ever, ostensibly bolstered by being home to the world's most globalized and most profitable companies. Globalized production may indeed have strengthened US corporations – most notably those rich in intellectual property, but has it also strengthened the state's domestic infrastructural power?

It is the domestic effects of the exercise of structural power (*qua* statecraft), the third face of infrastructural power, that most concern us. Taking up this issue, we appraise the extent to which the state's extractive and transformative capacities may have been weakened by Washington's internationalization of US IPRs, *despite* the growing economic power of its corporate actors. (There are, of course, other facets of projecting US structural power abroad, notably foreign investment rules and dispute settlement processes.)

Our argument emphasizes a paradox. The American state has been front and center of the process that has effectively internationalized US-style IPRs, giving them global reach through the World Trade Organization's (WTO) Trade-Related Aspects of Intellectual Property Rights agreement (TRIPS)[2] and its successive iterations. By negotiating trade agreements that extend US intellectual property rules into foreign jurisdictions, the state centered on Washington has internationalized its infrastructural power – and thereby achieved significant benefits for its multinational corporations. Yet, through these same actions (the exercise of structural power), US state authorities have fostered the conditions that are steadily diminishing its infrastructural power at home.

To advance our argument, we develop three propositions. First, we contest the conflation of US corporate power with US state power. Clearly, these two power entities have in many ways been in step with each other. Notably, the federal government has been a key actor in strengthening corporate power abroad through trade agreements that protect American IPRs. Authoritative accounts argue that TRIPS, instituted in 1995 with the launching of the WTO, was dictated by powerful MNCs that sought to mold international law to protect their markets (Drahos and Braithwaite, 2002; Sell, 2003). In effect, through coordinated representation of their interests via the Intellectual

Property Committee (IPC) that they formed with the purpose of 'globalizing enforceable intellectual property standards' (Drahos and Braithwaite, 2002, p. 71), it is claimed they 'made public law for the world' (Sell, 2003, p. 96). This enhanced MNC intellectual property rights globally, thereby safeguarding their investments and operations across multiple jurisdictions. Extending American intellectual property (IP) laws abroad through negotiation and consent represented the internationalization of the US state's infrastructural power. Thus externalized, the reach and writ of the American state into foreign jurisdictions also paved the way for massive growth in the profitability of its MNCs.

Second, we propose that whatever alignment may have existed in an earlier period, a growing divergence is now apparent between US corporate power and state power – understood here in the first conventional sense of *extractive* capacity. So, while US corporations (not solely, but chiefly IP-dominant companies) have massively increased their global profits, the state has not received a rising share of the winnings (aka rent) in the form of increased tax revenue.

Worse still for the state's extractive capacity are the *economy-wide effects*: IP-heavy companies have shown greater propensity to downsize labor and distribute production abroad, to retain profits offshore and to pare back investment and employment at home, resulting in sluggish economic growth, stagnant wages and a shortfall in federal revenues relative to non-discretionary outlays. Importantly, this problem has not been offset by America's structural power in other arenas.

Third, and most important, America's hegemonic power has never rested primarily on its extractive capacity – or on its structural (dollar) power: US military and commercial strength has been grounded in its '*transformative* capacity' – the state's ability to catalyze virtually all the major technological innovations that drive the modern postwar economy and underpin its prosperity. Radical innovations, which include communications satellites, microelectronics, computers, software, biotech, the Internet, even driverless vehicles, all owe their existence to a state that since World War II has based its national security strategy on the pursuit of technological supremacy. This security imperative has given rise to (a state with) an extraordinary appetite for risk, hence prepared to pour massive resources into long-term projects, often with uncertain outcomes. As mentioned, this capacity has resided chiefly in the national security state (*qua*, a cluster of federal agencies charged with security [or dual] missions), which centralize responsibility for science and technology.

Of major importance to our argument, transformative capacity in the US depends on collaboration with private enterprise with the capabilities to bring frontier technologies to market (via development of prototypes, testing, and scaling up) and the willingness to partner with the state in the pursuit of its transformative goals. Research shows that this capacity is now under stress –

and it is our argument that this is in no small measure due to the globalization of production, driven principally by IP-intensive firms. As production moves offshore, this has created large holes in the industrial ecosystem, which impede the translation of innovative ideas into marketable products, putting at risk the state's transformative capacity and thus its long-standing goal of technological supremacy and military primacy, as we elaborate below.

IPRS AND EXTRACTIVE CAPACITY

IPRs have enabled massive profit shifting, which has impacted on the state's extractive capacities in two main ways. First, profit shifting has weakened the reach of the state, making it harder to collect corporate tax (see Figure 3.2). Second, profit shifting has major flow-on effects throughout the economy that diminish the broader resource base available to the state. The flow-on effect of profit shifting is manifested above all in reduced corporate investment and thus domestic growth. This flow-on effect of profit shifting thus not only diminishes the state's domestic resource base, it also weakens the social contract as well-paid jobs disappear and income inequality widens (the Trump factor being one recent outcome).

Data covering several decades reveal four main trends: global company profits are ballooning, corporate tax revenue is plateauing, domestic investment is declining, and federal deficits are growing as the jobless rate grows.

Corporate Profits, Profit Shifting, and Tax Revenue

Since the mid-1980s, corporate profits have soared while corporate tax revenue has barely moved (Figure 3.2). This is the case whether we focus on before- or after-tax profits. The dips show recessions, but the overall trend is upward since the mid-1980s. While before-tax profits rose from 6.7 percent to just under 12 percent of gross domestic product (GDP) in the period since 1985, after-tax profits (the dotted line) doubled from around 4.4 percent to over 8.8 percent of GDP in 2015.

Indeed, as the solid line in Figure 3.2 indicates, the surging global profits of US corporations have not translated into surging tax revenues for the federal government. On the contrary, there is a growing gap between profits made and tax collected. This is evident also in the narrowing gap between before- and after-tax profits (dashed and solid lines); it shows that US corporations are holding onto a larger slice of their profits. Put simply, since the 1980s, corporate tax revenues have not kept pace with the dramatic increase in corporate profits.

Notably for our argument, IPR-intensive industries have led this profits charge, well documented by other scholars (see Schwartz, 2016b). Our

— —Corporate profits (before tax) ━━Corporate profits (after tax) ·····Corporate tax revenue

Source: Compiled by authors from Federal Reserve Bank of St Louis Economic Data (FRED) (for corporate profits, aggregated from US Bureau of Economic Analysis) and US Congressional Budget Office Data Tool (for corporate tax revenue).

Figure 3.2   *US corporate profits vs US corporate tax (as a percentage of GDP)*

summary of the highlights in Table 3.1 is indicative; it shows how global profits of firms in the most IP-intensive industries far exceeded the national average of 5.9 percent.[3] By comparison, in the four most profitable, most IPR-intensive US industries, profits as a percentage of global sales reached 21.4 percent in software and programming, 15.3 percent in computer services, 10.4 percent in computer hardware, and 8.9 percent in pharmaceuticals – the latter somewhat losing the edge as their blockbuster drugs come off patent.

Table 3.1   *Global profits by US firms in the four most IP-intensive industries (percentage of global sales)*

National (US) Average	Software and Programming	Computer Services	Computer Hardware	Pharmaceuticals
5.9	21.4	15.3	10.4	8.9

Source: Compiled with data from Schwartz (2016b, p. 234).

Super-profits are highly correlated with the extracting and monopoly-creating benefits of IP protection – hence why the *non-IP-intensive* companies that are often no less 'innovative' (that is, able to produce continuous incremental improvements to existing product lines) enjoy relatively lower profits (see Schwartz, 2016b).

More directly for our argument, super-profits are also the result of substantial profit shifting to escape the extractive reach of the US state. As several studies have observed, IPRs more readily enable profit shifting and US MNCs (abundantly in the IT sector) have been quick to take advantage by locating the bulk of their profits beyond the extractive reach of the US state. Indeed, IPR-intensive MNCs currently account for the bulk of the vast volumes of cash reserves (profits) that have been accruing to US firms in foreign jurisdictions over the past decade. According to the latest estimates, the accumulated untaxed foreign profits of US MNCs, mostly in the technology and pharmaceutical industries 'have now grown to a spectacular \$2.5 trillion, an amount equal to about 70 percent of the federal government's annual budget and 14 percent of the entire US economy' (Schwarz, 2017).

There is nothing novel about firms shifting their profit-generating assets and activities around the globe to reduce costs and maximize profits. What is 'new' is the intangibility factor. IPR-intensive firms are better placed than most to exploit profit-shifting opportunities thanks to the intangible nature of their most valuable assets. Unlike physical assets, patents, trademarks, and copyrights can be housed anywhere in the world. This makes it easy for IPR-intensive firms to shift these assets – and the substantial income they attract – to low-tax jurisdictions, creating what Seabrooke and Wigan (2017) refer to as global wealth chains (GWCs). For example, if an IP-rich company like Pfizer wishes to avoid paying up to 35 percent tax in the US, it can transfer ownership of its IP to a subsidiary based in a low- or no-tax jurisdiction (for example, see Palan, 1998). Then, when the US-based branch of Pfizer sells a drug, it pays a large licensing fee to the offshore subsidiary, turning the profits it made in the US into (accounting) losses. By virtue of such mechanisms, Pfizer reported no taxable federal income in the US between 2010 and 2012, despite booking 40 percent of its global sales in that country (Baxandall and Smith, 2013, p. 7). Pfizer is, of course, just one example. As Seabrooke and Wigan point out, both AOI (the Apple subsidiary that holds its intellectual property) and Google have managed to avoid being recognized as tax residents *anywhere* (2017, pp. 18–19). As a result, between 2009 and 2012, AOI paid no tax on an estimated income of around \$30 billion.

Profit shifting weakens the state's extractive capacity by reducing the federal corporate tax base. By retaining sizable profits abroad (mostly in low-tax jurisdictions), US corporations slash their tax bill at home and reduce federal revenue from corporate tax. This feeds into chronic revenue shortfalls and acrimonious clashes over budget deficits and government spending. Obviously, profits held overseas are profits not available to be spent on the provision of services at home, like health and education. They are also not available for investment in production and employment-generating activities. Since at least the early 2000s, America's IPR-intensive firms have led the drive to downsize local manufacturing, to offshore it to lower-cost locations and to distribute the savings to their shareholders. This has contributed to both a decline in corporate investment (described as 'the great stagnation' by Stewart and Atkinson, 2013) and in America's manufacturing base, discussed in detail below.

Reflecting this trend, between 1980 and 2011, total non-residential fixed investment as a percentage of GDP decreased from approximately 13 percent to 10 percent (Figure 3.3). As employment in both traditional and advanced manufacturing sectors – the largest source of so-called middle class (well-paid) jobs – has fallen from 22.1 percent in 1980 to 10.3 percent in 2012,[4] so too has the rate of participation in the labor force been on a clear downward trend, from 65.4 percent in 1987 to 62.7 percent in 2016, a drop from 65 to 62 million employed (Figure 3.4). The claim that this decline is due to automation is highly contentious rather than established – the auto industry being the least controversial since it accounts for some 4 percent of all industrial robots deployed worldwide. Massachusetts Institute of Technology economists Acemoglu and Restrepo (2017) find that US trade with China and Mexico, including offshoring, displaced three times as many jobs as did robots. Moreover, the automation claim rests on the false assumption that productivity has increased. As Eichengreen (2017) notes, 'total factor productivity, the best summary measure of the pace of technical change, has been stagnating since 2005 in the United States and across the advanced-country world'.

The upshot of weak investment and employment is stagnant income growth and a reduced tax base. In the context of stagnant or falling government revenues since 2000 (combined with the growth of non-discretionary spending) it is not surprising that the US federal deficit and debt has soared over this same period (Figures 3.5 and 3.6). These challenges have framed the government's most recent tax reforms, which are partly aimed at bringing corporate profits back home and kickstarting domestic investment. It is too early to evaluate the effectiveness of these measures – but their very existence bears testimony to the problems we identify. Apple has pledged to repatriate $252 billion in profits and incur a small one-off tax levy of $38 billion. Whether its simultaneously announced local investment and employment plans represent new commitments or business as usual is anything but clear, despite their rapturous reception by Fox media.[5]

The relevant question, then, is why in view of its global monetary power and the ability to borrow against its revenue shortfalls is the US is unable (or unwilling?) to increase federal spending when and where it is needed (viz. the decline in non-discretionary spending)? If the US government merely has to

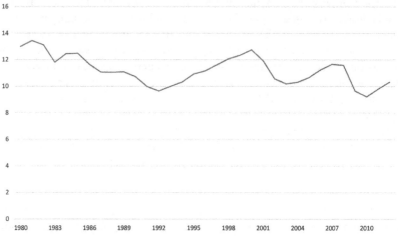

Source: Compiled by authors from US Bureau of Economic Analysis Data Tool: National
Accounts Historical Data (2013).

Figure 3.3   *Total non-residential fixed investment (as a percentage of*
              GDP)

issue Treasury bills to cover its revenue shortfalls, why then has federal spending (outside the mandatory categories of social insurance – health, welfare,
pensions and the like) fallen to an 'historic low'? At 11.3 percent of GDP,
total discretionary program spending (including education, R&D, energy,
transport, defense, and infrastructure) is already below its 40-year average of
12.0 percent of GDP and is projected to fall to 10.5 percent of GDP in 2027.[6]
If budget deficits are harmless, why do political perceptions so frequently
override hard deficit financing ability – viz. the repeated Congressional battles
over the budget and constant threats of sequestration (real and potential, for
example, the terms of the Budget Control Act of 2011 and the sequester
mechanism). Are these battles – which have real consequences – just a political exercise in which Republicans oppose social spending while Democrats
support it?

    Recent research by Hager (2017) suggests a more complex reason, and one
that lends a surprising new twist to 'elite network' accounts of America's
structural power. Hager's analysis reveals a startling fact: that since the
1980s, the wealthiest 1 percent of Americans have dramatically increased
their holdings of US government debt. Between 1980 and 2013, the share of
the super-rich in household sector holdings of public debt grew from around
one-third to 56 percent. At the same time, America's top 2500 corporations
increased their share in corporate holdings of US debt from 65 percent in

Source: Compiled by authors from Federal Reserve Bank of St Louis Economic Data (FRED) (aggregated from US Bureau of Labor Statistics Data).

Figure 3.4   Labor force participation

1977–81 to 82 percent in 2006–10 (2017, pp. 568–9). To be sure, foreign holdings of Treasury bills (T-bills) have also increased since the 1980s, with China's growing share receiving most attention. The fact remains, however, that it is Americans (67.5 percent) rather than foreign nations (32.5 percent) who are the majority holders of these bonds,[7] with the richest Americans massively over-represented in domestic holdings. It is worth noting that as the 1 percent's holding has increased, so too has the rate of return – the average yield on ten-year T-bills tracking at an impressive 5.5 percent over the 1980–2015 period, up from an average annual *loss* of 1 percent over the 30 years prior (Hager, 2016, p. 6).

Hager contends that their massive holdings of US debt gives America's super-rich a form of structural power, enabling them – through threat of exit – to powerfully shape public policy in line with their preferences. Unsurprisingly, the preferences of the 1 percent reflect their economic interests: as the government's major creditors, they prefer the government to commit itself to the principles of 'sound finance' and to make reliable debt servicing its primary policy priority (Hager, 2017, p. 559). They also prefer debt-servicing efforts to center on tax and spending cuts rather than tax increases, ferociously opposed by wealthy Americans since the 1980s. Faced with relentlessly growing costs (for infrastructure, education, health, and so on) and a structurally powerful,

Source: Compiled by authors from Federal Reserve Bank of St Louis Economic Data (FRED).

Figure 3.5   US federal debt (as a percentage of GDP)

tax-averse private elite, the US government has chosen to borrow from the 1 percent (by selling them T-bills) rather than to tax them (a point also made by Picketty, 2014, cited in Hager, 2017, p. 659). A consequence has been the growing alignment between the policy choices of the US government and its taxing- and spending-averse creditors. This helps to explain why the state's unique ability to borrow abroad has not enabled it to increase federal spending where needed (read: to offset tax income lost to profit shifting).

In sum, profit shifting has multiple ramifications that, in combination, work to erode an important dimension of infrastructural power: at issue here is the state's ability to extract and deploy the resources that strengthen the state's domestic economic base. Extractive capacity is a critical factor because it affects the ability of the US 'to confront societal challenges, from the cost of healthcare for a rapidly aging population, to new and ongoing infrastructure requirements, to strategies associated with climate change' (Bonvillian and Weiss, 2015, p. 6). Yet, ironically, the state's infrastructural power is not simply failing to be enhanced by the bounty promised by extension of IPRs (and indeed implied by the structural power of International Monetary System

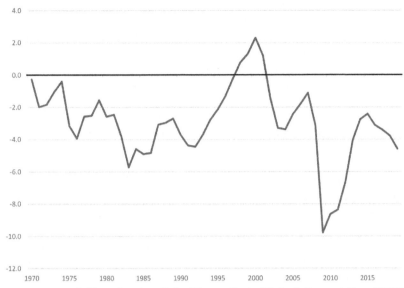

Source: Compiled by authors from Federal Reserve Bank of St Louis Economic Data (FRED).

Figure 3.6   *US federal deficit (as a percentage of GDP)*

domination), it is actually being eroded by it. Evidently, then, we cannot use the growing economic power (*qua* profits) of US MNCs as a proxy for the American state's economic power. On the contrary, there would appear to be greater divergence than ever between them. This is a perverse and unintended effect of the extent to which elite networks in the corporate and political spheres are so deeply entwined.

IPRS AND TRANSFORMATIVE CAPACITY

Turning now from profit shifting to production shifting, we examine the relationship of IPRs to the massive migration of production offshore. It is the impact of that migration on the state's transformative capacity that is our principal concern.

    Our argument stands the conventional claim on its head ('protection of IPRs is essential for innovation'). Instead, we propose that IPRs may actually do more to sever the link with, and thereby weaken, innovation. This point links directly to the debate on US power because transformative (that is, radical or breakthrough) innovation is key to the US strategy of technological supremacy, and the cornerstone of its military primacy.

The relationship between techno-supremacy and American primacy was forged in the earliest years of the Cold War, when strategists in the Pentagon acknowledged that they could never compete with the Soviets by relying on sheer quantity (of men and material). However, it was not until 1957 – when the Soviet Union sent shockwaves throughout America by successfully launching the world's first satellite – that technological supremacy, the so-called 'offset' strategy, became the primary and enduring goal of America's national security state. Pursuit of this strategy has catalyzed a formidable innovation engine that has enabled the unparalleled rise of the US as a high-tech hegemon. Still today, US officials routinely invoke (and pursue) technological superiority as the foundation of the nation's military and economic primacy (Weiss, 2014).

When tracing the origins of America's unmatched propensity for radical innovation, the American state and its transformative capacity sit at the center of the story.[8] Transformative capacity in the US context refers to the state's institutionalized capability for catalyzing the revolutionary innovations – most notably the general-purpose technologies – that spawn new industries. Since the end of World War II, this capacity has involved the cluster of federal agencies serving national security missions (defense, space, energy, health, and science), working in partnership with private actors in research labs and firms to bring breakthrough technologies to life. The concept of 'governed interdependence' captures the essence of these partnerships, in which strong (independently oriented) public and private actors collaborate for mutual benefit, but with the overarching goals and rules of participation set by the (national security) state.[9]

The key point is that US transformative capacity has long depended on the existence of private enterprises with the capabilities to bring frontier technologies to market, and the willingness to partner with the state in the pursuit of its transformative goals. But as offshoring has ballooned, and as pressures from financial institutions to offload production and focus on intellectual property have become endemic, even technology start-ups have embraced the offshoring business model (so-called 'China strategy'). We advance a two-step argument to show how the internationalization of IPRs has both aided and expedited the migration of US advanced manufacturing, and how this process of uncoupling erodes the capacity for the cutting-edge (whole-of-cycle) innovation that has underpinned the country's techno-industrial leadership. First, we examine America's offshoring trend, and how IP-heavy companies intensify the offshoring of production. Second, we show how this movement is impacting on firms' capabilities for innovation in the domestic space – and ultimately on the technological projects for which the mission agencies of the national security complex seek collaboration.

AMERICA'S OFFSHORING TREND

America's offshoring trend is well documented in the academic and policy literature. It began with the exit of labor-intensive industries in the 1970s, but gained real momentum in the following decades, extending into increasingly advanced manufacturing activities. By 2002, for the first time on record, the US began running trade deficits in *advanced* technology products (see Figure 3.7).[10] As a result, the US has seen a steady decline of its advanced manufacturing capabilities in a swathe of industries that are united by their dual military and commercial significance, as well as their IP intensity (discussed below).

The reality of America's advanced manufacturing challenges is not captured in official statistics that show the US maintaining or expanding its share in global manufacturing output. This is because official statistics do not take into account *imported* inputs in the way they calculate productivity and value added (Houseman et al., 2011). The reality is that while the US still accounts for the largest share of world high-tech manufacturing, that share has been declining markedly – from close to 40 percent in the late 1990s to less than 30 percent in 2014 – as other countries, especially China, increased their stake (see Figure 3.8; also Berger with MIT Task Force on Production, 2013). Similarly, the Information Technology and Innovation Foundation (ITIF) reports that over the 2000s, net manufacturing output declined in 16 of 19 manufacturing sectors, two key exceptions being computing and energy (Nager and Atkinson, 2015). Adjusting for inflated government data (which overstated the computing and energy sectors' output), ITIF found that US manufacturing value added fell by 11 percent in the same decade (ibid., p. 6).

By the mid-2000s, as the hemorrhaging of advanced manufacturing capabilities continued, researchers and policy advisers began voicing Cassandra-like[11] warnings (Berger, 2013; Bonvillian, 2018; Bonvillian and Weiss, 2015; Locke and Wellhausen, 2014; Manyika, Pacthod and Park, 2011; Pisano and Shih, 2009, 2011; President's Council of Advisors on Science and Technology [PCAST], 2011, 2012). A 2011 report by PCAST highlighted 'the risks this situation [the movement offshore of production facilities] has caused for the United States', concluding its report with just one line: 'A strong advanced manufacturing sector is essential to national security' (PCAST, 2011, p. 14).

The mounting concern over the migration of advanced production is not just about jobs but also innovation, since this feeds into future growth, jobs, and, not least, US strategic goals.

Continuing a steady decline, manufacturing shed more than 2 million jobs in the decade after 2004, and now employs a mere 8 percent of the US workforce. Indeed, one might venture that the general US pattern has been one of 'extreme offshoring': in pursuit of maximizing share price, American MNCs – espe-

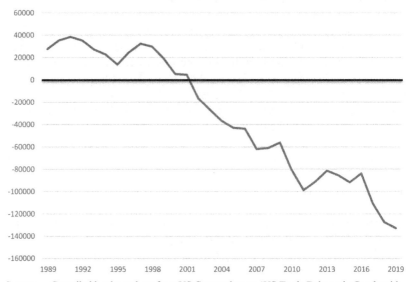

Source: Compiled by the authors from US Census data on 'US Trade Balance in Goods with
Advanced Technology Products', accessed 22 June 2020 at https://www.census.gov/foreign
-trade/balance/c0007.html.

*Figure 3.7   US trade balance in goods with advanced technology
products (in millions of US dollars)*

cially in the patent-heavy IT sector – have taken the 'downsize and distribute'
strategy further than any other advanced country, to the point where the size
of US manufacturing industry is now significantly smaller than in most other
advanced jurisdictions. As a sign of the times, a Martian wandering around
'Silicon' Valley might wonder at the name since so few semiconductors are
produced there anymore, let alone other forms of advanced hardware: a more
fitting name today might be 'App Valley', or 'dot-com Valley'.

HOW IPRS EXPEDITE OFFSHORING

The origins of America's offshoring trend lie in the growing competitive
pressures from East Asia that faced US firms in the 1970s. At that time, US
consumer electronics firms began outsourcing their manufacturing to Japanese
firms. US firms soon lost control of product design and 'were reduced to
affixing their brand names to products designed and manufactured by the
Japanese' (Sturgeon, 2002, p. 488). Eventually, those same Japanese firms
came to dominate the consumer electronics markets. Their similar prowess in

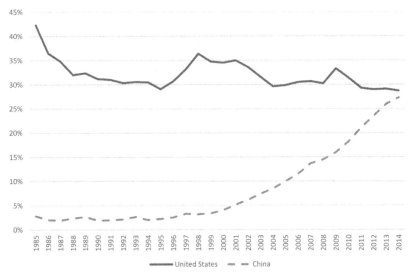

Source: Compiled by authors from National Science Board, 'Worldwide Distribution of Knowledge- and Technology-Intensive Industries', Science and Engineering Indicators, 2010 and 2016 editions.

Figure 3.8   *US percentage share in world high-tech manufacturing value added*

autos and semiconductors brought additional pressures to bear on US firms, who responded to the challenge by fragmenting their production processes. They created what are now referred to as 'intermediate' goods and services, like component parts and assembly tasks – and distributed the production of these discrete items to lower-cost foreign destinations.[12]

Since the 1980s, however, American offshoring has moved relentlessly up the value chain, to encompass ever more advanced manufacturing activities, notably integrated with higher-skilled services, such as IT support and industrial design services. Multiple factors have influenced this shift, including availability of relatively cheap and increasingly skilled labor in developing countries, technological advances such as digitization and the Internet, and declining transport costs. Such factors have allowed firms not just in the US but in all advanced countries to modularize and geographically distribute production – a key factor in the globalization of contract manufacturing and so-called 'modular production networks'.[13] However, nowhere has the offshoring trend been more extreme than in America.[14] Indeed, by the turn of this century, globalized modular production had become such a defining feature of the US advanced electronics (information technology) industry that by 2002 it was being heralded as 'a new American model of industrial organization' (Sturgeon, 2002).

Offshoring emerged as the default response of corporate executives under intense pressure from investors to rapidly reduce costs, boost profits, and focus on 'core competences' – even among those skeptical of embracing such a strategy. As bucking the trend often meant risking one's company or one's job, outsourcing overseas soon became 'a manhood test for corporate executives' (Pearlstein, 2012). Monocausal arguments for why this is the case are, of course, simplistic. Alongside finance, one might add to the list of 'extreme offshoring' enablers in America an additional ideational element. Over the past three decades, the relinquishment of manufacturing – even the more advanced variety – has been cast in an unquestioning, positive light. But in the case of America's IP-intensive MNCs, none of the 'push' or 'pull' factors by themselves could account for the massive migration of manufacturing in technology-intensive products that has left US shores since the late 1990s–early 2000s. For this movement to occur, the risk of IP theft had to be drastically reduced. Only the globalization of IPRs could counter this concern and create the conditions under which technology-intensive offshoring might flourish.[15]

By helping to neutralize the risk of reverse engineering and imitation by foreign firms, the globalization of IPRs would give American companies greater confidence to share their technology with overseas affiliates and subcontractors, and then source intermediate goods from them. IPRs would also encourage those foreign affiliates and subcontractors to upgrade their own capabilities, enabling them to offer an ever-widening range of cheaper intermediate goods to US firms.[16] Thus, as the 1980s progressed – and in the wake of its own domestic IP reforms – the US launched a sustained campaign to globalize its system of intellectual property rules and aggressively pursued this goal through both bilateral and multilateral channels. It was the legal structure of IPRs that made America's construction and control of global commodity chains possible. However, many of the physical capital-intensive activities that the US has since offshored to these chains have been IP intensive, and increasingly close to the technological frontier. This rebounds on the infrastructural power and capacity for transformative innovation, as we shall see.

As indicated previously, the US push to internationalize its laws on IPRs was not simply driven by the country's corporate sector. It also formed part of a joint strategy to keep world markets open for US MNCs (van Apeldoorn and de Graaff, 2015). By the 1980s, both government and corporate actors, for different reasons, saw the internationalization of IPRs as in their interests and began to pursue this mutually beneficial goal with equal gusto. The fact that corporate and public policy strategists inhabit(ed) the same networks and shared similar outlooks no doubt helped advance their project of global market opening. As a number of Asian countries (initially Japan, South Korea, and Taiwan) began to respond to American pressure to reform their IP regimes – which culminated in the 1994 TRIPs agreement – US high-tech firms stepped up the movement of production offshore.

Our argument is not that IPRs reform eliminates all concerns about intellectual property theft. Rather, it is our contention that the globalization of IPRs through trade agreements has played a critical role in this movement abroad by expanding the state's infrastructural powers to protect against intellectual property theft. The implications for the structure of US industrial production, trade, investment, employment and not least the tax base, have been profound. But the next chapter of our story takes a less travelled path. Here we turn to how the IPR-induced offshoring has impacted on innovation, and ultimately, the state's transformative capacity.

HOW OFFSHORING WEAKENS INNOVATION

Many insist that the US move away from making things is unambiguously positive, a mark of an economy's greater power, sophistication, and advancement. But a sizeable research effort is now deeply skeptical of the healthy economy verdict. As well as pointing to the negative slide in national wages, job quality and income distribution, mounting evidence suggests that the capacity for innovation itself (and thus the state's transformative capacity, the cornerstone of its ability to project power) is being diminished by the offshoring of manufacturing – especially IP-intensive advanced manufacturing. This is because in many industries, production and innovation are inextricably linked. So, as production declines, so does innovative capacity.

Although the US has been the undisputed leader of next-generation technologies, that status is now in question for a significant number of advanced industrial technologies. The problem goes well beyond a small number of highly specialized items designed to meet defense requirements. In the words of a leader of the US Joint Forces Command, the problem concerns the potential 'eradication of US industry capability' (Col. Michael Cole, cited in Yudken, 2010).

The argument is neither hypothetical nor limited to a small number of sectors. The most recent research reports a diminution of innovative capabilities in a sizable list of sectors critical to US commercial and military leadership in particular. These include semiconductors, electronic displays, energy storage, renewable energy production, computing and communications and advanced materials. In the area of energy storage and renewable energy production, for example, research has revealed that the US no longer has the critical skills, knowledge, or supply base to produce (and thus innovate at the cutting edge of) lithium ion and lithium polymer batteries (used in mobile phones and consumer electronics) or advanced rechargeable batteries, used in hybrid vehicles and solar cells (Berger with MIT Task Force on Production in the Innovation Economy, 2013; Bonvillian and Weiss, 2015; Manyika et al., 2011; Pisano and Shih, 2009, 2011; Wessner and Wolf, 2012). These studies also report that domestic capabilities are currently at risk in a wide range of areas, including optical communications components, core network equipment, advanced ceramics, carbon composite components for aerospace, and wind energy.

Three effects are apparent as the production of sophisticated products migrates abroad. First, the ability to create *next-generation* products diminishes. This is because in technology-intensive industries, innovating at the frontier often requires design engineers to constantly test, refine, and re-test new ideas in the *production process*. So, when firms cede their advanced manufacturing capabilities through offshoring, they often also cede their capacity for cutting-edge innovation (Pisano and Shih, 2009, 2011) and detailed industry case studies have revealed this dynamic to be well advanced in a range of US industries of both military and commercial significance, such as optoelectronics.[17] In a 2010 study, Fuchs and Kirchain found that as US optoelectronics firms have moved production offshore to reduce costs, so they have reduced domestic R&D centered on creating next-generation technologies. The same researchers found that in automobile production, where car bodies are made from fiber composites (which reduce weight and save energy), offshoring 'reduced the economic viability of the emerging technology and led firms to produce older generation technologies' (Carnegie Mellon Engineering News, 2011) For this reason, it seems meaningless to distinguish between 'manufacturing' or 'industrial firms' on the one hand, and 'IPR-intensive' or 'knowledge-based' firms on the other: advanced manufacturing firms are almost always IPR-intensive firms and the relationship between their productive and innovative (read: IP-creation) activities are mutually reinforcing.

But the effects of this production–innovation uncoupling do not stop there. In addition to constraining firms' abilities to innovate at the cutting edge of existing industries, it appears that offshoring has weakened the prospects for *pioneering new sectors* as well. Take the case of flexible electronics (so-called hybrid flexible electronics or HFE). As one of a handful of early-stage technologies with transformative potential, HFE meets the criteria of 'a general-purpose technology' capable of producing major impacts across a wide number of sectors in a manner similar to those flowing from microelectronics, the Internet and biotechnology (National Research Council [NRC], 2015, p. 11). In all these cases, the driving role of the state (*qua* the cluster of security-related mission agencies) has been paramount. The Defense Department is a key end user and has identified HFE as a dual-use technology ideal for military and commercial purposes. But the challenges are significant, not least because so much of the industrial ecosystem has been depleted.

In 2010, the National Science Foundation and the Office of Naval Research commissioned a report to probe the potential for the country to develop and commercialize the technology. But after examining European progress, the research team concluded that 'the relatively low prevalence of actual manufacturing and advanced systems research and development in the United States had led to an incomplete hybrid flexible electronics R&D scenario for this country' (NRC, 2015, p. 95). American scientists at labs like the Palo Alto Research Center are certainly working at the cutting edge of R&D in this field. But some of them are now publicly acknowledging that America's potential to dominate the HFE industry has been undermined by the migration of its manufacturing ecosystem to Asia – from local equipment manufacturers to material suppliers and technology developers. In the estimation of one senior Palo Alto researcher and manager, in the absence of this ecosystem – and the production capacity and expertise in volume production that comes with it – the barriers to entry to the HFE industry for the US are likely to be too high (see Wessner and Wolff, 2012, p. 85). And if new US companies are unable to scale up production, as in other industries, maintaining America's technological lead is likely to be impossible.

We have just touched on a third impact of the 'downsize and distribute' strategy practiced abundantly by IP-intensive firms: the *depletion of the industrial ecosystem*, the larger environment of the firm. A healthy industrial ecosystem anchors the routine interactions among networks of manufacturing firms, specialist suppliers and research institutes that generate innovation synergies among firms and sectors. However, researchers have discovered broad gaps emerging in that ecosystem, setting severe limits to the capacity for generating breakthrough innovations.[18] As the research leader of an important report *Making in America: From Innovation to Market* explained to a Congressional committee: 'The problem . . . is that by shifting the commercialization of their technologies abroad, US companies are creating gaping holes in the industrial ecosystem that enfeeble the capacity for future rounds of innovation' (Berger, 2013).

In its 2016 report on the state of advanced manufacturing, the National Science and Technology Council (NSTC) drew similar conclusions. The 'domino effect' of decades of offshoring, it observed, has now limited the private sector's ability to translate promising early-stage research into innovative high-value products. Innovation, once spread more generally throughout the economy by manufacturing-intensive growth, is now an activity increasingly 'isolated to the research community' (NSTC, 2016, p. vii).

A Department of Defense Advisory Group on Electronic Devices (AGED) issued a warning as early as 2002 that this uncoupling, especially in microelectronics, would undermine 'the ability of the US to research and produce the best technologies and products for the nation and the warfighter' (Department of Defense, 2002). Almost ten years on, an Industrial College of the Armed Forces (ICAF) report concluded that continued offshoring of the semiconductor industry posed direct risks to the nation's economy and national security (ICAF, 2011, p. 13).

According to William Bonvillian, former policy adviser and technology expert at MIT, 'the US is increasingly leaving hard technologies by the technology wayside'. Wall Street and venture capitalists prefer to fund the less risky software start-ups, and companies that can hive off the hardware and exploit their intellectual property. The upshot is that 'because innovation agencies like DARPA leverage the private sector for implementation, this will affect [their] ability . . . to use the entrepreneurial approach they have relied on for scaling up their hard technologies' (Bonvillian, 2018, p. 22). This disconnect has created a problem for America's techno-supremacy strategy.

CONCLUSION

To return to our starting point, we reject the idea that US corporate power can be used as a proxy for US state power. Corporate and state elites are indeed intertwined in blended networks of power and these clearly act as conduits for advancing US goals, but we must not blind ourselves to the possibility that shared projects do not always bring shared benefits. Our analysis highlights a power paradox: the vastly increased economic power of US MNCs has come about both by virtue of, and at the expense of, the US state itself. The US has internationalized its infrastructural power through trade agreements that have sought to globalize US IPRs (among other rules favorable to US business). This extension has delivered major benefits to its corporations. But in the same vein, it has created the conditions that are steadily chipping away at the state's infrastructural power at home.

Our argument leads us to conclude that whatever challenges to its power the US may face in the years to come, the most pressing in the near term would seem to be those of its own making, since these have been facilitated by government policies (tax rules, IP laws, financial regulations), and are therefore capable in principle of remedial action. More generally, recent studies have laid bare how US policy-makers have written the domestic rules that rig the system in favor of the wealthy few, and create massive inequality at home. Our story adds another (brief) chapter to that analysis by showing how the nation's policy elite in concert with elite economic actors have written the international rules that rig the system in favor of its IP-intensive companies; in doing so, their policies have unintentionally enabled massive profit and production shifting that increases income inequality, erodes the social contract, compromises technology leadership and weakens state power at home.

None of this means that the trends must continue in a downward direction. Policy changes and reversals could conceivably encourage the massive reshoring of profits, the revival of productive business investment at home, and the renaissance of the domestic supply networks that sustain the US innovation engine. But absent the requisite policy choices, we would expect US infrastructural power to gradually diminish, as political actors (in distinction to state institutions) continue to favor the interests of MNCs at the expense of the US state.

NOTES

1. This chapter is a condensed and re-oriented version of an article published in *Review of International Political Economy* (Weiss and Thurbon, 2018), with thanks to RIPE for their permission. The article considered the relationship from the point of view of the US state, whereas this chapter places focus on the MNCs. As frequent co-authors we rotate first authorship.
2. The essence of TRIPS was to wrest control of IPR from a weak organization – the World Intellectual Property Organization (WIPO) – to a strong one connected to trade, so that IPR violations could be met with trade sanctions. The WTO came into existence in 2001 largely as a means of housing TRIPS.
3. Following Schwartz (2016b, p. 235), these figures represent global profits as a percentage of global sales. This is a useful indicator of the degree to which firms are able to capture value from the value chains of which they are part (and thus able to exercise monopoly power through their IPR).
4. Federal Reserve Economic Data, accessed 25 June 2020 at https://fred.stlouisfed.org/series/USAPEFANA.
5. See, for example, Weissmann (2018).
6. See Kogan and Bryant (2019).
7. 2016 data from US Treasury Statistics, cited in Long (2016). While China's share of the overall total is significant (around 7 percent in 2016), it only just exceeds Japan's share, which gets little attention.
8. For the detailed argument, see Weiss (2014).
9. For a discussion of governed interdependence and its application to the US context, see Weiss (2014).
10. Since the deficits originated with Asia, Ireland and Mexico, none at the time advanced technology leaders, they apparently stemmed from US offshore manufacturing (Roberts, 2016).
11. In Greek mythology, Cassandra, who received the gift of prophecy, accurately predicted future events but was cursed never to be believed.
12. Firms can engage in offshoring by either establishing an affiliate in a foreign country or by arm's-length outsourcing to a foreign contractor.
13. Modular production networks are a constituent part of global value chains (GVCs); on the nature of GVCs and their governance see Gereffi, Humphrey and Sturgeon (2005).

14. Measured in the number of jobs lost to offshoring each year. See Aspray, Mayadas and Vardi (2006, p. 10).
15. A growing literature investigates the relationship between the strengthening of IPR in developing countries and the subsequent expansion of MNC activity, both in terms of expanding high-tech exports to developing countries and increasing foreign direct investment or subcontracting activities related to the manufacture of technology-intensive ('patent-sensitive') products. See, for example, Canals and Şener (2014); Co (2004); Ivus (2010); Javorick (2004); Şener and Zhao (2009); Smith (1999).
16. On the ways in which IPR encourage offshoring in patent-sensitive industries, see Canals and Şener (2014, p. 19).
17. Outsourcing is a viable business strategy for mature technologies with established production processes (for example, desktop computers, consumer electronics, active pharmaceutical ingredients, and commodity semiconductors). But in sectors where production processes are rapidly evolving (for example, capital goods, aerospace products, nanomaterials, energy equipment, OLED and electrophoretic displays, and complex pharmaceuticals), losing production can quickly erode any innovative edge (Alden, 2013). See also Bonvillian and Weiss (2015, Ch. 4); Pisano and Shih (2011, Ch. 4).
18. See recent studies and reports by Berger et al. (2013); Bonvillian (2018); Bonvillian and Weiss (2015); Manyika et al. (2011); NRC (2015); PCAST (2011, 2012); Pisano and Shih (2009, 2011); Locke and Wellhausen (2014).

REFERENCES

Acemoglu, D. and P. Restrepo (2017), 'Robots and jobs: evidence from US labor markets', MIT and Boston University, 17 March, accessed 10 January 2018 at https://economics.mit.edu/files/19696.
Alden, E. (2013), 'Why manufacturing really matters: Gary Pisano and Willy Shih on innovation', *CFR.org*, 4 February [blog], accessed 26 July 2020 at https://www.cfr.org/blog/why-manufacturing-really-matters-gary-pisano-and-willy-shih-innovation.
Aspray, W., F. Mayadas and M.Y. Vardi (2006), *Globalization and Offshoring of Software: A Report of the AGM Job Migration Taskforce*, Association for Computing Machinery report, accessed 26 July 2020 at https://www.acm.org/binaries/content/assets/public-policy/usacm/intellectual-property/reports-and-white-papers/full_final1.pdf.
Baxandall, P. and D. Smith (2013), *Picking Up the Tab 2013: Average Citizens and Small Businesses Pay the Price for Offshore Tax Havens*, accessed 26 July 2020 at https://calpirg.org/sites/pirg/files/reports/Picking%20Up%20the%20Tab%20vCA%20web_4.pdf.
Berger, S. (2013), 'Written testimony . . . before the Senate Committee on Banking, Housing, and Urban Affairs Subcommittee on Economic Policy December 11, 2013', accessed 17 March 2020 at http://web.mit.edu/pie/Senate%20testimony_Suzanne_Berger.pdf.
Berger, S. with MIT Task Force on Production in the Innovation Economy (2013), *Making in America: From Innovation to Market*, Cambridge, MA: MIT Press.
Bonvillian, W.B. (2018), 'DARPA and its ARPA-E and IARPA clones: a unique innovation organization model', *Industrial and Corporate Change*, **27**(5), 897–914.

Bonvillian, W.B. and C. Weiss (2015), *Technological Innovation in Legacy Sectors*, New York: Oxford University Press.

Canals, C. and F. Şener (2014), 'Offshoring and intellectual property rights reform', *Journal of Development Economics*, **108**(C), 17–31.

Carnegie Melon Engineering News (2011), *Innovation in an Offshoring Economy*, accessed 18 January 2017 at https://engineering.cmu.edu/alumni/magazine/winter_2011_2012/innovation_offshoring_economy.html.

Centeno, M.A. (1997), 'Blood and debt: war and taxation in nineteenth century Latin America', *American Journal of Sociology*, **102**(6), 1565–605.

Co, C.Y. (2004), 'Do patent rights regimes matter?', *Review of International Economics*, **12**(3), 359–73.

Cohen, B.J. (2015), *Currency Power: Understanding Monetary Rivalry*, Princeton, NJ: Princeton University Press.

Cohen, B.J. (2018), *Currency Statecraft*, Chicago, IL: University of Chicago Press.

Department of Defense, Advisory Group on Electronic Devices [AGED] (2002), *National Technology Leadership Forum, Microelectronics Study*, 24 September, Washington, DC: Department of Defense.

Drahos, P. and J. Braithwaite (2002), *Information Feudalism: Who Owns the Knowledge Economy?*, London: Earthscan.

Eichengreen, B. (2017), 'Two myths about automation', *Project-Syndicate.org*, 12 December, accessed 17 March 2020 at https://www.project-syndicate.org/commentary/two-myths-about-automation-by-barry-eichengreen-2017-12.

Fuchs, E.R.H. and R. Kirchain (2010), 'Design for location: the impact of manufacturing offshore on technology competitiveness in the optoelectronics industry', *Management Science*, **56**(12), 2323–49.

Fukuyama, F. (2014), 'America in decay: the sources of political dysfunction', *Foreign Affairs*, **93**(5), 5–26.

Gereffi, G., J. Humphrey and T. Sturgeon (2005), 'The governance of global value chains', *Review of International Political Economy*, **12**(1), 78–104.

Haas, R.N. (2013), *Foreign Policy Begins at Home: The Case for Putting America's House in Order*, New York: Basic Books.

Hager, S.B. (2016), *Public Debt, Inequality, and Power: The Making of a Modern Debt State*, Oakland, CA: University of California Press.

Hager, S.B. (2017), 'A global bond: explaining the safe-haven status of US Treasury securities', *European Journal of International Relations*, **23**(3), 557–80.

Hall, J.A. (1985), *Powers and Liberties*, Oxford: Blackwell.

Helleiner, E. (2014), *The Status Quo Crisis: Global Financial Governance After the 2008 Meltdown*, Oxford: Oxford University Press.

Hobson, J.M. (1997), *The Wealth of States: A Comparative Sociology of International Economic and Political Change*, Cambridge, UK: Cambridge University Press.

Houseman, S.N., C. Kurz, P.A. Lengermann and B.J. Mandel (2011), 'Offshoring bias in US manufacturing', *Journal of Economic Perspectives*, **25**(2), 111–32.

Industrial College of the Armed Forces [ICAF] (2011), *Electronics Industry Final Report: Semiconductors and Defense Electronics*, Washington, DC: National Defense University.

Ivus, O. (2010), 'Do stronger patent rights raise high-tech exports to the developing world?', *Journal of International Economics*, **81**(1), 38–47.

Javorick, B. (2004), 'The composition of foreign direct investment and protection of intellectual property rights: evidence from transition economies', *European Economic Review*, **48**(1), 39–62.

Johnson, S. and J. Kwak (2013), *White House Burning: Our National Debt and Why It Matters to You*, New York: Penguin Random House.

Kogan, R. and K. Bryant (2019), 'Program spending outside Social Security and Medicare historically low as a percent of GDP and projected to fall further', *Policy Futures*, 8 March, Center on Budget and Policy Priorities.

Konings, M. (2011), *The Development of American Finance*, Cambridge, UK: Cambridge University Press.

Lazonick, W. (2014), 'Profits without prosperity', *Harvard Business Review*, **92**(9), 46–55.

Locke, R.M. and R.L. Wellhausen (2014), *Production in the Innovation Economy*, Cambridge, MA: MIT Press.

Long, H. (2016), 'Who owns America's debt?', *CNN.com*, 10 May, accessed 7 April 2020 at https://money.cnn.com/2016/05/10/news/economy/us-debt-ownership/index.html.

Lucas, J. (1998), 'The tension between despotic and infrastructural power: the military and political class in Nigeria, 1985–1993', *Studies in Comparative International Development*, **33**, 90–113.

Mann, M. (1984), 'The autonomous power of the state: its origins, mechanisms and results', *European Journal of Sociology*, **25**(2), 185–213.

Manyika, J., D. Pacthod and M. Park (2011), 'Translating innovation into US growth: an advanced-industries perspective', *McKinsey.com*, 1 May, accessed 17 March at http://www.mckinsey.com/insights/public_sector/translating_innovation_into_us_growth_an_advanced-industries_perspective.

Nager, A. and R. Atkinson (2015), 'The myth of America's manufacturing renaissance', Information Technology and Innovation Foundation (ITIF), accessed 17 March 2020 at http://www2.itif.org/2015-myth-american-manufacturing-renaissance.pdf.

National Research Council [NRC] (2015), *The Flexible Electronics Opportunity*, Washington, DC: National Academies Press.

National Science and Technology Council [NSTC] (2016), *National Network for Manufacturing Innovation Program Strategic Plan*, Washington, DC: Executive Office of the President, Advanced Manufacturing National Program Office.

Nye Jr., J.S. (1990), *Bound to Lead: The Changing Nature of American Power*, New York: Basic Books.

Palan, R. (1998), 'Trying to have your cake and eating it: how and why the state system has created offshore', *International Studies Quarterly*, **42**(4), 625–43.

Pearlstein, S. (2012), 'Outsourcing: what's the true impact? Counting jobs is only part of the answer', *Washington Post*, 1 July, accessed 17 March 2020 at https://www.washingtonpost.com/business/economy/outsourcings-net-effect-on-us-jobs-still-an-open-ended-question/2012/07/01/gJQAs1szGW_story.html.

Pisano, G.P. and W.C. Shih (2009), 'Restoring American competitiveness', *Harvard Business Review*, **87**(7/8), 114–25.

Pisano, G. and W. Shih (2011), *Producing Prosperity: Why America Needs a Manufacturing Renaissance*, Boston, MA: Harvard Business Review Press.

President's Council of Advisors on Science and Technology [PCAST] (2011), *Report to the President on Ensuring Leadership in Advanced Manufacturing*, accessed 26 July 2020 at https://obamawhitehouse.archives.gov/sites/default/files/microsites/ostp/pcast-advanced-manufacturing-june2011.pdf.

President's Council of Advisors on Science and Technology [PCAST] (2012), *Report to the President on Capturing Domestic Competitive Advantage in*

Advanced Manufacturing, accessed 26 July 2020 at https://www1.eere.energy.gov/ manufacturing/pdfs/pcast_july2012.pdf.

Roberts, P.C. (2016), 'The offshore outsourcing of American jobs: a greater threat than terrorism', Centre for Research and Globalization, accessed 17 March 2020 at http:// www.globalresearch.ca/the-offshore-outsourcing-of-american-jobs-a-greater-threat -than-terrorism/18725.

Schwartz, H.M. (2016a), 'Strange power over credit; or the enduring strength of US structural power', in R. Germain (ed.), *Susan Strange and the Future of Global Political Economy*, Abingdon: Routledge, pp. 69–92.

Schwartz, H.M. (2016b), 'Wealth and secular stagnation: the role of industrial organization and intellectual property rights', *Russell Sage Foundation Journal of the Social Sciences*, **2**(6), 226–49.

Schwarz, J. (2017), 'Corporations prepare to gorge on tax cuts Trump claims will create jobs', *The Intercept*, 5 January, accessed 17 March 2020 at https://theintercept.com/ 2017/01/05/corporations-prepare-to-gorge-on-tax-cuts-trump-claims-will-create -jobs/.

Seabrooke, L. and D. Wigan (2017), 'The governance of global wealth chains', *Review of International Political Economy*, **24**(1), 1–29.

Sell, S.K. (2003), *Private Power, Public Law: The Globalization of Intellectual Property Rights*, Cambridge, UK: Cambridge University Press.

Şener, F. and L. Zhao (2009), 'Globalization, R&D and the iPod cycle', *Journal of International Economics*, **77**(1), 101–8.

Smith, P.J. (1999), 'Are weak patent rights a barrier to US exports?', *Journal of International Economics*, **48**(1), 151–77.

Soifer, H. and M. vom Hau (2008), 'Unpacking the strength of the state: the utility of state infrastructural power', *Studies in Comparative International Development*, **43**(3), 219–30.

Starrs, S. (2013), 'American economic power hasn't declined – it globalized! Summoning the data and taking globalization seriously', *International Studies Quarterly*, **57**(4), 817–30.

Stewart, L.A. and R.D. Atkinson (2013), 'The greater stagnation: the decline in capital investment is the real threat to US economic growth', Information Technology and Innovation Foundation, October.

Stoner-Weiss, K. (2002), *Local Heroes: The Political Economy of Russian Regional Governance*, Princeton, NJ: Princeton University Press.

Strange, S. (1988), *States and Markets*, London: Continuum.

Sturgeon, T.J. (2002), 'Modular production networks: a new American model of industrial organization', *Industrial and Corporate Change*, **11**(3), 451–96.

Tilly, C. (1975), *The Formation of National States in Western Europe*, Princeton, NJ: Princeton University Press.

Van Apeldoorn, B. and N. de Graaff (2015), *American Grand Strategy and Corporate Elite Networks: The Open Door Since the End of the Cold War*, Abingdon: Routledge.

Wade, R. (1996), 'Japan, the World Bank, and the art of paradigm maintenance: the East Asian miracle in political perspective', *New Left Review*, **217**(May/June), 3–36.

Weiss, L. (2003), *States in the Global Economy: Bringing Domestic Institutions Back In*, Cambridge, UK: Cambridge University Press.

Weiss, L. (2006), 'Infrastructural power, economic transformation, and globalization', in J.A. Hall (ed.), *An Anatomy of Power: The Social Theory of Michael Mann*, Cambridge, UK: Cambridge University Press, pp. 167–86.

Weiss, L. (2014), *America Inc.? Innovation and Enterprise in the National Security State*, Ithaca, NY: Cornell University Press.

Weiss, L. and J.M. Hobson (1995), *States and Economic Development*, Cambridge, UK: Polity Press.

Weiss, L. and E. Thurbon (2018), 'Power paradox: how the extension of US infrastructural power abroad diminishes state capacity at home', *Review of International Political Economy*, **25**(6), 779–810.

Weissman, J. (2018), 'No, Apple is not creating 20,000 jobs because of the tax bill', *Slate.com*, 17 January, accessed 20 March 2020 at https://slate.com/business/2018/01/no-apple-is-not-creating-20-000-jobs-because-of-the-tax-bill.html.

Wessner, C.W. and A.W. Wolff (eds) (2012), *Rising to the Challenge: US Innovation Policy for Global Economy*, Washington, DC: National Academies Press.

Yudken, J. (2010), *Manufacturing Insecurity: America's Manufacturing Crisis and the Erosion of the US Defense Industrial Base*, 14 April, report prepared for Industrial Union Council.

Zhu, T. (2003), 'Building institutional capacity for China's new economic opening', in L. Weiss (ed.), *States in the Global Economy: Bringing Domestic Institutions Back In*, Cambridge, UK: Cambridge University Press, pp. 142–60.

4. Corporate influence and environmental regulation in shipping: navigating norms and influence pathways in the International Maritime Organization

Christian Hendriksen

In early April 2018, an endgame took place in the International Maritime Organization (IMO) – the intergovernmental organization (IGO) tasked with regulating international shipping. In accordance with the Paris Agreement, the IMO had to agree on the overall direction of climate regulation of the global shipping industry, with 13 April as the deadline for such an agreement. Climate change negotiators from other parts of the UN system were flying in to continue the climate discussion in the IMO, but they were all surprised at what they found at Albert Embankment in London where the IMO is situated: row after row of industry associations with their own name flags sitting right next to state delegations, and state delegations that were filled with multinational corporation (MNC) employees who were participating as national delegates. Climate negotiators coming from outside the IMO were scratching their heads as they were wondering how this could possibly be an IGO if MNCs played such a prominent role in the negotiations.

The IMO has worked like this since its inception in the 1950s when it was established as a technical agency tasked with developing standards for the global shipping industry. Because of this mandate, MNCs in the shipping industry have played a crucial role in the development of international maritime regulation, even when large environmental disasters in the 1970s and 1980s spurred the IMO to develop stronger environmental regulation. In 2020, the legacy of this mandate still underpins the strong presence of MNCs in the IMO, even if the regulation today involves much more than simply technical standards. However, what makes MNC influence in the IMO interesting is the dynamics of influence pathways as they shift from relationships between MNCs and specific states to MNC engagement in IMO deliberation. Crucially, as this chapter shows, MNCs not only build on national structural or discursive power to influence states' policy positions, but also must conform to IMO deliberative norms in order to influence the IMO process from within.

This chapter explains which pathways MNCs can use to influence the regulatory process of the IMO and how the dynamics of influence change when MNCs end up participating in the IMO process. MNC influence in the IMO is channeled either through business associations permanently represented in the IMO or through states where individual MNCs or national business associations gain access as state delegates. However, both pathways relate to the dynamics of interests within the industry, between MNCs and governments, and between states themselves. The importance of the shipping industry in specific countries is a source of structural power, but the prevalence of the industry as legitimate political actors in the IMO also has a strong element of discursive power.

To provide the context of the interests within the industry, the chapter explains in brief how the main lines of interest divisions are structured in international shipping and between states. Then the chapter explains the structure of international shipping regulation and how the IMO as an institution is set up to formally allow for MNCs to exercise influence on the drafting of regulation. This is then related to the way influence is exerted via business associations and individual states, respectively, and the chapter ends with a consideration of the theoretical and normative lessons that can be drawn from the influence of MNCs on international shipping regulation. The chapter takes departure in a distinction between public and private entities as it fits with their respective roles in the IMO.

THEORIZING MNC INFLUENCE ON INTERNATIONAL REGULATION: EXISTING PERSPECTIVES

The literature on MNCs' participation in international treaty development is limited – in particular, when treaty development and amendment is anchored in an IGO like the IMO. Some scholars have provided extensive explanations of the relationship between specific firms and governments in international trade policy development (Sell, 1999; Woll, 2008), and this stream of research has shown that both material and ideational links between MNCs and states are important explanatory elements of MNCs' political influence. More recent research has highlighted the role of international business associations and individual MNCs as normative entrepreneurs (Flohr et al., 2010; Nasiritousi and Linnér, 2016). In international environmental governance, a few scholars have explored the role of private actors (including MNCs) in treaty negotiations (e.g., Rietig, 2016; Vormedal, 2008), but there has been scant research on the specifics of MNC influence when the development of treaty law is anchored in an IGO. Some scholars have highlighted the lack of theorizing of the influence by MNCs on international regulation (Culpepper, 2015, pp. 394–7; Dür, 2008, pp. 560–2; Young, 2012, pp. 666–9), emphasizing the challenge of theorizing interactions directly between policy-makers and MNC representatives without direct empirical access or reliable interview sources. Consequently, there is a lacuna of theorizing on the dynamics of MNCs' political influence on legally binding international regulation anchored in IGOs.

Because of this lacuna, the case of MNC influence on international environmental shipping regulation is a suitable opportunity to expand the theoretical repertoire of the global power of MNCs. While macro-level theoretical perspectives have been successful in developing new and critical accounts of the role of global corporations across issues, policy arenas, and institutional contexts (Fuchs, 2007; Mikler, 2018; Wilks, 2013), the specifics of MNC influence when they are directly participating in treaty development has been subject to less scrutiny. Kevin Young (2012) has argued that macro-level theories can be incongruent with case-specific research (Mattli and Woods, 2009), which calls for new theories explaining industry and MNC influence at a lower scale. The case of the IMO fits into this research ambition nicely. First, the international shipping regulation agreed by the IMO is legally binding, making it different from the proliferation of non-binding standards governing international conduct. Second, states and MNCs both have interests at stake. Changes in ship design, compliance or operational measures can be costly, and there are stark differences between MNCs in terms of their adaptability. Third, MNCs and business associations are directly participating in the regulatory process within the IMO, and it is possible to observe this participation. This means that it is possible to go beyond merely theorizing the question of access (Bouwen, 2002b; Dür and Mateo, 2013) and take departure in the MNCs' actual participation in the discussions of the IMO. By developing novel theoretical insights based on the case of international shipping regulation it is possible to add to the discussion on the political power of international firms.

THE STRUCTURE OF THE MARITIME INDUSTRY AND GLOBAL SHIPPING REGULATION

Material interest structures are important factors when explaining MNC–state relationships, regardless of whether the material interests are taken as objective or subjective (Elbra, 2014; Woll, 2008). The following sections explain the details of the structure of interests in the industry and states. This is important as context for the dynamics of industry influence in itself, but it is also relevant to highlight that states and MNCs have divergent interests, and this gives rise to contestation in the IMO.

MNC Interests

Global shipping as an industry can be understood as consisting of various markets – principally container, tanker (oil), bulk goods, and specialized cargo – with various functions for MNCs across different market segments (Stopford, 2009; United Nations Conference on Trade and Development [UNCTAD], 2018). The functional differences for different MNCs range from actual ship ownership to brokerage, and these functional differences in the business models of MNCs correspond to differences in material interests. For example, MNCs that primarily own and operate their own fleet shoulder the cost of compliance measures, while MNCs that only charter (i.e., lease) vessels do not carry the investment costs of compliance. Variance in the types of MNCs and their respective business models create differences in interest between different firms.

Additionally, different MNCs differ in their effective capacity to handle changes in the business environment. Most importantly, technological 'laggards' (Falkner, 2008, pp. 33–4) are less prepared to anticipate and implement regulatory changes that stipulate changes to the technology used by the MNCs compared to technological leaders who can identify and use new technology more efficiently or effectively than their laggard competitors. Even if regulation does not directly stipulate the use of new technology, the changes in the cost structure of the firms may indirectly coerce MNCs to adopt new technology faster than anticipated. This differential interest rooted in the capabilities of different types of firms (Oliver and Holzinger, 2008) gives rise to the different political interests of MNCs, which means that changes in international environmental regulation of the shipping industry has clear MNC winners and losers.

State Interests

In the context of shipping regulation, states can be roughly divided depending on whether their main interests are environmental protection, financial income from shipping registration, or protection of national industry concerns. For some states – in particular, Western European states – environmental concerns are important for public health reasons and marine environment integrity, and these concerns often synergize well with the more advanced capabilities of nationally based MNCs that allow the firms to implement compliance solutions at a lower cost relative to their non-European competitors. A good example of this is Denmark, Finland, and Germany with local branches of engine-designing MNCs. The technological sophistication of these MNCs with regard to competitors located outside Europe enables them to make new engine designs in accordance with new environmental requirements at higher speed and lower costs than non-European competitors. The reverse logic is true for states with state-owned MNCs, like China, or countries with high ownership concentration of technological laggards, like Greece, where it is in their interest to either limit development of stronger environmental protection or couple it with technology transfer.

Several important states represent the majority of locations where vessels (measured by tonnage, i.e., vessel size) are registered. In sum, Panama, the Marshall Islands, Liberia, Hong Kong, Singapore, and Malta have a total of 63 percent of the world tonnage registered (UNCTAD, 2018, p. 35), which is an important source of income for the flag states because of registration fees. States where flag registration income is important for the state finances have a clear interest in keeping standards low to enable a continuous expansion of the industry. While environmental concerns are generally less of a priority for these states, individual states have concerns related to their national situation. The Marshall Islands are at risk of succumbing to rising sea levels because of the climate crisis and this dictates their position on issues related to climate change, while Singapore's geographical position near the important shipping lane of the Strait of Malacca makes Singapore interested in reducing pollution from shipping for both public health and biodiversity concerns.

The International Regulatory System: Why the IMO Is Important

The foundation of international shipping regulation lies in the characteristics of the industry, the legal basis for international treaties and the formal designation under the UN Law of the Sea of the IMO as the organization tasked with regulating international shipping. This section provides an overview of how international shipping is regulated, with a focus on the dynamics that are instrumental in making the IMO the primary site of political contestation in environmental regulation. Because of the nature of international shipping and historical developments since the inception of the IMO, regulation made by the IMO is legally binding internationally, and it is important to understand these dynamics before explaining how MNCs utilize the different pathways to influence international regulation.

Under the Law of the Sea, states have different rights and responsibilities depending on their role relative to a given ship. In this system, a vessel's 'flag' denotes the state jurisdiction, and the rules of that jurisdiction apply to all vessels flying that particular flag – that is, the 'flag state'. This makes it beneficial for MNCs to shift vessel flag registration to more favorable jurisdictions even if the MNC vessels never physically visit that jurisdiction. After a series of environmental disasters in the late twentieth century, the European states forced other flag states to follow international standards on pollution based on the threat of exclusion from European ports (DeSombre, 2006), which has

translated into global implementation of the treaties on environmental regulation developed by the IMO.

The IMO was originally set up as a technical agency under the UN umbrella
in the 1950s with the mandate to develop technical, environmental, and
safety-related standards for international shipping. Although the IMO has
been reformed several times since its inception, the basic structure has not
fundamentally changed. The IMO is governed by a Council that reports to the
Assembly, but the policy development takes place in the specialized committees and subcommittees. For environmental policy, the Marine Environment
Protection Committee (MEPC) and its subcommittee Pollution Prevention
and Response (PPR) constitute the formal institutional space for regulatory
development. Within this space, only states are formally considered to have
decision-making power in line with the IMO's status as an IGO.

In parallel with environmental disasters, the IMO developed a treaty
system governing pollution from international shipping called MARPOL (the
International Convention for the Prevention of Pollution from Ships). This
treaty system outlines principles of international environmental protection
and has several annexes that cover specific issues such as oil spill prevention
(Annex I, entered into force in 1983) and air pollution (Annex VI, entered into
force in 2005). These annexes constitute the specific requirements and obligations for vessels that fly the flag of a jurisdiction bound by the treaty. Perhaps
the most well-known example is the requirement for newbuild tankers to be
fitted with double hulls (Regulation 19 of MARPOL Annex I), which was an
amendment of Annex I decided in 1992 that took effect in July 1993.

Each annex to MARPOL, as well as any new treaty developed by the
IMO, stipulates the requirements for entry into force, and it usually requires
a combination of a number of member states representing a certain percentage
of total world tonnage. However, once a treaty or annex enters into force, it
legally applies to all IMO member states, which means that it becomes an obligation for all IMO flag states to inscribe the regulation into national law and
enforce the regulation on vessels flying that flag. A set of minor states or states
representing a minority of tonnage cannot avoid the regulation, and failure to
implement or effectively enforce it is a violation of the UN Law of the Sea.
This makes international rules developed by the IMO globally binding on all
international shipping.

Unlike most other committees of IGOs, the MEPC does not need Assembly
or Council approval for agenda setting or revision of legally binding instruments. Decisions in the MEPC about amendments to existing annexes to
MARPOL take effect 16 months after the last day of the MEPC session where
it was agreed, which means that the process of decision-making that takes
place in the MEPC is important since it formally does not require any other
body to approve of its output.

Since the early 2010s, most of the agenda of the MEPC has revolved around reducing air pollution, limiting invasive species from ships' ballast water, and developing climate change regulation. Some of the most important regulatory changes have involved reducing the NOx and sulfur emissions from ships. Although both sulfur and NOx emission control involves the reduction of pollutants emitted through gas exhaust from ships, abatement of the two pollutants differ substantially. Sulfur emission levels depend directly on the sulfur content of the fuel used, and it is possible either to reduce the sulfur content or clean the exhaust gas similarly to how stationary power plants clean exhaust. NOx emissions, on the other hand, depend on the combustion characteristics of the engine rather than the fuel and it is much more difficult to clean NOx from exhaust gas, so regulating NOx emissions requires engine design standards that tie into onboard cleaning systems. Ballast water management with the aim of preventing spread of invasive species involves mandating vessel plans for handling ballast water and specifications for water treatment systems, both of which can be disruptive for operations or simply expensive. Reduction of greenhouse gases from vessels has been an extremely contentious issue in the IMO since the Paris Agreement, and the issue is characterized by not only entrenched state positions, but also a lack of technical solutions even in the short term. In all these issues, different segments of the industry often have competing interests and states may want stronger environmental controls despite the implication on the cost of compliance for shipowners.

With the broad lines of international maritime regulation and interests covered, the next section delves into the details of MNC influence in the IMO via their different potential pathways.

PATHWAYS FOR MNC INFLUENCE IN THE IMO

The following sections analyze three pathways through which MNCs can influence the environmental regulation of the IMO, as indicated in Figure 4.1. Methodologically, the empirical basis for this analysis is the author's participant observation in the IMO from early 2017 through late 2018 complemented by interviews with state delegates, and the analytical method is inspired by process tracing (Beach and Pedersen, 2019).

MNCs' Influence in Their Own Right

Large shipowner MNCs are important economic actors, and their ability to influence international environmental regulations or standards in their own right hinges on the MNCs' ability to translate their economic importance into state concerns. The largest firms are found in liner shipping, with Maersk, MSC, CMA-CGM, and COSCO together controlling almost half the global

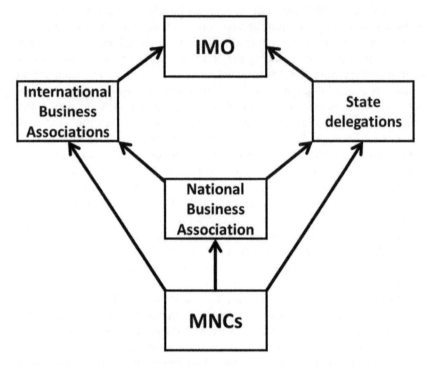

Figure 4.1   Pathways for MNCs' influence in the International Maritime
Organization

market share for container shipping (UNCTAD, 2018), which makes them integral to the functioning of global trade. Their structural importance in the global economy is a potential pathway of influence for MNCs in their own right, as states seek to protect the industry due to its ability to enable cost-efficient international trade. Invariably, IMO state delegates in environmental negotiations refer to the need for balancing environmental concerns with trade concerns. The imperative of protecting trade and global economic growth directly stems from the societal importance of the industry as the enabler of global trade, and this allows shipping MNCs to influence international regulation in their own right.

However, MNCs' different business models mean there are large variations in each individual MNC's attitude towards more stringent environmental regulation. For example, MNCs that are capable of adapting to new abatement requirements have a competitive interest in raising standards to outcompete less capable competitors. This competitive dynamic makes it unattractive for other firms to engage in environmental self-regulation to improve standards

(Falkner, 2008; Oliver and Holzinger, 2008) since that would play to their competitors' strengths. This variance of business interest in private regulation is evident in the limited extent of private regulation in shipping; different eco-rating schemes and industry-led benchmarking initiatives have been established, but have not yet had an effect on the industry, nor have they replaced traditional regulation (Poulsen, Ponte and Lister, 2016). Due to this fragmentation, the industry does not have widespread self-regulation schemes even if their importance in the global economy would allow shipping MNCs to set up systems of self-governance.

Differences in the business models of shipping firms are also a barrier to the potential extent of their power as actors in their own right. Although the common denominator is the MNCs' importance for global trade, the differences that arise from the fragmentation of their business interests prevents them from imposing clear imperatives even on states that are dependent on them for trade and revenue. A clear example of this is the industry's attitude to the transformation towards zero-emissions propulsion. Large swathes of the industry are opposed to creating regulation intended to force shipowners towards zero-emissions shipping because it creates huge compliance costs. However, large shipping MNCs with strong internal technological capabilities have allied with supporting industries and with states that are threatened by rising sea levels. This division has meant that states seeking to defend the MNCs and their role in international trade are left with a fragmented set of ideas, capacities, and interests in respect of what the industry actually wants.

These dynamics give rise to the high degree of industry organizing into different specialized business associations instead of large firms exercising political influence in their own right. There are exceptions to this, such as the economic importance of Maersk in the Danish political system, and the close collaboration between East Asian shipyards and their host governments in Korea and Japan. This is because the firms are so important for the national economies that their host governments *choose* to predominantly defend the interests of those MNCs in their specific national interests. But, in most other cases, the main pathways of influence of the MNCs is through their instrumental participation in IMO discussions, either as part of business associations or via member state delegations.

MNCs' Influence via Business Associations

The maritime industry exercises some of its influence on global regulation through powerful business associations. These business associations organize, with some overlap, the different segments of the industry, and serve both as political agents and as service providers for their members. Depending on the organization, they either have direct corporate memberships (e.g., the Baltic and International Maritime Council [BIMCO] or the World Shipping Council [WSC]) or are constituted by other industry associations at the national level (e.g., the International Chamber of Shipping [ICS] or Active Shipbuilding Experts' Federation [ASEF]). These associations are formally recognized non-state participants in the proceedings of the IMO and its component bodies, with speaking and submission rights on par with state delegates. In total, more than 80 business associations (Linné and Svensson, 2016) from the industry are recognized in the IMO, representing shipowners, shipyards, equipment and engine manufacturers and other parts of the industry. Maritime business associations are thus important vehicles of influence for MNCs.

As business associations are institutionally part of the machinations of MEPC and PPR, they are potentially extremely influential. Since the IMO has very strict rules on the secrecy of proceedings in plenary as well as working group sessions, there is no way for press representatives or other IMO delegates to refer to the details of discussions in the IMO. Some of the most important regulatory decisions have been drafted in working groups with the direct participation of some of the largest business associations who had an economic stake in the outcome of the regulatory process, but without directly observing the proceedings or systematically reconstructing events through testimonies after the fact, the influence of these business associations during IMO proceedings is a black box phenomenon. This makes it all the more relevant to look inside the proceedings of the IMO, as this is where it would be theoretically expected that industry actors could influence regulation the most (Culpepper, 2011; Fuchs, 2007; Mattli and Woods, 2009).

The business associations influence the draft regulation by leveraging their technical expertise and reinforce the idea that they contribute to solving regulatory problems rather than provide undue interference with the regulatory work (Ronit and Schneider, 2000). The concentration of technical knowledge in most business associations outweigh the capabilities of the IMO secretariat as well as even the largest state administrations. For example, the ICS draws on its members' data sources, and as it represents around 80 percent of world merchant tonnage, this is more direct data than any individual state could hope to collect. The business associations then use this information as supporting arguments for their positions, both in submissions and in verbal interventions. For example, during MEPC 73 in October 2018, a business association made a verbal proposal during the proceedings based on a dataset the representative had in front of him, and which no public authorities had seen. The majority of the states then suggested postponing a final decision on the issue in order to allow the business association to make a formal proposal at MEPC 74 the following year. The proposal was passed exactly as presented by the business association in question.

Business associations not only act as transmitters of MNC viewpoints. Their constituent firms may differ in their interests due to their different business models, and in some instances, the business associations must enter IMO deliberations without a clear agreement among their members. This can also happen when there is a shift in the strategic outlook of member MNCs, evident in the transition by the ICS and the WSC towards a more ambitious stance on climate change regulation. In practice, business association delegates must assess the interests of their MNC members on the spot during IMO deliberations, because the direction of the discussion was unanticipated, because there was disagreement among members, or because the mandate given was very broad.

It seems that the business associations could potentially capture the regulatory process due their presence, but this is not necessarily the case. Although the industry representatives have more data and can afford to have technical experts as consultants, the state delegates are also technical experts themselves and often have decades of experience working directly with the issues being discussed. These delegates may not have the same data or knowledge base available to them as industry representatives, but they are often capable of assessing whether the technical reasoning deployed by business associations holds water in the policy discussions. Since business associations are careful not to lose credibility, they make sure to present information that is truthful, in line with theoretical expectations from studies of national or EU-level lobbying (Bouwen, 2002a; Chalmers, 2013). In one interview, a senior business association representative lamented that not all business associations substantiated their arguments with rigorous analysis or data. The *raison d'être* of the participation of business associations in the IMO proceedings is to produce viewpoints from industry based on expertise or data, so when some associations neglect this they cast the foundation of industry participation in the IMO into doubt. This is consistent with observations of IMO sessions where industry actors only succeeded in influencing discussions when they substantiated their positions with technical or data-based reasoning.

The IMO as an organization holds strong deliberative norms (Müller, 2004; Risse and Kleine, 2010) that structure the possible influence of private actors on the regulation agreed by MEPC and PPR. The majority of delegates – in particular, veteran delegates with many years of experience in the IMO – share these norms, and they find it inappropriate to make interventions or submissions that do not contribute to solving the regulatory problem at hand. Business associations then must use their knowledge to contribute to drafting better regulation, while other delegates consider it inappropriate if the business associations make interventions or submissions that do not appear to contribute to solving the problem at hand. For example, in one instance, a business association made an intervention by only highlighting that their members found the new regulation increased uncertainty; as this comment did not con-tribute to moving forward, the states ignored it. Another business association, on the other hand, pooled experiences with compliance measurements from their member base and successfully persuaded the state delegates to change parts of the regulation to accommodate the problems the industry experienced. The deliberative norms both enable and constrain the influence that business associations can achieve by deploying their technical expertise, and it is neces-sary for the business associations to understand what kind of interventions the state delegates find appropriate or not if they seek to leverage their members' experiences.

MNCs' Influence via Member States

Instead of engaging the IMO through their business associations, MNCs can influence draft regulations by using state delegations as pathways of influence. This pathway is viable when MNCs gain a close relationship with state dele-gates, allowing them to influence the state position before IMO sessions and joining the delegation as participants themselves.

While MNCs have an interest in influencing states before IMO sessions, it is difficult for them to leverage their economic weight if they do not have a significant economic presence in a given polity. Firms that do not operate in the liner shipping segment often have fewer permanent staff members and route their wealth chains (Seabrooke and Wigan, 2017) through small flag states primarily for tax reasons. Their territorial presence in a given state is thus negligible and limits the ability of MNCs to use both implicit threats based on structural power and instrumental provision of information to gain access to national policy-makers or IMO delegation leaders, with the possible exception of large flag states that rely heavily on vessel registration as a source of income.[1] However, MNCs that are active in the liner shipping market or are part of the supporting industries have more assets that are bound in large coor-dinating headquarters (such as Maersk) or production and research divisions (such as the engine developer MAN Energy Solutions or any of the large ship-yards). These MNCs are more strongly territorially bound to a specific location compared to the less labor-intensive MNCs that are active in tanker or bulk shipping and, accordingly, they have more concentrated resources in a given state and a stronger economic link that underpins their influence efforts.

In addition to MNCs' economic presence, some states have large concentra-tions of shipowners. Greece, Germany, and China collectively hold ownership of just below 40 percent of the total global merchant fleet by deadweight tonnage (UNCTAD, 2018). This makes the respective national shipowner firms (and their national business associations) important political actors not only because of their structural position in the economy, but also because the shipowners enjoy a prominent discursive position with regard to the national governments even if the productive assets of the MNC in question are not located within the national jurisdiction. In this way, states' definition of policy position and overall interest in environmental issues in the IMO are shaped in an interaction with national industry players that help shape the defining interests of the state (Elbra, 2014; Woll, 2008), and individual MNCs can leverage this discursive-structural power to influence states' positions before the start of IMO deliberations.

However, the ability of MNCs to directly become part of the state delegation to IMO constitutes a more direct form of potential influence. As state delegation leaders are free to choose the composition of their delegations, MNCs can leverage their national power resources or draw upon their discursive position in the national polity to become part of a state delegation. When this happens, MNCs come under the auspices of the national delegation at the discretion of the delegation leader, and depending on the practices of the delegation in question, MNC employees are allowed to speak on behalf of the state in working groups or continuously provide advice to the state delegates during discussions. In some instances, other delegations asked specifically to hear the viewpoints of MNC representatives who were part of state delegations because they were experts in their field. Other delegations sometimes allowed MNC employees to lead the discussion on certain issues, whereby the MNCs in question effectively acted as state representatives. These close relationships also strengthen the MNCs' ability to influence state positions in anticipation of IMO debates, where the close social networks and mutual trust are important ways for MNCs to use state delegations as influence pathways.

MNCs that use state delegations as a pathway of influence draw heavily on their discursive position in the domestic arena in question, because their position as legitimate political actors and status as participants in the state delegation is rooted in state delegates' belief that their presence and role is appropriate. In interviews, state delegates consistently noted that they found it completely appropriate to have industry participants – both MNC and business associations – engage closely in the discussions, both in their own right and as part of state delegations. In particular, delegates highlighted that their own limits on expertise on a given issue that requires specialized knowledge made it natural for them to turn to MNC and business association representatives. During some discussions in 2017 and 2018, MNC employees that were part of a state delegation brought digital blueprints with them, which they could use to explain their suggestions to their delegation leader and other delegates during IMO sessions. In one instance, a Chair directly asked an MNC employee from a state delegation for suggestions for changes to draft regulatory text, and upon making changes asked the employee whether he was satisfied with it. State delegates understood these kinds of interaction to be completely unproblematic since MNC representatives were seen as bringing valuable knowledge to the table. This allowed the MNCs to conform as discursively legitimate participants in the regulatory process in line with the deliberative norms.

Across state delegations, there is idiosyncrasy in terms of the different delegations' relationship with industry associations or specific MNCs. One example highlights this. In 2018, two national delegations – one Western European and one North American – decided to enact a policy whereby no industry representatives would participate in their delegations, and this relatively sudden change surprised industry delegates who otherwise thought they could join those delegations. Perhaps surprisingly, large flag states like Panama, Liberia, and the Marshall Islands consistently have none or few MNC representatives as part of their delegations, as these states instead rely on experienced state experts or collaborate with the large business associations that participate under their own flags. On the other end are states like Denmark and Norway who have many MNC employees and business association representatives on their delegations as advisers. However, regardless of each individual state delegation's approach to whether MNCs (or national business association representatives) should be allowed to join the delegation, all state delegations accept that other states may decide to have many industry representatives on board. This creates a favorable basis for industry influence because of the deliberative norms, as industry representatives are generally seen as contributing to the quality of environmental policy discussions. Despite the differences in national relationships between MNCs and states, resistance to industry participation evaporates in the working groups of the IMO, as long as MNC representatives contribute constructively to the discussion.

It is evident that MNCs have two clear pathways into the IMO. Either they use their international business associations who represent the different industry segments, or they approach national delegations directly in order to join the delegations as advisers. This does not include efforts outside the IMO to persuade governments to change their position, but since the regulatory process in the IMO working groups requires direct participation to influence the discussion, it is important for MNCs to use their pathways to participate directly in the discussions. Once the door closes and the sessions begin, MNCs and their business associations engage in a different process with the aim to influence the regulatory outcomes.

ALL PATHWAYS LEAD TO DELIBERATION: THE DYNAMICS OF INFLUENCE IN THE IMO

As MNCs influence the IMO deliberations directly through either of their potential pathways, the power dynamics shift from being a matter of struggling to get a seat at the table to being a matter of legitimate political interaction.

Participation in the deliberation does not automatically translate into influence, but the MNCs use their possible pathways to contribute to the drafting process by conforming to the working norms of the IMO. All industry proposals whether verbal or written are evaluated by state representatives along three dimensions. First, state delegates assess whether the kind of input provided is legitimate at all. Input by MNCs is legitimate if states perceive it as being contributive in nature relative to the discussion at hand, which in practice implies a strong emphasis on technical information supported by evidence collected by MNCs themselves. For example, during PPR 5, a representative from a business association representing individual MNCs used their collective industry experience to argue why a specific state proposal was problematic for the achievement of the overall aim of already agreed-upon regulation, and their technical substantiation of their argument resulted in several states agreeing with the business association.

Second, state delegates assess whether the substance of the proposal is reasonable. Most state delegations are staffed by officials with a background in engineering or naval architecture, and even when MNCs are undisputed experts on a given issue, state representatives are usually capable of assessing whether a proposal makes sense from a technical point of view. This dynamic requires MNCs to substantiate their proposals to convince state delegates that their points are valid. Of course, states evaluate these claims with an eye on the economic relationship between MNCs and the states themselves, but since both the ownership and registration of vessels is concentrated in specific countries, as noted earlier, the majority of states in any given discussion do not have a direct material link to the MNCs in a given industry segment, which implies the MNCs must mobilize technical arguments and analyses to convince the rest of the states. For example, a business association made a proposal on behalf of their MNC members to postpone entry into effect of a certain provision for the industry. Most state delegates did not believe the technical justification made sense, but two states voiced support in the plenary for the proposal against the majority. These two states were economic homes to many of the MNCs that were members of the business association. The proposal quickly fell because these limited economic relationships were insufficient to sway the entirety of the MEPC.

Third, the MNCs and their business associations must focus their efforts on issues that state delegates believe to be less salient, since state delegates believe it is illegitimate to allow MNCs to influence highly politicized issues. Even if industry proposals are contributive to the regulatory problem and they are perceived as technically sound, state delegates only accept proposals that originate from industry actors if the extent of the proposal is proportional to how salient the delegates believe the issue is. In issues where state delegates believe there is a high degree of public attention, or issues where broader political concerns dictate the states' positions, state delegates do not accept influence by industry – whether individual MNCs or business associations – because they perceive firms as illegitimate political actors in high politics. One senior business association representative explained this limit as a 'glass ceiling' where industry representatives simply had to acknowledge that the discussion had shifted into political territory with no room for industry influence.

MNCs can use either pathway to support the efforts made by their business associations or sympathetic states. The most important activity is their ability to present their own in-house data as part of a discussion in a working group. As long as state delegates believe the work of the industry to be contributive, it is an effective instrument to put first-hand data or experience on the table during a discussion. For example, in one instance, a working group Chair specifically asked a specific state to put one of their MNC advisors on the microphone. The Chair quizzed the MNC employee about their points of view on the issue at hand, and the proposals by the employee were written into the draft regulation. In another instance, an MNC employee facilitated a meeting between two state delegations during an IMO session where the employee successfully persuaded one of the states to support the MNC proposal by mobilizing their internal test data. When MNCs are part of business association delegations, they can make similar contributions during discussions or act as liaisons between delegations. This is where the bureaucratic capacity of individual MNCs becomes important. Maersk had four individual employees present at MEPC 74 in 2019, with three attached to the Danish delegation and one positioned in the WSC. This kind of presence across delegations allows for coordination of interventions or transmission of information during IMO sessions. Maersk's major competitors (MSC, CMA-CGM, and COSCO) each had one employee attached to the delegations of Liberia, France, and China, respectively. In sum, MNCs with the appropriate capabilities can utilize their role as political participants to support the legitimate contributions of either business associations or state delegations.

CONCLUSION

The case of industry influence in the IMO shows that MNCs' pathways of influence can happen through close collaboration with business associations and state delegations, but ultimately rest on MNC representatives' ability to participate in deliberations in a legitimate fashion. If MNC representatives show up and think that their presence in the IMO automatically warrants influence, then they leave the meeting halls empty-handed. The point is that their pathways of influence not only entail getting a seat at the table, but also participating in deliberations in a way that legitimizes industry influence.

MNCs can leverage their instrumental power or build on their structural position in specific states, but when MNC representatives are physically present in the IMO discussions, they are capable of mobilizing their expertise and data to swing discussions in their favor. With the long history of the IMO working in this way, the institutionalization of MNCs and business associations as legitimate participants in the work of the IMO is a strong basis for MNC influence in the IMO. As both MNCs and business associations continuously participate in the regulatory work, they deepen the institutionalization of their own participation, which in turn makes their participation more legitimate. This constitutes a form of self-reinforcing discursive power, whereby the legitimate contributions of MNCs and business associations strengthen their own discursive position. It deepens the power of MNCs in the IMO as state delegates potentially take their participation for granted to an even higher extent.

MNCs can build on their structural or discursive power in individual states to shift both the national position, enable them to participation in the IMO sessions, and make state delegates more predisposed to accept MNCs and business associations as legitimate political actors. The IMO is not unique in this sense. The International Civil Aviation Organization (ICAO) is the parallel IGO governing international air transport, and in ICAO, MNCs and business associations have similar access compared to the IMO. What makes the IMO stand apart is the strong organizational deliberative norms. MNCs must 'play by the rules' to maintain their legitimacy as political actors and successfully influence regulation, and although MNCs' national position matters, the deliberative norms structure their strongest potential for influence. MNCs that are effective at influencing states in changing their positions may not necessarily be effective at participating in IMO deliberations, and future research on the political role of MNCs should explore the activities, power bases, and capabilities of MNCs to understand how the firms exercise influence.

An important lesson from the IMO is that the manifestation of private actors' structural and discursive power in a global industry can manifest in the working rooms of international deliberations. When a Chair asks an MNC employee how to phrase the draft regulation or when state delegates engage in serious discussion with business associations, it is the observable manifestation of an institutionalized relationship between industry and state actors that is applicable across the global maritime industry. The specific deliberative norms of the IMO relate to macro-level ideas about the appropriate role of shipping MNCs in global shipping regulation, and the constant participation of private actors in the regulatory process entrench this institutionalized relationship. It is possible to view this entrenchment as a deepening of the discursive power of firms; the more state delegates take the political of MNCs for granted, the deeper the discursive power of the maritime industry.

The IMO as a case also adds to the normative discussion on the limits of potential industry power in global governance. An obvious concern here is the extreme potential for industry access to the regulatory process where even state delegations can freely choose to let MNC employees speak on their behalf in working groups. However, the dynamics of influence in deliberations complicate the matter since access does not imply influence, and even if MNC access to the IMO regulatory process is tightened, MNCs are still able to exercise influence over national positions as in every other global policy issue. One solution could be more transparency of the process. In 2019, the IMO began discussing whether to reform the procedural rules and potentially open up media access to working groups and make the decisions more transparent. Adding to this is the almost paradoxical stance of state delegates, as the consensus among state delegates is that industry presence is highly valued and that it would result in lower quality of regulation should industry participation be limited. In other words, the case of the IMO hits the core of the normative discussion on the legitimate extent of MNCs' political power.

One of the lessons from the shipping case is that not all pathways are equal. Deep relationships between individual MNCs and state delegations are much stronger than simply using the business associations, because the business associations must accommodate a variety of business models. In some state delegations, the lines dividing MNC and state employees seem to have almost disappeared, and the identity of the delegation fuses into one. Such relationships are the epitome of business discursive power, since state delegates take industry participation for granted and assume their goals align with broad public interest. However, this strong position in the national context only translates into influence in the IMO when the MNCs understand how to participate in a legitimate way. This finding calls for a deeper look into the relationship between MNCs' global power as manifest in the relationship with specific states, and MNCs' global power as manifest in their participation in international negotiations.

With the complex interplay between industry and state interests, the different pathways of influence for MNCs, and the important institutionalized norms that govern deliberations in the IMO, this case contributes to explaining how and why MNCs exercise influence in global governance. The lessons and challenges raised by international shipping regulation are applicable in every setting where it is worth examining industry influence or questioning the extent of their power, and researchers can use the IMO as a relevant case for expanding our understanding of global corporate power.

NOTE

1. For Liberia in 2011, the business of ship registry brought in US$18–22 million relative to a total gross domestic product of about US$1.5 billion (Reed, 2011).

REFERENCES

Beach, D. and R.B. Pedersen (2019), *Process-Tracing Methods: Foundations and Guidelines*, 2nd edition, Ann Arbor, MI: University of Michigan Press.

Bouwen, P. (2002a), 'Corporate lobbying in the European Union: towards a theory of access', *Social Sciences*, **9**(3), 365–90.

Bouwen, P. (2002b), 'Corporate lobbying in the European Union: the logic of access', *Journal of European Public Policy*, **9**(3), 365–90.

Chalmers, A.W. (2013), 'Trading information for access: informational lobbying strategies and interest group access to the European Union', *Journal of European Public Policy*, **20**(1), 39–58.

Culpepper, P.D. (2011), *Quiet Politics and Business Power*, Cambridge, UK: Cambridge University Press.

Culpepper, P.D. (2015), 'Structural power and political science in the post-crisis era', *Business and Politics*, **17**(3), 391–409.

DeSombre, E.R. (2006), *Flagging Standards: Globalization and Environmental, Safety, and Labor Regulations at Sea*, Cambridge, MA: MIT Press.

Dür, A. (2008), 'Measuring interest group influence in the EU: a note on methodology', *European Union Politic*, **9**(4), 559–76.

Dür, A. and G. Mateo (2013), 'Gaining access or going public? Interest group strategies in five European countries', *European Journal of Political Research*, **52**(5), 660–86.

Elbra, A.D. (2014), 'Interests need not be pursued if they can be created: private governance in African gold mining', *Business and Politics*, **16**(2), 247–66.

Falkner, R. (2008), *Business Power and Conflict in International Environmental Politics*, Basingstoke: Palgrave Macmillan.

Flohr, A., L. Rieth, S. Schwindenhammer and K. Wolf (2010), *The Role of Business in Global Governance: Corporations as Norm-Entrepreneurs*, Basingstoke: Palgrave Macmillan.

Fuchs, D. (2007), *Business Power in Global Governance*, Boulder, CO: Lynne Rienner Publishers.

Linné, P. and E. Svensson (2016), 'Regulating pollution from ships', in K. Andersson, S. Brynolf, J.F. Lindgren and M. Wilewska-Bien (eds), *Shipping and the Environment: Improving Environmental Performance in Marine Transportation*, Berlin/Heidelberg: Springer, pp. 75–121.

Mattli, W. and N. Woods (2009), 'In whose benefit? Explaining regulatory change in global politics', in W. Mattli and N. Woods (eds), *The Politics of Global Regulation*, Princeton, NJ: Princeton University Press, pp. 1–43.

Mikler, J. (2018), *The Political Power of Global Corporations*, Cambridge, UK: Polity Press.

Müller, H. (2004), 'Arguing, bargaining and all that: communicative action, rationalist theory and the logic of appropriateness in international relations', *European Journal of International Relations*, **10**(3), 395–435.

96 *MNCs in global politics*

Nasiritousi, N. and B.-O. Linnér (2016), 'Open or closed meetings? Explaining nonstate actor involvement in the international climate change negotiations', *International Environmental Agreements: Politics, Law and Economics*, **16**(1), 127–44.

Oliver, C. and I. Holzinger (2008), 'The effectiveness of strategic political management: a dynamic capabilities framework', *Academy of Management Review*, **33**(2), 496–520.

Poulsen, R.T., S. Ponte and J. Lister (2016), 'Buyer-driven greening? Cargo-owners and environmental upgrading in maritime shipping', *Geoforum*, **68**(January), 57–68.

Reed, J. (2011), 'Ship registry: steady source of funds', *Financial Times*, 7 December, accessed 3 May 2016 at https://next.ft.com/content/66601d70-1ab3-11e1-bc34-00144feabdc0.

Rietig, K. (2016), 'The power of strategy: environmental NGO influence in international climate negotiations', *Global Governance*, **22**(2), 269–88.

Risse, T. and M. Kleine (2010), 'Deliberation in negotiations', *Journal of European Public Policy*, **17**(5), 708–26.

Ronit, K. and V. Schneider (2000), *Private Organisations in Global Politics*, Abingdon: Routledge.

Seabrooke, L. and D. Wigan (2017), 'The governance of global wealth chains', *Review of International Political Economy*, **24**(1), 1–29.

Sell, S.K. (1999), *Multinational Corporations as Agents of Change: The Globalization of Intellectual Property Rights*, Albany, NY: State University of New York Press.

Stopford, M. (2009), *Maritime Economics*, 3rd edition, Abingdon: Routledge.

United Nations Conference on Trade and Development [UNCTAD] (2018), *Review of Maritime Transport 2018*, accessed 18 March 2020 at https://unctad.org/en/PublicationsLibrary/rmt2018_en.pdf.

Vormedal, I. (2008), 'The influence of business and industry NGOs in the negotiation of the Kyoto Mechanisms: the case of carbon capture and storage in the CDM', *Global Environmental Politics*, **8**(4), 36–65.

Wilks, S. (2013), *The Political Power of the Business Corporation*, Cheltenham, UK and Northampton, MA, USA: Edward Elgar Publishing.

Woll, C. (2008), *Firm Interests: How Governments Shape Business Lobbying on Global Trade*, Ithaca, NY: Cornell University Press.

Young, K. (2012), 'Transnational regulatory capture? An empirical examination of the transnational lobbying of the Basel Committee on Banking Supervision', *Review of International Political Economy*, **19**(4), 663–88.

5. Private sustainability governance and global corporate power

Kate Macdonald

Private sustainability standard-setting systems have come to occupy a central position within the institutional landscape of global business regulation. Such initiatives include well-known consumer labels such as Fairtrade and Rainforest Alliance, alongside multi-stakeholder roundtables and working groups promoting sustainable production standards such as the Forest Stewardship Council, Fair Labor Association, and a range of single-commodity sustainability roundtables. These private regulatory systems have been variously characterized as examples of non-state market-driven governance (Cashore, 2002), transnational private governance (Auld, Renckens and Cashore, 2015; Bartley, 2011) or civil regulation (Vogel, 2010). Despite significant variation in their regulatory agendas and institutional designs, such initiatives share the central aim of improving the social and environmental impact of global business activity through developing shared regulatory norms and associated systems for supporting and verifying compliance.

Together with traditional governmental and inter-governmental regulation, such schemes now play a prominent role in regulating the social and environmental effects of global business activity across a wide range of sectoral contexts, including industrial production, agricultural supply chains, and processes of natural resource management. Increasing reliance on private regulatory mechanisms has often been interpreted as evidence of a wider systemic shift towards more complex and pluralist modes of global regulatory governance that rely in unprecedented ways on the initiative and capacities of both state and non-state actors (Braithwaite, 2008; Grabosky, 2013; Hale and Held, 2011).

The proliferation of such new forms of private governance has been received with enthusiasm by some observers, who have viewed global sustainability governance schemes as bolstering the effectiveness of global business regulation by facilitating learning, normative change, and collaborative engagement in processes of regulatory implementation (Bäckstrand, 2006; Mena and Palazzo, 2012; Scherer and Palazzo, 2011). Multi-stakeholder variants of private sustainability governance that facilitate extensive civil society participation and third-party monitoring of standards implementation have often been embraced with particular optimism, as potential means of supporting more inclusive and legitimate global business regulation by facilitating collaboration between MNCs and civil society interests (Abbott, 2012; Cashore, 2002). Such approaches have been argued to offer useful means of supporting balanced representation of corporate interests alongside groups focused on labor, social or environmental concerns, and promoting deliberation amongst diverse stakeholder voices in the design and implementation of regulatory processes (Bäckstrand, 2006; Meidinger, 2007).

While such accounts recognize the pervasive character of corporate power, they do not view such power as an insurmountable obstacle to regulatory effectiveness and legitimacy. Instead, corporate power is assumed to be amenable to institutional control through appropriately inclusive or representative modes of institutional design. Indeed, to some extent, corporate power is regarded at least implicitly as a core enabling condition for the effectiveness of private systems of regulatory governance. On this view, the corporate concentration of large retail and processing MNCs that occupy dominant positions within buyer-led supply chains not only confers power on these firms, but also makes them vulnerable to social and regulatory pressures (Schleifer, 2016). Social and environmental movements can thus use private sustainability governance schemes as a vehicle through which to harness the power of lead firms in global supply chains as a means of pressuring other supply chain actors (often located in sites of commodity production in the Global South) to comply with stronger social and environmental production standards.

Yet, decades after the first pioneering private sustainability governance initiatives were created, evidence of their capacity to tackle social and environmental harms associated with the activity of MNCs remains limited and uneven. Critics have interpreted such findings as highlighting the fundamentally limited capacity of private sustainability governance to support effective and legitimate social and environmental regulation – many attributing such failings to the capture of private governance by powerful corporate interests (Cheyns and Riisgaard, 2014). Although private sustainability governance processes are usually managed by third-party organizations that are legally independent from the businesses that they seek to regulate, multiple forms of structural, material, and discursive power have been argued to undermine their practical autonomy from business interests – eroding their effectiveness and legitimacy. At the same time, such private governance schemes have been viewed as vehicles through which the structural power of corporate interests can be legitimized and reproduced, as processes of sustainability certification serve discursively to insulate companies from societal pressure for stronger regulation (Bloomfield, 2012; LeBaron and Lister, 2015).

These debates provide the backdrop to this chapter's analysis of the dynamics and consequences of corporate power within private sustainability governance. Speaking directly to the core themes of this book as outlined by Mikler and Ronit in Chapter 1, the chapter's central aim is to explore the multiple *pathways* through which corporate power is exercised within processes of private sustainability governance, and the implications of such power for regulatory effectiveness and legitimacy. To develop this theoretical analysis, the chapter brings together insights from several literatures that are rarely brought into explicit engagement. Of particular importance are insights from institutionalist scholarship on global environmental governance and transnational business regulation, and literature on global business power that is grounded more centrally in critical political economy traditions. To support the theoretical synthesis of these disparate bodies of work, analysis also draws on a broad synthesis of evidence from the rich empirical scholarship on private sustainability governance, with a particular focus on examples of private regulatory schemes operating in Latin America and Southeast Asia.

The chapter begins by unpacking the multiple sources and pathways of business power exercised within processes of private sustainability governance – reflecting on the implications of such power for the capacity of competing business and societal stakeholders to influence the design and implementation of regulatory processes. The effectiveness and inclusiveness of private sustainability governance is shown to be weakened as a result of power exercised by corporations, business associations, and wider business networks *directly* within the decision-making processes of individual private regulatory organizations, and *indirectly* through interactions with state, market, and civil society actors in wider fields of regulatory contestation. However, while private regulatory systems are frequently harnessed as means of reinforcing or legitimizing corporate power, they can also provide organizational and discursive vehicles through which such power can be *contested* by pro-regulatory coalitions. The chapter therefore argues that it is possible to acknowledge the potent and multi-dimensional character of corporate power within private sustainability governance, while also recognizing the potential for such power to be resisted, contested, and sometimes even actively appropriated in support of strengthened social and environmental regulation of MNCs.

CORPORATE POWER AND THE LIMITS OF PRIVATE SUSTAINABILITY REGULATION

We begin by teasing apart some of the principal dimensions and pathways of business power that have been shown to operate within processes of private sustainability governance across a range of economic sectors, geographical locations and institutional models of private governance. As we will see, such power often imposes significant constraints on the potential of private sustainability governance to support effective and inclusive processes of social and environmental regulation of MNCs.

Scholarship on business power has often focused on two central analytical distinctions through which varying forms of business power have been differentiated (see also Mikler and Ronit, Chapter 1). The first of these is a distinction between *instrumental* power, involving observable power relations between agents, and *structural* power, constituted within broader socio-economic or discursive orders and relationships (Fuchs, 2007; Fuchs and Lederer, 2007; Mikler, 2018). Second, such analyses have frequently distinguished between *material* power, based on access to economic and organizational resources or a dominant structural position within wider systems of social, economic, or organizational relationships, and *discursive* power, which is embodied within particular normative and cognitive orders, and expressed through a variety of communicative practices, discourses, or narratives (Cheyns and Riisgaard, 2014; Fuchs and Lederer, 2007; Holzscheiter, 2005). Scholarship on private sustainability governance has identified multiple forms of business power that span these categories – different dimensions of power often interacting in support of business efforts to control the design and operation of private regulatory processes.

Perhaps most readily observable are the material forms of power that enable business interests to dominate many decision-making processes through which individual private regulatory schemes are governed. As numerous authors have documented, corporate access to extensive economic and organizational resources is often associated with disproportionate influence and voice within processes of private sustainability governance (Fuchs and Lederer, 2007).[1] MNCs and other large companies have access to a range of financial, organizational, and human resources that support their influence within collaborative decision-making processes, such as money, staff, access to specific forms of legal and technocratic expertise, and fluency in the working languages of global regulatory schemes (Bennett, 2017; Boström and Hallström, 2010; Ponte and Gibbon, 2011). Such power imbalances have been shown to generate systematic under-representation of marginalized groups, including workers, trade unions, farmers groups, indigenous people, and other communities whose land claims conflict with those of agricultural or extractive firms (Fransen and Kolk, 2007; Nelson and Tallontire, 2014; Utting, 2002). Such disparities are associated not only with distorted processes of bargaining and deliberation, in which marginalized voices are often excluded, but also with the narrowing of regulatory agendas to focus on issues of particular concern to actors in the Global North (Cheyns and Riisgaard, 2014).

In analyzing such material sources of business power, early literature on private regulation often emphasized the role of industry or trade associations in shaping private regulatory processes – drawing on numerous examples of private regulatory schemes established and controlled by business associations in sectors such as chemicals, mining, electronics, apparel, toys, coffee, and cocoa (Ronit and Schneider, 1999; Vogel, 2010). Domestic structures of business organization have been viewed as potentially important determinants of regulatory processes and outcomes through effects on interest group mobilization, information flows, and patterns of access to authoritative regulatory actors and forums (Büthe and Mattli, 2013). The influence of private regulatory initiatives controlled by business associations has tended to wane over time, as civil society demands for more inclusive rule-making processes have pushed many businesses towards participation in multi-stakeholder regulatory programs. Nonetheless, recent literature has highlighted emerging trends towards increased assertiveness of business associations in producing countries, leading in a number of cases to the development of competing systems of regulatory standards initiated by producer associations and governments in the Global South (Schouten and Bitzer, 2015).

Regardless of the degree of engagement by trade or industry associations, powerful individual corporations often take on central roles within private regulatory processes. Corporate capacity to exercise disproportionate influence within private standard-setting processes is often particularly pronounced for those major retail or processing companies who occupy a dominant structural position as 'lead firms' within global supply chains (Dauvergne and Lister, 2010; Fuchs and Kalfagianni, 2010). Such firms exercise structural power over private standard-setting processes as a result of their 'gatekeeping' power over networks of suppliers (van der Ven, 2018). Such power depends in part on the centrality and connectedness of lead firms within diffuse production networks, enabling them to control the degree to which sustainability standards achieve market uptake by exerting leverage on their networks of suppliers to participate in a particular scheme.[2] Voluntary sustainability governance initiatives further depend on business participation for support in the dissemination and implementation of private regulatory norms, and in many cases also for operating revenue derived from membership or licensing fees. The structural power of lead firms in global supply chains often enables such firms to push the costs of standards compliance onto suppliers, generating regressive distributional effects, and excluding the participation of smallholder producers as a result of prohibitive entry barriers (Gibbon, Ponte and Lazaro, 2010; Ponte, 2008; Selwyn, 2015). Moreover, the structural power of lead firms over rule-making processes is often used to dilute regulatory standards (Fuchs and Lederer, 2007; Jaffee and Howard, 2010), though it can sometimes operate instead to strengthen standards, particularly where lead firms themselves face high levels of scrutiny over their supply chain sustainability practices. For example, van der Ven (2018) showed how Walmart used its structural position within aquaculture supply chains to strengthen Best Aquaculture Practices standards, while others have documented similar dynamics in the cases of large retailers and supermarkets who have been essential to the growth of prominent sustainability standards such as the Forest Stewardship Council, Marine Stewardship Council, and Fairtrade (Barrientos and Smith, 2007; Bartley, 2018).

Corporate power over private standard-setting processes is often further intensified by the exercise of discursive power in shaping which (and whose) forms of knowledge and expertise are conferred legitimacy within the bureaucratic and technocratic procedures of private regulatory systems. It has often been argued that such processes tend to privilege technical or legal forms of knowledge over the knowledge or experiences of marginalized workers, small producers, or aggrieved land users (Cheyns, 2014). Such dynamics have been documented in deliberative forums focused on standard setting, in processes of monitoring and audit, and in the context of specific disputes between companies and affected people. For example, reliance on technical forms of evidence to evaluate land rights claims has been shown to downplay the value of testimonies from communities and associated reference to traditional markers such as trees and rivers – reinforcing local power imbalances (Cheyns and Riisgaard, 2014; Silva-Castañeda, 2012). In standards development processes, the exclusion of marginalized forms of knowledge has been linked to a disproportionate focus on measurable features of safety, such as use of chemicals, at the expense of more intangible issues relating to livelihood inequalities or insecurity (Nelson and Tallontire, 2014; Raynolds, 2014). There is often particular fear that by exaggerating levels of neutrality and consensus within private regulatory systems, such inequalities of discursive power are masked, exposing marginalized groups to greater manipulation and control by powerful business actors (Edmunds and Wollenberg, 2001; Moog, Spicer and Böhm, 2015). While at times such exclusion may be unintended – resulting from the dominance of technical modes of knowledge within wider cultural and organizational fields – at other times the privileging of technical knowledge may be intensified through strategic forms of rhetorical action exercised by business actors seeking to gain advantage in particular negotiation or mediation processes (Fuchs and Lederer, 2007).

In addition to material and discursive power exercised in the design and implementation of private regulatory standards, business power also shapes the pathways through which private regulatory initiatives interact with other regulatory actors within the wider regulatory fields in which they are embedded (de Bakker, Rasche and Ponte, 2019; Gereffi, Humphrey and Sturgeon, 2005; Henderson et al., 2002). While such interactions sometimes take the form of direct relationships of collaboration or competition between regulatory actors (Eberlein et al., 2014; Overdevest and Zeitlin, 2014), flows of power often play out through more diffuse processes, reflected in shifting distributions of power between competing regulatory actors, coalitions, or discursive narratives.

One frequently expressed fear is that corporate-dominated private regulatory systems can serve to reinforce and extend the discursive power of business within wider regulatory fields – legitimizing and reproducing corporate power and crowding out more enforceable or radical forms of regulation or social mobilization. According to this view, efforts by business actors to control discourses and regulatory agendas within private regulatory systems, and their representation within wider public discourses as legitimate forums for social and environmental regulation, can stabilize and reproduce weak forms of regulation. It is feared that this 'can effectively de-rail serious political struggles in more conventional political arenas and marginalize the state as a potential enforcement mechanism' (Moog et al., 2015, p. 470; see also LeBaron and Lister, 2015). As well as undermining potentially stronger forms of state regulation, there is fear that such forms of discursive power can support processes of depoliticization: 'undermin[ing] the ability of concerned citizens to effectively politicize underlying conflicts [and] defanging critiques as they are channeled into restricted arenas of well-mannered deliberation' (Moog et al., 2015, p. 470).

The risk is not only that such discursive processes will crowd out strengthened state regulation or more radical forms of social organizing; critics also fear that corporate-controlled private regulatory systems will have detrimental effects on competing sustainability governance schemes that seek to impose more stringent social and environmental standards on MNCs and other business actors. To some extent, individual standard-setting schemes can control the market segments, production locations or supply chains in which they operate (Bloomfield and Schleifer, 2017), preserving some autonomy for more stringent schemes such as Fairtrade to promote more radical or transformative efforts at change (Raynolds, 2014). Nonetheless, a number of scholars have documented cases in which fragmentation and competition between private regulatory schemes can lead firms to forum shop for the least costly standards (Fransen, 2011; Gulbrandsen, 2005; Raustiala and Victor, 2004). Conversely, cases have also been documented in which competition has generated pressures for upwards convergence, at least in relation to specific issues targeted by civil society campaigns, relating both to the stringency of substantive standards, and procedural requirements for transparent and independent auditing (Overdevest, 2010; Smith and Fischlein, 2010). Battles for discursive power play a crucial role in determining the outcomes of such interactions. The more readily 'weaker' regulatory systems can establish themselves as legitimate and credible alternatives, the harder it is for more demanding regulatory systems to survive within a competitive marketplace.[3]

While many critical analyses have focused on power struggles within global regulatory fields, others have highlighted the potential for private sustainability governance to reinforce the power of elite networks of corporate and state actors at the *national* level, in jurisdictions in which production is located. For example, Peña's (2014) analysis of a number of global sustainability governance schemes operating in Brazil showed how networks of state and business elites operated as national champions or gatekeepers for these schemes – supported by powerful local business associations. Their ability to control domestic uptake of international standards through their dominant position within neo-corporatist state–society relations at the national level enabled them to gain voice and influence within international standard-setting processes in exchange for their support as brokers in diffusing and legitimizing the standards at the national level. Likewise, Selfa, Bain and Moreno's (2014) analysis of Bonsucro's operation in the Colombian sugarcane industry showed how this multi-stakeholder sustainability governance scheme consolidated and legitimized established national networks of business and state elites, enabling local producers to consolidate their power at the national level and expand their control over contested land and water resources. By presenting sustainability certification as an apolitical and value-neutral set of standards, while disregarding political debates regarding state complicity in unequal access to land, these authors argued that corporate participation in Bonsucro helped to discursively legitimize a process of intensified sugarcane production, and associated dispossession of rural communities (see also Schouten and Glasbergen, 2011 on the palm oil case).

PRIVATE SUSTAINABILITY REGULATION AND THE CONTESTATION OF CORPORATE POWER

The above examples illustrate the diversity of pathways through which private sustainability governance can extend or reinforce corporate power – often undermining the stringency and inclusiveness of global regulatory processes, while serving to depoliticize such distributional effects. However, as the following section explores, the interaction of private regulatory systems with power struggles in wider regulatory fields may also create opportunities for the contestation and re-politicization of corporate power, as the entry of private sustainability governance processes into existing regulatory contests opens up new spaces for material and discursive contestation, 'creat[ing] new grounds upon which, and around which, struggles over the ethical and social responsibilities of corporations take place' (Moog et al., 2015, p. 471).

One well-documented pathway through which private regulatory processes may be appropriated as means of contesting corporate power – even when standard-setting processes themselves remain dominated by corporate interests – involves efforts by civil society organizations (CSOs) to harness corporate commitments to private standards as a basis for 'accountability politics' (Keck and Sikkink, 2014). Such a strategy involves an effort to harness formal corporate commitments to voluntary standards, together with increased transparency of corporate social and environmental performance, as a basis for exposing persistent distance between normative discourse and established practice – increasing pressure for substantive behavioral change (LeBaron and Lister, 2015). For many critically minded non-governmental organizations (NGOs), willingness to engage with or endorse private sustainability governance systems has remained conditional on their capacity to support such efforts to hold corporate power to account (Macdonald, 2014).

Private sustainability governance processes may also support the contestation of corporate power to the extent they help to open up new spaces for discursive contestation, or shift the balance of discursive and material power, in ways that enable pro-regulatory actors or coalitions to gain ground within ongoing regulatory struggles. Even where private sustainability governance schemes remain corporate-dominated, 'counter-hegemonic' coalitions operating outside these schemes (Levy, 2008), such as coalitions of NGOs, smallholders, or trade unions, can sometimes use these multi-stakeholder forums as a way of building discursive and material leverage in support of demands for strengthened regulation on particular issues. For example, in the Indonesian palm oil sector, Diprose, Kurniawan and Macdonald (2019) showed how the involvement of international NGOs in the Roundtable on Sustainable Palm Oil (RSPO) helped facilitate civil society influence over Indonesian policy debates surrounding both Free, Prior and Informed Consent for communities affected by new palm oil plantations, and protections for High Conservation Value land. The multi-stakeholder deliberative forum provided by the RSPO created discursive spaces within which these agendas could gain increased visibility and credibility, while support from powerful buyers of palm oil such as Unilever and Nestlé increased the material leverage of pro-regulatory coalitions. Others have documented examples in which private certification systems have supported local demands for higher wages, freedom of association, or strengthened enforcement of state regulation by providing a focal point for strengthened civil society mobilization and associated market pressure (Overdevest and Zeitlin, 2014; Sundstrom and Henry, 2017).

The contestation of corporate power can also be facilitated by audit or grievance-handling mechanisms within private sustainability governance schemes, where workers or communities engaged in conflicts with companies are able to harness these in support of their claims (Haines and Macdonald, 2019; Köhne, 2014). For example, some Indonesian NGOs who participated in complaints to the RSPO reported that their ability to access company representatives and local government officials was enhanced both by the personal and organizational networks they developed through engagement with RSPO processes, and the greater visibility and credibility that these mechanisms provided to structurally marginalized community and civil society voices. Others reported further benefits in the form of increased rights consciousness and horizontal networking capacity amongst worker and community organizations (Macdonald and Balaton-Chrimes, 2016). In some cases, evidence gathered in the course of preparing, investigating, and evaluating grievance claims can be deployed as advocacy tools in broader struggles for improved labor standards or claims over contested land. Often, however, the production of such evidence has depended on support provided to local communities by national and international NGOs – for example, in the form of support for participatory land mapping processes (Macdonald, 2020; Macdonald and Balaton-Chrimes, 2016).[4]

While the above examples highlight the potential role of counter-hegemonic coalitions that directly challenge corporate power, a distinct pathway through which corporate power can be appropriated in support of strengthened social and environmental regulation emerges when corporate participation in private regulatory schemes produces a shift in corporate interests. This can enable pro-regulatory coalitions to harness corporate support for strengthened regulation on specific issues without directly destabilizing established distributions of power. For example, the palm oil company Golden Agri-Resources (GAR) was incentivized to engage with potential reforms to its sustainability and human rights practices as a result of sustained civil society campaigning against GAR's contributions to deforestation, and subsequent processes of dialogue and pressure from civil society and key supply chain buyers (Unilever and Nestlé), who are major players within the RSPO (Macdonald and Balaton-Chrimes, 2016). This process led not only to changes in the company's internal policies, but also its engagement in wider coalitions of businesses and CSOs within Indonesia seeking to influence government policy on protection of High Conservation Value land.[5] Likewise, in the garments sector, the multi-stakeholder Ethical Trading Initiative (ETI) has at times played an important role supporting advocacy for legislative reform within the UK. For example, the ETI was reported to play a role in the successful push to include a 'transparency in supply chains' component in the Modern Slavery Act 2015 (UK), and in persuading the UK parliament to pass the Gangmasters (Licensing) Act 2004 (UK) (Connor, Delaney and Rennie, 2016). Such examples have, however, depended on relatively unusual circumstances in which all three categories of participant within ETI's tripartite governance structure (UK trade unions, UK civil CSOs, and major UK businesses) have agreed on a shared policy platform.

Frequently, efforts by pro-regulatory coalitions to challenge established configurations of business power have met with direct resistance from organized business interests. In seeking to protect entrenched sources of power, business actors often draw on material, institutional, and discursive support from political and bureaucratic elites. Resistance to global regulatory agendas by coalitions of business and state actors in jurisdictions where production is located has often drawn on *discursive* claims about the inappropriateness or insensitivity of global sustainability standards to local cultural contexts, and the inability of foreign standard-setting bodies to properly understand such local contexts. Such claims often draw on practical concerns about compliance capacity, in the form of technical barriers to compliance, excessive compliance costs associated with demanding prescriptive rules, or strict auditing procedures involving costly data or auditing requirements (Auld et al., 2015; Strambach and Surmeier, 2018). Such claims are then frequently linked to broader struggles over the epistemic and moral authority of global standards and standard-setting bodies (Haines, Macdonald and Balaton-Chrimes, 2012; Macdonald, 2020).

Elite state–business networks also wield significant *material* power as a result of their capacity to act as gatekeepers for the national dissemination of global regulatory standards, as discussed above. Not only does this provide an important potential source of structural power to large producers who choose to participate in global regulatory schemes, it also provides a pathway through which the implementation of global regulatory standards can be directly resisted, where demanding requirements are considered to threaten powerful state and business interests in producing countries. Several authors have documented the response of large producers and government regulators to both the Roundtable for Responsible Soy in Brazil and the RSPO in Indonesia and Malaysia. In each of these cases, elite state–business networks viewed their interests as being undermined by the efforts of northern CSOs and retailers to promote increasingly demanding regulatory standards on issues such as protection of High Conservation Value land, controls on greenhouse gas emissions, and respect for the Free Prior and Informed Consent of communities to the conversion of customary lands for plantation of commercial crops. In response, powerful networks of state and business actors have shifted their support away from global regulatory schemes and towards rival national sustainability certification programs that place fewer restrictions on established business practices (Hospes, 2014; Macdonald, 2020).[6]

NGOs engaging in these ongoing regulatory struggles often confront difficult dilemmas as they attempt to engage with private sustainability governance schemes as potentially useful vehicles for supporting their agenda-setting or accountability agendas, while maintaining sufficient 'critical distance' (Boström and Hallström, 2010) from the schemes to protect their own credibility and symbolic resources, and preserve their capacity to pursue broader campaigning activities, even where these bring them into conflict with certified companies. If this balance is not able to be managed, then the risk is that the NGOs 'become tools for the expansion and legitimization of the standard and its related certified companies . . . rather than being empowered by using the standard as a tool for their continuing political protest, campaigning and monitoring of corporate conduct' (ibid., p. 56).

Although the above discussion has highlighted various examples of pathways through which private sustainability governance systems have facilitated the contestation of corporate power, such illustrations should therefore not distract from a broader picture in which such examples have usually remained localized and weakly institutionalized while dominant power structures have persisted largely unthreatened. The effects of these dynamic contests on the strengthening or weakening of global regulatory standards depend on path-dependent processes of political struggle, through which discursive contests over epistemic and representational legitimacy interact with material power struggles between competing coalitions of actors at both local and global scales.

CONCLUSION

Private systems of global sustainability governance have been variously characterized as means of facilitating, legitimizing, or taming the power of MNCs. Some observers have lauded these schemes as innovative regulatory tools for promoting global sustainability norms, while others have perceived them as tools of global corporate power – reproducing the structural power of business in global markets and commodity-producing nations, while operating discursively to insulate companies from societal pressure for stronger regulation. Such debates have significant implications for analysis of the political influence of corporations within global politics, and the new forms of global governance in which global corporations – alongside other non-state actors – now play a prominent role.

Taking such debates about corporate power within evolving systems of global governance as an entry point, this chapter has explored the multiple pathways of both direct and indirect influence through which corporate power is asserted, resisted, and contested through engagement with processes of private sustainability governance. Rather than viewing private sustainability governance schemes as discrete regulatory mechanisms and adopting a corresponding focus on the direct exercise of corporate power, the chapter has shown how MNCs and other business actors can also exercise power more indirectly, through the ripple effects that private regulatory schemes generate for wider regulatory struggles between business, civil society, and state actors (Köhne, 2014). Under these circumstances, indirect pathways of corporate influence take on particular significance as the power of individual firms or industry associations is facilitated or amplified by interactions with wider networks of state and civil society actors within contested regulatory fields.

At times, companies can use their involvement in processes of private sustainability governance as means of reinforcing and extending their power in wider regulatory fields – drawing on structural sources of market power, discursive processes of legitimation, and alliances with powerful political and bureaucratic actors in key regulatory jurisdictions. Such interacting pathways of corporate power frequently constrain the regulatory agendas and voices that are given expression in systems of global sustainability governance. However, business involvement in private regulatory processes can also generate opportunities for resisting and contesting dominant business interests, as companies confront countervailing sources of state, community, and civil society power (Levy and Newell, 2002; Moog et al., 2015).

Patterns of business influence have been shown to vary significantly depending on the specific temporal, geographical, and sectoral contexts in which processes of private sustainability governance are embedded. The balance between corporate power and that of its challengers depends on varied sources of structural and material power in a particular sector, location, and issue; on the organizing capacity of competing groups; and on the discursive power wielded by competing alliances of business, state, and civil society actors in specific sectoral and jurisdictional contexts. Moreover, such distributions of power evolve dynamically as political opportunities and strategies shift and interact over time. Outcomes of regulatory struggles therefore hinge on a shifting balance between competing sources of structural, material, and discursive power within and between the multiple institutional and social fields in which these regulatory struggles play out.

The institutional designs and regulatory strategies adopted by individual private regulatory schemes can also importantly influence the course of these struggles. While corporate domination of private regulatory processes has often been attributed to weaknesses of transparency, inclusiveness, or accountability of private governance arrangements (Auld and Gulbrandsen, 2010; Bäckstrand, 2006; Koenig-Archibugi and Macdonald, 2013), the capacity of such institutions to accommodate conflictual or oppositional modes of regulatory engagement can also influence their effects on either enabling or stifling constructive processes of regulatory contestation. Rather than viewing the legitimacy of private regulation as depending primarily on participatory and consensus-based decision-making, the chapter's analysis has suggested the potential value of more explicitly acknowledging both power inequalities through which private regulatory systems are constituted and the legitimacy of more overtly politicized processes of regulatory contestation (Cheyns and Riisgaard, 2014). Recognition of the potentially constructive value of regulatory contestation could help to foster debate over appropriate forms of evidence used in audit or grievance processes – resisting technocratic approaches to the collection and evaluation of evidence that view such processes as political, neutral, and closed to contestation. Such an acknowledgment may also provide a productive basis for defending adversarial forms of civil society campaigning carried out in parallel with audit or mediation processes coordinated by multi-stakeholder governance schemes – countering frequent corporate claims that such processes should remain confidential and sheltered from public scrutiny (Macdonald and Balaton-Chrimes, 2016).

The dynamism and unpredictability of complex processes of regulatory contestation may also help to make sense of why many communities, workers, and CSOs continue to engage with private sustainability governance processes, in spite of persistent evidence of corporate domination. Even where marginalized groups fail to achieve their primary goals, sometimes the normative or institutional changes associated with such processes of contestation can feed into future campaigning and alliance-building – supporting further systemic change. Conversely, corporate actors often respond to challenges with 'counterstrategies that entail a degree of local accommodation and compromise around specific issues' while protecting and even reinforcing underlying structures of corporate power (Levy, 2008, p. 957). It is therefore often difficult, at least in the short term, to differentiate between 'strategies that lead to co-optation of challengers and the blunting of efforts for more systemic change and dynamic strategies that use the shifting terrain of compromise as the staging ground for another round of contestation' (ibid.).

While corporate power continues to impose significant constraints on the regulatory potential of private sustainability governance, such governance initiatives may be viewed in a more optimistic light if they are also recognized at least as *potential* entry points for teasing open cracks in prevailing formations of corporate power. Where resistance to corporate power can be facilitated and legitimized, affected communities, workers, and civil society supporters can sometimes organize effectively to resist efforts by business to control the agendas, procedures, and associated effects of private sustainability governance, instead harnessing these as means of supporting broader struggles for strengthened social and environmental regulation of global business activity.

NOTES

1. Major NGOs and wider networks of 'experts' based in the Global North have also been shown to exercise disproportionate influence in many schemes, compared with more marginalized actors based in the Global South.
2. Such power is therefore likely to be lower where production is more highly concentrated amongst a few large firms, enabling private regulatory schemes to work directly with large-scale producers, and reducing the gatekeeping power of lead firms (Lowder, Skoet and Raney, 2016; van der Ven, 2018). Such power is

further constrained in sectors where structural power is gradually shifting towards firms located in major producing countries, as increasing volumes of South–South trade and rising demand for food and other resource and agricultural products in emerging economies shifts market power away from big brand buyers in the Global North (Schleifer, 2016).

3. Such field-level discursive struggles also interact in important ways with the more direct and material forms of power discussed above. For example, the increasing role of corporate actors within the Fairtrade system has threatened to undermine Fairtrade's progressive foundations not only through Fairtrade's competitive interactions with less demanding certification standards, but also through internal tensions that arise when it attempts to extend its ideals of partnership and personalized trust to the regulation of hired labor enterprises, and to trading chains between plantations and large corporate buyers (Bacon, 2010; Low and Davenport, 2006; Raynolds, 2009).

4. Of course, such efforts by pro-regulatory coalitions are not met passively by business actors. Köhne (2014) has shown how companies involved in contesting community grievances mediated by the RSPO attempted to use RSPO processes to legitimize their own forms of evidence, undermining community claims and strengthening their own negotiating positions. Others have documented cases in which companies have sought to shut down broader advocacy processes carried out in parallel with such mediation processes by imposing confidentiality provisions on audit and grievance investigation processes (Macdonald and Balaton-Chrimes, 2016).

5. There are also examples of such coalitions feeding into broader efforts to influence government policy at the national level. For example, the international Palm Oil Innovation Group (POIG) – which was formed in 2013 and involves collaborative work amongst a number of international NGOs and palm oil producing companies – is one example of a broader network of actors that has been facilitated in part through the network infrastructure supported by the RSPO.

6. In both Indonesia and Malaysia, there have been prominent attempts to establish government-controlled rivals to the RSPO. In Indonesia, development of the Indonesian Sustainable Palm Oil (ISPO) system has been ongoing since 2011, and a Malaysian Sustainable Palm Oil (MSPO) certification scheme was established in 2014.

REFERENCES

Abbott, K.W. (2012), 'Engaging the public and the private in global sustainability governance', *International Affairs*, **88**(3), 543–64.

Auld, G. and L.H. Gulbrandsen (2010), 'Transparency in nonstate certification: consequences for accountability and legitimacy', *Global Environmental Politics*, **10**(3), 97–119.

Auld, G., S. Renckens and B. Cashore (2015), 'Transnational private governance between the logics of empowerment and control', *Regulation and Governance*, **9**(2), 108–24.

Bäckstrand, K. (2006), 'Multi-stakeholder partnerships for sustainable development: rethinking legitimacy, accountability and effectiveness', *Environmental Policy and Governance*, **16**(5), 290–306.

Bacon, C.M. (2010), 'Who decides what is fair in Fair Trade? The agri-environmental governance of standards, access, and price', *The Journal of Peasant Studies*, **37**(1), 111–47.

Barrientos, S. and S. Smith (2007), 'Mainstreaming fair trade in global production networks', in L. Raynolds, D. Murray and J. Wilkinson (eds), *Fair Trade: The Challenges of Transforming Globalization*, New York: Routledge, pp. 103–21.

Bartley, T. (2011), 'Transnational governance as the layering of rules: intersections of public and private standards', *Theoretical Inquiries in Law*, **12**(2), 517–42.

Bartley, T. (2018), 'Transnational corporations and global governance', *Annual Review of Sociology*, **44**, 145–65.

Bennett, E.A. (2017), 'Who governs socially-oriented voluntary sustainability standards? Not the producers of certified products', *World Development*, **91**(C), 53–69.

Bloomfield, M.J. (2012), 'Is forest certification a hegemonic force? The FSC and its challengers', *The Journal of Environment and Development*, **2**(4), 391–413.

Bloomfield, M.J. and P. Schleifer (2017), 'Tracing failure of coral reef protection in nonstate market-driven governance', *Global Environmental Politics*, **17**(4), 127–46.

Boström, M. and K.T. Hallström (2010), 'NGO power in global social and environmental standard-setting', *Global Environmental Politics*, **10**(4), 36–59.

Braithwaite, J. (2008), *Regulatory Capitalism: How it Works, Ideas for Making it Work Better*, Cheltenham, UK and Northampton, MA, USA: Edward Elgar Publishing.

Büthe, T. and W. Mattli (2013), *The New Global Rulers: The Privatization of Regulation in the World Economy*, Princeton, NJ: Princeton University Press.

Cashore, B. (2002), 'Legitimacy and the privatization of environmental governance: how non-state market-driven (NSMD) governance systems gain rule-making authority', *Governance*, **15**(4), 503–29.

Cheyns, E. (2014), 'Making "minority voices" heard in transnational roundtables: the role of local NGOs in reintroducing justice and attachments', *Agriculture and Human Values*, **31**(3), 439–53.

Cheyns, E. and L. Riisgaard (2014), 'The exercise of power through multi-stakeholder initiatives for sustainable agriculture and its inclusion and exclusion outcomes', *Agriculture and Human Values*, **31**(3), 409–23.

Connor, T., A. Delaney and S. Rennie (2016), 'The Ethical Trading Initiative: negotiated solutions to human rights violations in global supply chains?', *Non-Judicial Redress Mechanisms Report Series*, No. 18.

Dauvergne, P. and J. Lister (2010), 'The power of big box retail in global environmental governance: bringing commodity chains back into IR', *Millennium*, **39**(1), 145–60.

de Bakker, F.G., A. Rasche and S. Ponte (2019), 'Multi-stakeholder initiatives on sustainability: a cross-disciplinary review and research agenda for business ethics', *Business Ethics Quarterly*, **29**(3), 343–83.

Diprose, R., N.I. Kurniawan and K. Macdonald (2019), 'Transnational policy influence and the politics of legitimation', *Governance*, **32**(2), 223–40.

Eberlein, B., K.W. Abbott and J. Black et al. (2014), 'Transnational business governance interactions: conceptualization and framework for analysis', *Regulation and Governance*, **8**(1), 1–21.

Edmunds, D. and E. Wollenberg (2001), 'A strategic approach to multistakeholder negotiations', *Development and Change*, **32**(2), 231–53.

Fransen, L. (2011), 'Why do private governance organizations not converge? A political-institutional analysis of transnational labor standards regulation', *Governance*, **24**(2), 359–87.

Fransen, L.W. and A. Kolk (2007), 'Global rule-setting for business: a critical analysis of multi-stakeholder standards', *Organization*, **14**(5), 667–84.

Fuchs, D. (2007), *Business Power in Global Governance*, Boulder, CO: Lynne Rienner Publishers.

Fuchs, D. and A. Kalfagianni (2010), 'The causes and consequences of private food governance', *Business and Politics*, **12**(3), 1–34.

Fuchs, D. and M.M. Lederer (2007), 'The power of business', *Business and Politics*, **9**(3), 1–17.

Gereffi, G., J. Humphrey and T. Sturgeon (2005), 'The governance of global value chains', *Review of International Political Economy*, **12**(1), 78–104.

Gibbon, P., S. Ponte and E. Lazaro (eds) (2010), *Global Agro-Food Trade and Standards: Challenges for Africa*, New York: Springer.

Grabosky, P. (2013), 'Beyond responsive regulation: the expanding role of non-state actors in the regulatory process', *Regulation and Governance*, **7**(1), 114–23.

Gulbrandsen, L.H. (2005), 'Sustainable forestry in Sweden: the effect of competition among private certification schemes', *Journal of Environment and Development*, **14**(3), 338–55.

Haines, F. and K. Macdonald (2019), 'Non-judicial business regulation and community access to remedy', *Regulation and Governance* [online early view], https://doi.org/10.1111/rego.12279.

Haines, F., K. Macdonald and S. Balaton-Chrimes (2012), 'Contextualising the business responsibility to respect: how much is lost in translation?', in R. Mares (ed.), *The UN Guiding Principles on Business and Human Rights: Foundations and Implementation*, Leiden: Brill, pp. 107–28.

Hale, T.N. and D. Held (eds) (2011), *Handbook of Transnational Governance*, Cambridge, UK: Polity Press.

Henderson, J., P. Dicken and M. Hess et al. (2002), 'Global production networks and the analysis of economic development', *Review of International Political Economy*, **9**(3), 436–64.

Holzscheiter, A. (2005), 'Discourse as capability: non-state actors' capital in global governance', *Millennium*, **33**(3), 723–46.

Hospes, O. (2014), 'Marking the success or end of global multi-stakeholder governance? The rise of national sustainability standards in Indonesia and Brazil for palm oil and soy', *Agriculture and Human Values*, **31**(3), 425–37.

Jaffee, D. and P.H. Howard (2010), 'Corporate cooptation of organic and Fair Trade standards', *Agriculture and Human Values*, **27**(4), 387–99.

Keck, M.E. and K. Sikkink (2014), *Activists Beyond borders: Advocacy Networks in International Politics*, Ithaca, NY: Cornell University Press.

Köhne, M. (2014), 'Multi-stakeholder initiative governance as assemblage: Roundtable on Sustainable Palm Oil as a political resource in land conflicts related to oil palm plantations', *Agriculture and Human Values*, **31**(3), 469–80.

Koenig-Archibugi, M. and K. Macdonald (2013), 'Accountability-by-proxy in transnational non-state governance', *Governance*, **26**(3), 499–522.

LeBaron, G. and J. Lister (2015), 'Benchmarking global supply chains: the power of the "ethical audit" regime', *Review of International Studies*, **41**(5), 905–24.

Levy, D.L. (2008), 'Political contestation in global production networks', *Academy of Management Review*, **33**(4), 943–63.

Levy, D.L. and P.J. Newell (2002), 'Business strategy and international environmental governance: toward a neo-Gramscian synthesis', *Global Environmental Politics*, **2**(4), 84–101.

Low, W. and E. Davenport (2006), 'Mainstreaming Fair Trade: adoption, assimilation, appropriation', *Journal of Strategic Marketing*, **14**(4), 315–27.

Lowder, S.K., J. Skoet and T. Raney (2016), 'The number, size, and distribution of farms, smallholder farms, and family farms worldwide', *World Development*, **87**(C), 16–29.

Macdonald, K. (2014), 'The meaning and purposes of transnational accountability', *Australian Journal of Public Administration*, **73**(4), 426–36.

Macdonald, K. (2020), 'Private sustainability standards as tools for empowering Southern pro-regulatory coalitions? Collaboration, conflict and the pursuit of sustainable palm oil', *Ecological Economics*, **167**(January), article 106439.

Macdonald, K. and S. Balaton-Chrimes (2016), 'The complaints system of the Roundtable on Sustainable Palm Oil (RSPO)', *Non-Judicial Redress Mechanisms Report Series*, No. 15.

Meidinger, E. (2007), 'Competitive supragovernmental regulation: how could it be democratic?', *Chicago Journal of International Law*, **8**(2), article 7.

Mena, S. and G. Palazzo (2012), 'Input and output legitimacy of multi-stakeholder initiatives', *Business Ethics Quarterly*, **22**(3), 527–56.

Mikler, J. (2018), *The Political Power of Global Corporations*, Cambridge, UK: Polity Press.

Moog, S., A. Spicer and S. Böhm (2015), 'The politics of multi-stakeholder initiatives: the crisis of the Forest Stewardship Council', *Journal of Business Ethics*, **128**(3), 469–93.

Nelson, V. and A. Tallontire (2014), 'Battlefields of ideas: changing narratives and power dynamics in private standards in global agricultural value chains', *Agriculture and Human Values*, **31**(3), 481–97.

Overdevest, C. (2010), 'Comparing forest certification schemes: the case of ratcheting standards in the forest sector', *Socio-Economic Review*, **8**(1), 47–76.

Overdevest, C. and J. Zeitlin (2014), 'Assembling an experimentalist regime: transnational governance interactions in the forest sector', *Regulation and Governance*, **8**(1), 22–48.

Peña, A.M. (2014), 'Rising powers, rising networks: Brazilian actors in private governance', *Oxford Development Studies*, **42**(2), 217–37.

Ponte, S. (2008), 'Greener than thou: the political economy of fish ecolabeling and its local manifestations in South Africa', *World Development*, **36**(1), 159–75.

Ponte, S. and P. Gibbon (2011), *Governing Through Standards: Origins, Drivers and Limitations*, Basingstoke: Palgrave Macmillan.

Raustiala, K. and D.G. Victor (2004), 'The regime complex for plant genetic resources', *International Organization*, **58**(2), 277–309.

Raynolds, L.T. (2009), 'Mainstreaming Fair Trade coffee: from partnership to traceability', *World Development*, **37**(6), 1083–93.

Raynolds, L.T. (2014), 'Fairtrade, certification, and labor: global and local tensions in improving conditions for agricultural workers', *Agriculture and Human Values*, **31**(3), 499–511.

Ronit, K. and V. Schneider (1999), 'Global governance through private organisations', *Governance*, **12**(3), 243–66.

Scherer, A.G. and G. Palazzo (2011), 'The new political role of business in a globalized world: a review of a new perspective on CSR and its implications for the firm, governance, and democracy', *Journal of Management Studies*, **48**(4), 899–931.

Schleifer, P. (2016), 'Private governance undermined: India and the Roundtable on Sustainable Palm Oil', *Global Environmental Politics*, **16**(1), 38–58.

Schouten, G. and V. Bitzer (2015), 'The emergence of Southern standards in agricultural value chains: a new trend in sustainability governance?', *Ecological Economics*, **120**(C), 175–84.

Schouten, G. and P. Glasbergen (2011), 'Creating legitimacy in global private governance: the case of the roundtable on sustainable palm oil', *Ecological Economics*, **70**(11), 1891–9.

Selfa, T., C. Bain and R. Moreno (2014), 'Depoliticizing land and water "grabs" in Colombia: the limits of Bonsucro certification for enhancing sustainable biofuel practices', *Agriculture and Human Values*, **31**(3), 455–68.

Selwyn, B. (2015), 'Commodity chains, creative destruction and global inequality: a class analysis', *Journal of Economic Geography*, **15**(2), 253–74.

Silva-Castañeda, L. (2012), 'A forest of evidence: third-party certification and multiple forms of proof – a case study of oil palm plantations in Indonesia', *Agriculture and Human Values*, **29**(3), 361–70.

Smith, T.M. and M. Fischlein (2010), 'Rival private governance networks: competing to define the rules of sustainability performance', *Global Environmental Change*, **20**(3), 511–22.

Strambach, S. and A. Surmeier (2018), 'From standard takers to standard makers? The role of knowledge-intensive intermediaries in setting global sustainability standards', *Global Networks*, **18**(2), 352–73.

Sundstrom, L. and L. Henry (2017), 'Private forest governance, public policy impacts: the Forest Stewardship Council in Russia and Brazil', *Forests*, **8**(11), 445.

Utting, P. (2002), 'Regulating business via multistakeholder initiatives: a preliminary assessment', in United Nations Research Institute for Social Development [UNRISD] (ed.), *Voluntary Approaches to Corporate Responsibility: Readings and a Resource Guide*, Geneva: UNRISD.

van der Ven, H. (2018), 'Gatekeeper power: understanding the influence of lead firms over transnational sustainability standards', *Review of International Political Economy*, **25**(5), 624–46.

Vogel, D. (2010), 'The private regulation of global corporate conduct: achievements and limitations', *Business and Society*, **49**(1), 68–87.

6. MNCs and their role in global business associations

Karsten Ronit

Multinational corporations (MNCs) are major actors in the global economy and occupy a prominent position in a range of markets.[1] In many policy fields, public authorities acknowledge their interests, and a major objective for some institutions is to adopt rules that enable globalization and facilitate the operation of corporations, while for others a goal is to control, and to varying degrees set barriers for, their activities. Indeed, public authorities struggle with how to balance these concerns.

Obviously, MNCs are not a politically idle force that merely stand by and observe the adoption of legislation and comply with regulation; or for that matter in silence violate the rules going against their interests. Different pathways of influence are available to MNCs. They leverage political institutions in domestic and international settings to bring about favorable regulation; or at least to avoid measures that negatively influence their competitiveness. Because they need to observe the regulations in a range of different countries, on top of which comes regulation in the form of inter-state agreements, often within the framework of intergovernmental agencies, MNCs have strong incentives to take action in different institutional contexts. In fact, the broad presence of these firms enables them to harness major economic and informational resources to develop political strategies, factors that qualify them as global political actors.

However, business is consistently portrayed as acting through individual firms, which tends to overlook their capacities to develop relevant collective action. An endless number of studies on global politics refer to MNCs *and* non-governmental organizations (NGOs) as if the political actions of business were entirely driven by single corporations, whereas the actions of civil society were launched via cooperation in various movements. This stands in sharp contrast to reality. Business is capable of developing advanced forms of collective action at the global level, and there is a rich tradition of associability in which MNCs also find their place. As such, the membership of business associations is one of the many available pathways for corporations in the global business community and, in turn, their positioning in associations may have repercussions on their influence in relation to states, intergovernmental organizations and various actors in civil society. In a broader context, this emphasis on organized business is not only a corrective to the general understanding of global politics as populated by disorganized business and organized civil society but also a perspective that opens up an avenue for the further scrutiny of the complex and institutionalized role of MNCs in global politics and their many pathways of influence. Acknowledging the multiple options of political engagement available to MNCs, numerous intriguing questions regarding the role of MNCs in global business associations become relevant. We may start exploring some of the basic opportunities for MNC membership in global associations and query whether membership is granted to single corporations and under which circumstances direct membership models are applied; or whether there is a practice of indirect membership achieved through national associations. For obvious reasons, we cannot examine the whole population of global business associations, whose number is significant. Instead, we limit the analysis to studying peak associations that must coordinate business interests in a very broad sense. Given this encompassing task, these bodies may prefer to build on already negotiated positions that are best represented through national associations and, in other words, we may surmise that it is relatively difficult for MNCs representing individual and highly specific corporate interests in such highly aggregated organizations.

In this chapter, I first examine the existing literature to clarify how MNCs are perceived as determined political actors who have not only shaped the conditions for politics through their strong role in global markets but also engage in political actions in the global realm to influence public policy adopted by intergovernmental agencies and other political institutions. One particular goal is to find guidelines to tease out the principles of MNC membership of associations and to establish an analytical framework. The following chapter concentrates on the role of MNCs in a particular type of global business association, namely the peak associations, as key vehicles for the representation of business. The conclusion sums up the major findings and shows that, despite the complex mechanisms of membership, MNCs can work through global associations and use them as important pathways of influence.

THEORETICAL APPROACHES TO MNCS AS POLITICAL ACTORS: A BRIEF DISCUSSION

There are many ways to address the behavior of MNCs and their political activities in the global realm, each bringing some facets to attention. While there is a tradition in economics and management studies to examine the position of MNCs in the global economy (Dunning and Lundan, 2008), it is also recognized that MNCs – in addition to states – deserve critical scrutiny in the analysis of global society and politics (Baars and Spicer, 2017; May, 2006; Mikler, 2013; Nölke and May, 2018; Strange, 1988). Indeed, this perspective on corporations and political action goes back decades in the study of capitalism but is sidelined in conventional approaches (Cohen, 2019). Although MNCs are prominent actors that transcend the boundary of economy and move into the political arena, MNC behavior is complex and demands further operationalization.

A major understanding of MNCs in global politics is rooted in the study of domestic politics. Like many other actors, MNCs can work through their 'own' governments but typically have relations with multiple governments. Theoretical approaches that give significant weight to the role of states in international relations see states as relevant vehicles for the organization and promotion of corporate interests (e.g., Gilpin, 2001), a view in many ways concomitant with the two-level games approach (Putnam, 1988). Accordingly, states represent national interests in international contexts, and they are influenced by a diverse range of domestic interests, including powerful corporations. However, there is considerable variation as to whether states are just bound to speak for powerful corporate interests or whether these interests must work actively in a case-by-case fashion to persuade governments and help form particular strategies. Either way, states draw on forces in domestic society, and corporate actors must rely on states to get their interests effectively represented in the international realm.

Although states and MNCs can be structurally and institutionally integrated at domestic levels (Mikler, 2018), MNCs can also use their influence in national business associations to promote their interests in global contexts. Other lines of research therefore move beyond state-centered frameworks and primarily raise questions about the international behavior of MNCs. A key aspect is the structural power of business in international contexts (for an overview, see Fuchs, 2007, pp. 119–44). Because businesses, and especially large corporations, are important in the global economy and can be seen as drivers of, for instance, prosperity, welfare, employment, innovation and many other things, a number of international institutions are compelled to adopt policies functional to this development, and ostensibly some institutions were originally designed to further business-friendly agendas. This is discussed in studies on intergovernmental bodies engaging in a variety of economic, financial, competition, and trade policies (Backer, 2011; McKeen-Edwards and Porter, 2013; Ruggie, 2013; Sell, 2003). Accordingly, these bodies tend to further pro-market paradigms in the process of globalization and in ways that are particularly beneficial to MNCs and their transboundary operations.

However, there is some variation as to how the role of business is examined in the context of intergovernmental organizations. Some studies are occupied with how agendas, ideas and interests are shaped and become conducive to the globalization and institutionalization of markets (Kahler and Lake, 2009; Porter and Ronit, 2010), while other studies are mainly concerned with the practical work of intergovernmental agencies (Hoekman and Mavroidis, 2015; Woods, 2007). It is interesting to note that a range of efforts are launched to meet the interests of MNCs, but it is not always clear whether the MNCs themselves assume an active role.

Evidence of political action is found at the corporate level, however, as in the voluminous literature on 'corporate social responsibility' (Carroll, 2008; Chandler, 2019; Scherer, Palazzo and Matten, 2014; Vogel, 2005), often designed with the dual purpose of improving the competitiveness of firms in markets and forestalling public regulation. Indeed, when major interests are at stake, firms respond to challenges and define their own strategies. Corporations become actors in their own right, and influence is not just achieved through benevolent governments or intergovernmental organizations.

Seeking to establish some generalized patterns of corporate action and to explain the possible benefits of individual action (e.g., Coen, 1997; Hillman and Hitt, 1999; Lawton, Doh and Rajwani, 2014; Yoffie, 1987), firm-centered models are developed to embrace a variety of political strategies (Mitnick, 1993). While such theoretical guidance offers new insights and helps us to move beyond anecdotal evidence, further operationalization is required to capture the global activities of MNCs.

It is clearly helpful to regard MNCs as actors present in global markets as well as in global politics, and as having their own resources and strategies to leverage political institutions. Although not necessarily in agreement, these strategy-orientated literatures stress how MNCs have an intrinsic political orientation; are present in global markets that enable them to retrieve knowledge and formulate global strategies; actively engage in issues to further or forestall public regulation; do not simply rely on benevolent political institutions; leverage individual governments; and exchange with global institutions.

Such factors are exceedingly important in analyzing corporations, but existing literatures do not explore all the political dimensions at the global level. Indeed, the emphasis on the political action of large corporations stresses important power relations, but it is also an under-institutionalized approach. While contributions highlighting the autonomous strategies of corporations tend to ignore the multiple forms of coordinated action through MNCs, other literatures have grappled with collective action in global business. Some of these studies take an interest in entities such as 'elites' and 'social classes' and examine coordinated action in contemporary contexts (Jessop and Overbeek, 2019; Heemskerk and Takes, 2016; Robinson and Harris, 2000; van der Pijl, 1998). These entities are supposed to coordinate interests at highly aggregated levels, but it is a key question how cohesive such forms of collective action actually are, which organizations are involved, and how they can be studied empirically.

There is a variety of other actors in the business community (Schmitter, 1991), many of whom are engaged in global politics. One of the primary vehicles for the organization and representation of business interests is the business association that abounds in many sectors of the economy (Ronit, 2018). Individual and collective action may be seen as two different alternatives available to business (e.g., Wilks, 2013; Woll, 2016), and it is worthwhile to investigate such options in different sectors and in different countries and to explain how these patterns unfold. The choice is not necessarily between contrasting strategies, however, and an integrated approach is therefore required to capture the many and varied links between MNCs and business associations and, in a further perspective, their many relations with institutions in their environment.

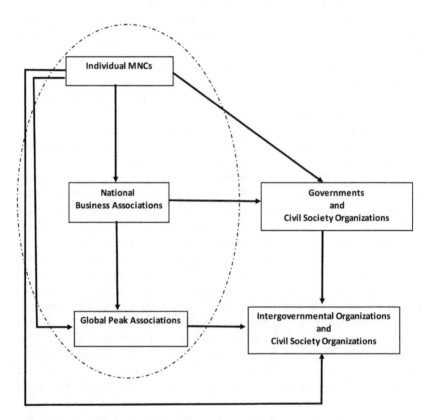

Figure 6.1   Pathways of MNC influence in relation to global peak associations

Very rarely have studies tried to examine such links (e.g., Martinelli, 1991). While MNC studies have largely ignored their participation in business associations, the literature on business associations has generally omitted the special role of MNCs. However, different cleavages in business associations, such as variation in firm size, are discussed as important factors of heterogeneity that complicate collective action (Schmitter and Streeck, 1981 [1999]). We must therefore identify and explore many links, which requires a differentiated understanding of membership. The clarification of membership is a first and necessary step to examine these links and, in a further perspective, it enables us to examine the role of MNCs in the complex life of associations.

In principle, several kinds of membership can be envisaged and help us understand the pathways of MNC influence and links with other actors. A general model (sketched in Figure 6.1) suggests that MNCs can join national associations through which they become members of international associations. Many relations within the business community must therefore be mapped, analyzed and theorized to document how corporations become involved in collective action. However, a further avenue of international (including global) engagement is manifested in cases where MNCs join international associations and are able to represent their interests authentically without depending on interest being mediated through national member associations.

The remainder of this chapter analyzes the affiliations of MNCs with global associations and how indirect and direct forms of membership are applied. This focus on membership is not in conflict with the other lines of research briefly outlined above, such as, for instance, that corporations and states may share a number of key interests, that corporations need to be active on domestic political scenes, or that multiple options for individual action might be available. However, the exploration of links between corporate and associational actions at the global level adds new perspectives to existing scholarship.

MNCS IN GLOBAL BUSINESS ASSOCIATIONS: EXPERIENCES FROM THE PEAK LEVEL

The global business community abounds with associations. In this chapter, I concentrate on organizations at the peak level; that is, associations organizing business on a trans-industry basis and addressing general concerns for global business, but each in their own way and depending on different institutional contexts.

Of key importance is the basic commitment of global peak associations. In principle, they aim to represent the general and unified view of the business community in a whole range of issues, and they neither cater to business in particular countries or industries nor do they act for particular groups of corporations. While this does not rule out peak associations possibly becoming captured by special interests in the business community, attention to selected member groups is not an official goal and would eventually jeopardize their general purpose. Indeed, other associations representing industries or other subsets of business interests work to represent specific interests (Ronit, 2019). Many other organizations and channels are therefore available for members, including MNCs, a factor that may diminish the burden on peak associations. These relations require additional studies and are beyond the scope of this chapter.

Consequently, an organizational structure to facilitate relatively smooth decision-making processes and to define strategies backed by business is required. Instead of the global peak associations sorting out the different positions of a heterogeneous business community, national bodies are tasked with finding suitable compromises among different subsets of members and transferring them to the global level, reducing the transaction costs of business through prior coordination. The most viable solution is to rely on and create a number of strong intermediate structures responsible for the organization and coordination of corporate interests. As Figure 6.1 illustrates, such a division of labor is typical of international federations in which international associations build on national associations to synthesize a plethora of national interests.

Indeed, this private associability model resembles the model in international relations whereby states meet in intergovernmental organizations and, seemingly, private organizations acquire a kind of parallel legitimacy with national associations as building blocks. This model is also logical in a historical perspective. National associations first developed to organize and represent members in domestic contexts. These entities later amalgamated to form overarching international bodies in business or civil society. While these federations have become quite pervasive in business, and global peak associations have a solid historical basis, there are interesting exceptions and novel trends that offer special opportunities for MNCs.

However, it would be incorrect to argue that MNCs do not coordinate at all. Being represented in many countries, one of the major tasks of these corporations is obviously to find a common denominator and represent the firm as a unitary actor on the global scene, although national embeddedness may complicate this (Geppert and Dörrenbächer, 2011). Given the supreme coordination function of peak associations in business, however, it may seem dysfunctional to involve MNCs as direct members. Essentially, the primary role of the global peak associations is not to coordinate interests across firms – a key goal of national associations – but rather to coordinate national businesses.

In terms of case study design, this gives rise to important reflections. Given the broad commitments of global associations, it is more likely that they will accommodate national associations that are supposed to bring already coordinated positions into the peak associations rather than accepting individual firms as direct members who have no real coordinated interests beforehand and cannot represent the same broad interests. In other words, the classical federated model of organizing interests is 'most likely', and the direct membership model is 'least likely', according to case study terminology (Gerring, 2009). As a case study, this chapter also investigates a number of embedded subunits (Yin, 2014), where the units are various peak associations in global business. Although these very large associations share a number of similar tasks, variation is possible. Should encompassing organizations for business apply other principles and not focus on national associations as members, it is likely that direct membership models are prevalent in organizations that speak for narrower elements of global business.

In fact, MNCs represent significant parts of the world economy and could therefore be relevant to include as direct members, and it is possible that this group of firms would in some cases also prefer direct participation. Although the introduction of direct membership would contradict established principles and traditions, the organization of global business is complex and dynamic, and various principles may co-exist in the peak associations. Detailing the membership formats in the various peak associations is therefore necessary to analyze the many pathways of influence.

Today, there is a very limited number of associations that are founded and governed by private business interests, aspire to become global and organize members from different regions of the world, cover business on a trans-industry basis, and are active across an array of issues (Ronit, 2016). Today, the group that best fulfills these multiple criteria, albeit with certain reservations, consists of the International Chamber of Commerce (ICC), International Organization of Employers (IOE), Business at OECD (Business and Industry Advisory Committee to the Organization for Economic Cooperation and Development – BIAC), World Economic Forum (WEF), World Business Council for Sustainable Development (WBCSD), Global Business Coalition (GBC) and BRICS Business Council (BBC).[2] These organizations represent (or at least host an ambition to represent) general business interests and not just specific industries. They do this in very different ways, however, and with different emphases in their work.

International Chamber of Commerce (ICC)

Founded in 1919, the ICC is the oldest of today's peak associations in global business. Acting through its secretariat in Paris, it also possesses the strongest resources. It is active in a wide number of policy fields and represents interests before a variety of intergovernmental agencies. At the same time, it is in a position to provide members with many services to enhance their competitiveness in the market. Recognizing the domains of other associations, its ambition is clearly to be the primary organization of global business, but this also requires very broad compromises.

Essentially, the ICC builds on chambers of commerce (ICC, 2019). Such chambers can be entities under private as well as public law, and their legal status varies across countries. Chambers of commerce are found in different contexts at domestic levels, from the local chamber representing the business in a particular town to the national chamber representing business in a broad sense, and the ICC thus brings different chambers together in a global framework.

The key membership category is the national chamber of commerce (called committee), sometimes referred to as a 'chamber of commerce and industry' to indicate the organization of the multiple business activities. There are also local chambers. These are usually admitted in cases where there is no eligible national body to join.[3] Today, as shown in the figure above, individual corporations can join: 'In countries where an ICC national committee has yet to be formed, companies, banks, law firms, chambers of commerce, individuals, associations and other associations can join ICC by becoming a direct member' (ICC, 2018). These opportunities are primarily available in smaller economies and where the collective organization of business is weak.

The national chamber is a body embracing a variety of business entities, such as local chambers of commerce or different groups of firms, or single corporations on some occasions. It is interesting to note that the ICC does not simply admit already existing entities into the organization. Active effort is also made to create new national chambers, and as chapters of the ICC they usually also carry the ICC name followed by the name of the given country, signaling that they are local bodies of the encompassing global association. This suggests neither a very strict control of national activities and organizational formats nor an ambition to arrive at a uniform design, and different ways of organizing interests are accepted. In domestic contexts, the ICC name is not always used, also an indication that national traditions are accepted as long as they fit the overall ICC pattern.

In some cases, single corporations play a strong role in the national committees. An interesting case is the United States Council for International Business (USCIB). Domestically, this association operates in a direct membership format and we find a long list of American corporations with an international presence; in other words, a significant number of MNCs. This model is rather unusual for chambers of commerce affiliated with the ICC but gives this group of corporations a stronger position in their national chamber (and again in the ICC as a whole). If specific corporations want to play an active role in the peak association, they must generally work through the respective national chambers. Affiliated through multiple chambers, because MNCs are active in many countries, there are therefore many opportunities for influencing the organization's strategy. This may give them a strong position in the ICC as a whole (Louis, 2016, pp. 243–6).

International Organization of Employers (IOE)

Established in 1920 to represent the interests of employers, the IOE also has solid traditions. Right from the outset, it was institutionally integrated into the International Labour Organization (ILO), today a UN organization, together with unions and member states, but it has relations with many other agencies. Its task is not to engage in and negotiate collective agreement with unions, a role taken by its members in domestic contexts, but in a broad sense to influence the regulations affecting employers. Its major ambition is not to represent global business in the same way as the ICC but instead to be the global organization of employers and, in this capacity, the association is unchallenged by other global business associations.

The organization includes employer organizations from a large number of countries (IOE, 2019), some of which were instrumental in creating the IOE but many of which have been added since. Indeed, together with ILO, the IOE has been very active in creating national associations of employers, especially in developing countries.

While almost all the members are national employer organizations, chambers of commerce and industry or other relevant bodies are admitted in a few cases where specific employer organizations are missing. Only one member per country is usually accepted to bring already coordinated interests into the association. The key role of national associations is reflected in the whole history of the IOE, where the philosophy is to represent employers before intergovernmental agencies and definitely not through single corporations. The ILO has made a strong contribution to this model, wherein exchanges are restricted to representative associations (as opposed to single corporations) regardless of size. Overall, this model facilitates decision-making in the ILO, where its three member groups (employers, workers and governments) each in their own way coordinate at the national level.

National employer associations organize in different ways, most building on a federated structure. Firms, including MNCs, are typically organized in various sector associations for industries, product groups or employers or are affiliated via territorial associations that organize firms in particular regions. In these contexts, large corporations are compelled to coordinate with other enterprises. We also find cases of direct firm affiliation with national employer associations, however, a model that obviously gives the MNCs stronger influence on the national association, thereby also enabling stronger input into the IOE.

Although emphasis is on the collective level, the IOE has discussed various ideas to facilitate greater participation for corporations, a difficult balancing act. Since 2013, the IOE has offered partnership status to individual corporations that is different from the ordinary membership held by associations. Indeed, the organization has especially responded to requests from MNCs to develop new ways of collaboration. It is important that the old principles are still given primacy, however, and a reference is needed from the relevant national member association for corporations to obtain partnership. This 'IOE Partner Initiative' (IOE, 2018), as it is called, enables partners to deliver input to specific bodies of the organization, thereby legitimizing IOE consultation with individual corporations. Moreover, it provides opportunity to meet in networks to share experiences in relation to occupational safety and health, industrial relations and youth employment. Finally, the corporations can draw on the IOE and benefit from numerous individualized services. While this new partnership may challenge the established pattern of participation in different ways, it is too early to assess the consequences it will have for the association.

Business at OECD (BIAC)

The BIAC was created in a different era than its two predecessors, between which there was some division of labor. Founded in 1962 as Business and Industry Advisory Committee to the OECD, the mission of the BIAC was, and remains, to represent interests emerging from commodity and labor markets in the Organisation for Economic Co-operation and Development (OECD).[4] The BIAC thus unites producer and employer interests.

The BIAC has a complex membership structure (BIAC, 2019a). In its constituency, we find full members representing nationwide business interests through producer and employer associations, in most cases one association per country, and business therefore follows the principles of organizing through national associations joining the global association, as sketched in Figure 6.1. The same applies to the observer organizations that emanate from countries not affiliated with the OECD. We also find a number of international business associations, ranked as 'associate expert groups', that are of interest to the BIAC's work in the OECD and vice versa. The emphasis is on collective entities, and there is no membership category for single corporations.

Depending on the internal structure of the participating organizations, of which the full member associations have the highest status, MNC involvement can vary in terms of how complicated it may be. Where national associations, for instance, build on the direct membership of corporations, either alone or in addition to other mechanisms of participation, corporations will have a stronger role in the development of an associational strategy and ultimately also in its engagement with the BIAC. Where this opportunity is missing, however, direct opportunities for influence are limited. Because MNCs are present in all OECD countries, there can be multiple chances of simultaneous leverage, and we need to analyze the internal mechanisms of national associations to grasp these processes.

Obviously, the associate expert groups do not have the same rights in the BIAC and play a far more peripheral role. Many expert organizations are listed – some European, some global – and they all represent specific industries with an interest in the work of the OECD (and the BIAC) and vice versa. These associations are often organized in a direct membership format, enabling the participation of many MNCs that tend to dominate particular industries. They will have a stronger position in determining the strategies of industry associations and therefore may use such opportunities more effectively when communicating with the BIAC.

Many BIAC activities are carried out by its policy groups. Numbering more than 20, these bodies cover a rich variety of policy fields and provide an important background for the official policy formulation of the association, both in very traditional issues and in new areas. Interestingly, the BIAC refers to the involvement of 2800+ persons who are drawn from its different members (BIAC, 2019b), and a significant portion of these experts very likely come from large corporations. Indeed, MNCs have the resources to employ staff in the work of these groups, an opportunity not always open for smaller enterprises. Additionally, MNCs have experiences from many countries that are useful in the deliberation and formulation of global policies. Without being a part of the official mechanisms, this suggests that the participation of MNCs in the work of these committees may be very solid and that they even have good opportunities for defining relevant strategies.

World Economic Forum (WEF)

Formed in 1971, the WEF did not start out as a global outlet, but rather as a European entity under the name 'European Management Forum' and mainly catered to European issues. It did not begin life as an extroverted body setting important agendas, mainly concerned instead with servicing business. Much has changed. Today, the WEF is probably the best-known global business association, at least in the general public, a position often envied by other associations in the business community. The organization has a peculiar organizational format and does not portray itself as a business association proper. While maintaining its focus as a business association, it is a hybrid organization that engages in different experiments. It combines many functions (WEF, 2019a), such as delivering think-tank analyses, creating partnerships between different stakeholders, and staging an annual summit that looks like a UN event. Amid these different tasks, however, the key function is to bring businesses together and speak on behalf of global business in different issue areas and institutional contexts. Accordingly, business funding and business membership are crucial to the organization.

Unlike the other peak associations discussed thus far, we do not find national business associations as members, a principle that is otherwise thought to furnish global associations with coordinated opinions from a complex constituency. Instead, only single firms are members, thus completely avoiding national bodies, an opportunity also anticipated in Figure 6.1. Hence, the organization cannot speak with authority for global business as such, as it cannot represent an array of national opinions in business but only certain segments of corporate interests.

The association manages a diversity of membership categories for firms (WEF, 2019b). These categories have been adapted over time, reflecting organizational reforms; hence, the number of firms in these categories has also changed. The most privileged status is held by firms in the 'strategic partners' class, today totaling a little more than 100 'leading global companies'.[5] As they have access to more platforms in the organization, fees are higher, suggesting a certain hierarchy among member corporations.

WEF's membership list encompasses a varied group of MNCs. Some countries are particularly well represented, US corporations being especially numerous. Interestingly, however, the MNCs are not only based in the most affluent parts of the world, and we also notice several Southern MNCs. It is striking to note, however, that MNCs from some countries, including Russia and China, remain poorly represented. In terms of their industrial origins, however, firms come from many different industries, but it is difficult to see whether there is a deliberate strategy to involve or even balance different industries.

The unilateral participation of large firms obviously provides them with excellent opportunities to dominate policy-making in the organization, but MNCs are not necessarily in agreement just because of their size and uniting the different MNCs headquartered in different countries and originating in different industries is required. However, the WEF does not function in the very same way as most of the other peak associations, and it is less keen to define its strategies through complex decision-making. Indeed, the organization does not represent members in a strict sense. For instance, participation is quite limited in the work of intergovernmental agencies where a coordinated stance is expected, although relations have expanded over time. Its strength lies more in its ability to identify major problems confronting global business and to set important agendas.

World Business Council for Sustainable Development (WBCSD)

While there are many similarities between the World Economic Forum and the World Business Council for Sustainable Development, the WBCSD did not begin as a regional entity. It can trace its roots as a global association back to 1992 and attained its present form three years later. It has a rather specific profile, distinguishing itself from all other peak associations in global business by focusing on a cluster of sustainability concerns (WBCSD, 2020a), which suggests that its recruitment policy cannot be the same as in the WEF. It includes industries across a wide spectrum of global business, and although its policy portfolio is rather specific, it now encompasses a growing number of issues.

National business associations do not link up with the WBCSD. While some national bodies specialize and seek to coordinate business interests in the area of sustainability policies, there are generally no national entities that could function effectively as domestic chapters of the WBCSD. Consequently, interests are not coordinated at the national level and fed into the organization, for which reason the WBCSD is the first place to negotiate and formulate a cohesive global strategy.

The only membership category of the WBCSD is individual corporations (WBCSD, 2020b), and membership first becomes relevant when corporations with activities in many countries need a global platform. The typical member is therefore an MNC. Members have an interest in formulating global policies through active participation in various decision-making structures. They also benefit from the various services of the organization in this framework. There are many MNCs with a strong environmental and energy policy profile, as they provide solutions to further sustainability in its various dimensions, but we also find many members that are not particularly associated with sustainability as such, but encounter various general sustainability challenges and contribute from this perspective. In such cases, they do not provide solutions for other corporations and industries. Indeed, many corporations join the WEF as well as the WBCSD and benefit from both organizations. Because the two organizations are not engaged in the exact same fields and a division of labor exists between them, they do not engage in strong competition, and MNCs have reason to retain membership in both associations. This obviously provides many MNCs with opportunities to influence the strategies of both associations.

The WBCSD is a global association and draws members from many parts of the world, including developing countries; it is not merely an organization for the affluent North. Corporations headquartered in the Global North predominate, however, and these countries are particularly well represented. The US and UK rank high on the list, which is likely due in part to the number of MNCs in these countries.

Global Business Coalition (GBC)

Formerly known as the B20 Coalition but as the GBC since 2016, this association is strongly influenced by its institutional environment. A special organization was needed to represent general business interests in the world, or at least in the G20 countries, before the G20 summits. Indeed, there was no other relevant vehicle tailored to this particular context and choosing between the different associations already analyzed might have stirred up conflicts in the business community. The various institutional legacies of, for instance, the ICC or IOE would have risked spilling over into interest representation in the G20 context.

The GBC members are all peak associations from the G20 countries with a few additions (GBC, 2019a),[6] and the organization thus tends to replicate the G20 membership by organizing the business communities of these countries. The organization is not currently able to organize business in all countries, however, and several important associations are missing, such as from China and Russia. This is not least attributable to the conflicts between Russia and the US/EU, but other problems have also influenced the problems pertaining to the cohesive organization of business.

The national associations are supposed to represent highly coordinated interests, mainly on the producer side and in all kinds of issues debated in the G20 framework. MNCs are not present as members of the GBC, but this does not rule out important input from MNCs. In principle, there are various opportunities to influence the GBC's strategy; first, because the interests of large corporations may be articulated by individual national associations and, second, because large corporations can be active in all member associations and therefore have multiple input opportunities into the GBC. However, when national member associations of the GBC do not organize single corporations as members, MNCs will have to work through the various territorial and sectoral entities that are members of the affiliated national peak associations.

Although MNCs are in a unique position to set agendas and bring in experiences from different regions, thereby playing important roles in facilitating global strategies in the association, this work must be coordinated to be effective. The MNCs must also align with many other business interests in the respective national contexts, endeavors that do not necessarily lead in the same direction for all the national member associations of the GBC. National strategies will therefore not be equally beneficial for MNCs as a specific segment of business. Without having a formal role in the GBC there are many ways to participate, but there are also barriers blocking or moderating their potential influence.

BRICS Business Council (BBC)

The last of the global business associations examined in this chapter is the BBC. This organization, an inherent part of the BRICS process, is the most recent of the peak associations seeking to represent business interests across different industries, continents and policy fields. Encouraged by the BRICS member states, which require strong business integration, BBC was founded by private business actors in Brazil, Russia, India, China and South Africa. A primary purpose of the organization is to deliver input to the BRICS summits, somewhat akin to the role of the GBC in the context of the G20. However, BRICS and the BBC are both in a more formative stage and still operating within a less institutionalized framework, meaning that their organizational development is difficult to predict.

The business associations in Brazil, Russia, India, China and South Africa play an important role in the organization but, officially, the BBC operates with special national chapters (BBC, n.d.a). These do not really figure as independent associations and, as such, the chapters are not active at the domestic level, serving instead as a platform for organizing work in relation to the global body, thereby adding further complexity to the figure on the pathways of influence in global business associations.

In these national chapters, however, special rights are also granted to individual firms. Five corporations from each member state are selected to participate in the leading body of the BBC, which gives them a key role in developing national business strategies and the BBC's voice.[7] However, we also find examples of participation from among the ordinary national associations, including Russia and South Africa (BBC, n.d.b). The basic criterion for participation is not that these corporations have real global coverage but that they are supposed to have a role in the trade between the BRICS countries. They are positioned to take responsibility for parts of the BRICS process and to facilitate the active involvement of national business communities, so the idea is not simply to have corporations represent individual corporate interests.

It is still difficult to evaluate the balance between the national associations, the national chapters and the selected corporations that enjoy unique membership status, and each country adopts its own practices, further adding to the complexity of the picture. All the member countries already have peak associations representing the general concerns of business; a lack of domestic associability is therefore not an argument for granting individual corporations a prominent role. Leading corporations spearheading the BBC can, however, give stronger credibility to the BRICS process and encourage the further active involvement of corporations.

Although the emphasis is on delivering input to the summits, BBC is also active between these meetings, and its small secretariat, together with different working groups, coordinates activities in numerous policy fields. The secretariat alternates between the different countries according to the hosting of the summits, giving rise to different management models; for instance, while the Federation of Indian Chambers of Commerce and Industry (FICCI) was organizing the work of the BBC, the same function was carried out by one of the five Chinese corporations in the Chinese chapter of the BBC. A lack of uniformity seems characteristic of these rotating chair arrangements, and it is difficult to evaluate how the relevant national associations and individual corporations will shape future arrangements.

MEMBERSHIP PROFILES COMPARED

Global business associations at the peak level have different membership profiles. First, members define admission criteria – and members are not quite the same across associations – and these criteria have been laid down in their by-laws and adjusted slightly over time. Second, these choices are influenced by the role of the associations in their broader institutional environment and with the assignment to represent business in specific policy fields and in relations with particular intergovernmental organizations. These conditions temper rivalries and imply that the associations treated in this analysis are not available to all sections of business and, vice versa, the associations cannot appeal exactly to the same sections of business.

Some bodies operate exclusively with national associations as members, while others are open to individual corporations. This variation is illustrated in Table 6.1, where membership categories are indicated with emphasis on national associations or corporations, as well as modifications of these principles. It is important to note that the categories of both national associations and individual corporations must always be further qualified as there are indeed different entities within these two broader categories.

Among national associations, we find organizations with different tasks, such as producer associations (joining the GBC, BBC) and employer associations (joining the IOE), and some of them are mixed, taking responsibility for both functions (joining the BIAC). In addition, we also find chambers (joining the ICC), special legal entities that organize business in their own ways and, in some cases, they are identical with producer and employer associations. In all these cases, corporations have the opportunity to influence the strategies of global peak associations through membership of national associations.

Among individual corporations, we also find variation and different kinds of membership. A special distinction can be drawn between corporations with a broad and almost unrestricted approach to policy engagement (joining the WEF) versus corporations with a special emphasis on various sustainability issues (joining the WBCSD).

Table 6.1   *Membership of global peak associations*

Global Associations	Forms of Individual and Collective Membership				
	Selected corporations	Corporations	Chambers of commerce	Producer associations	Employer associations
ICC	✓		✓		
IOE	✓				✓
BIAC				✓	✓
WEF		✓			
WBCSD		✓			
GBC				✓	
BBC	✓			✓	

A point of no small concern is the role of the fees, which are essential to operate associations and boost their capacities. High fees are obviously a challenge but companies with considerable resources, such as MNCs, have clear advantages. Although associations working in a direct firm format are open to individual corporations in general, corporations tend to belong to a special league of multinationals, and the benefits of membership and participation are enjoyed in the meeting between corporations of similar size. In the WEF and WBCSD, this tends to privilege Northern MNCs but also provide opportunities for some Southern MNCs. However, associations with individual corporations as members cannot represent the same broad sections of global business.

CONCLUSION

Research on MNCs and business associations is strongly segregated. While studies of firms, including MNCs, are central in, for instance, economics, business administration and management, certain aspects of business associability are examined in areas of, for instance, economic and political sociology and comparative politics. Approaches in international political economy and transnational relations give space to MNCs as well as business associations, but especially corporations have attracted scholarly interest. Unified approaches are therefore required to examine how the behavior of MNCs *and* associations are interwoven in global politics and how different pathways of influence are available to MNCs.

This chapter has examined one of the pathways of influence available to MNCs, namely the global business associations that operate as key vehicles of interest representation in the business community. Indeed, MNCs join associations to advance their own specific strategies and to assist in defining general business interests.

Instead of only scrutinizing the behavior of single corporations *or* exclusively examining the conduct of business associations, greater emphasis must be put on the role of corporations *in* associations; in this case, peak business associations at the global level. Starting with the basic properties of membership, we may begin to unravel this complex relationship. Indeed, MNC membership opens a range of important avenues for leadership functions and for participation in various kinds of committee work and, thus, for defining associational strategies. The rules governing membership are therefore 'high politics', because the inclusion of members and their status in the organizations have significant consequences for which kind of business interests are taken into consideration and how associational strategies are formulated and, eventually, how global business associations are involved in the shaping of global politics.

This study on the relations between MNCs and global peak associations shows that MNCs are mainly represented through a range of national business associations. These traditional bodies on the domestic scene are very important in bringing coordinated positions to the global level, thereby saving transaction costs associated with the complex processes of interest intermediation in global associations. Organizations, such as the ICC, IOE, BIAC, GBC and, to some extent, the BBC, can act on behalf of a wide group of businesses by embracing different regions and countries, different industries and different-sized firms. This generally implies that MNCs must join via national associations to seek influence on the formulation of broad business strategies in global politics.

However, this study also shows that there are other pathways of MNC influence in global peak associations. The direct membership of MNCs and other corporations is granted through various processes of application, consultation and invitation. Global associations, such as the IOE, offer certain opportunities for direct engagement, although they are essentially based on national associations, but some associations are based on MNC membership alone. This membership model exists in the WEF and WBCSD, two of the most recent peak associations and, in certain respects, also in the BBC.

The emergence of better opportunities for direct membership reflects the stronger demand for novel forms of participation, indicating a recent trend in peak associations where the diversification of the pathways of influence is important. Nevertheless, the traditional model of participation remains dominant, and MNCs generally must join national associations if they want to be active in global peak associations and use them as relevant platforms in global politics.

NOTES

1. Reference is made in this chapter to multinational corporations (MNCs). Alternative concepts include transnational corporations and multinational enterprises, which have slightly different meanings.
2. This choice excludes associations that do not fully meet these criteria. Let us briefly mention two examples. The APEC Business Advisory Council (ABAC) includes businesses from Asia, North and South America and Australia in the Asia Pacific Economic Community (APEC) and, thus, it is not simply regional with emphasis on one continent or transcontinental involving two continents, as it spans several parts of the world (ABAC, 2020). It is by definition geographically limited, however, and does not aspire to become global. The organization was created in 1995 by the member states of APEC, and the states' 'economic leaders' appoint the members of the ABAC, a mix of associations and companies across member states, and its status as an independent association is unclear. Hence, the ABAC cannot be seen in all respects as a global peak association for business. Another example of an important international – but not global – entity organizing business is the Trans-Atlantic Business Council (TABC), established in 2013 and coordinating business in North America and Europe (TABC, 2019). It lists companies as members. The TABC must be considered an independent association but not one with global ambitions.
3. As a special arrangement, the World Chambers Federation (WCF), an independent organization as well as a section of the ICC, organizes local chambers of commerce but does not recruit individual corporations.
4. Over the past few years, the organization has increasingly shifted to the name Business at OECD, often followed by (BIAC). In this chapter, the acronym is used.
5. These changes render it difficult to follow developments. For earlier accounts, see Ronit (2016; 2018, p. 40). Currently, the WEF has defined no less than six member categories for business.
6. In January 2019, the Egyptian and Moroccan peak business associations were admitted into the GBC, a new step suggesting an ambition to adopt a broader profile and to move beyond the G20 countries (GBC, 2019b, 2019c).
7. Nominally, the respective governments appoint these business leaders but based on recommendations from the national associations. In South Africa, a reconstitution of the national chapter has been necessary to restore the influence of organized business (Malope, 2018).

REFERENCES

APEC Business Advisory Council [ABAC] (2020), 'Founding and structure', accessed 28 July 2020 at https://www2.abaconline.org//page-content/2521/content/.
Baars, G. and A. Spicer (eds) (2017), *The Corporation: A Critical, Multi-Disciplinary Handbook*, Cambridge, UK: Cambridge University Press.

Backer, L.C. (2011), 'Private actors and public governance beyond the state: the multinational corporation, the Financial Stability Board, and the global governance order', *Indiana Journal of Global Legal Studies*, **18**(2), 751–802.

BRICS Business Council [BBC] (n.d.a), 'About the BRICS Business Council', accessed 23 February 2019 at http://www.brics-info.org/about-the-brics-business -council/.

BRICS Business Council [BBC] (n.d.b), 'Members of Business Council', accessed 28 July 2020 at http://www.brics-info.org/members/members-of-business-council -russia/ and http://www.brics-info.org/members/members-of-business-council -south-africa/.

Business and Industry Advisory Committee [BIAC] (2019a), 'Our members', accessed 6 April 2019 at http://biac.org/our-members/.

Business and Industry Advisory Committee [BIAC] (2019b), 'Business at OECD', accessed 8 May 2019 at http://biac.org/quick-facts/.

Carroll, A.B. (2008), 'History of corporate social responsibility: concepts and practices', in A. Crane, D. Matten and A. McWilliams et al. (eds), *The Oxford Handbook of Corporate Social Responsibility*, Oxford: Oxford University Press.

Chandler, D. (2019), *Strategic Corporate Social Responsibility: Sustainable Value Creation*, 5th edition, Newbury Park, CA: Sage.

Coen, D. (1997), 'The evolution of large firm political action in the European Union', *Journal of European Public Policy*, **4**(1), 91–108.

Cohen, B.J. (2019), *Advanced Introduction to International Political Economy*, 2nd edition, Cheltenham, UK and Northampton, MA, USA: Edward Elgar Publishing.

Dunning, J. and S.M. Lundan (2008), *Multinational Enterprises and the Global Economy*, 2nd edition, Cheltenham, UK and Northampton, MA, USA: Edward Elgar Publishing.

Fuchs, D. (2007), *Business Power in Global Governance*, Boulder, CO: Lynne Rienner.

Geppert, M. and C. Dörrenbächer (2011), 'Politics and power in the multinational corporation: an introduction', in C. Dörrenbächer and M. Geppert (eds), *Politics and Power in the Multinational Corporation: The Role of Institutions, Interests and Identities*, Cambridge, UK: Cambridge University Press.

Gerring, J. (2007), 'The case study: what it is and what it does', in C. Boix and S.C. Stokes (eds), *The Oxford Handbook of Comparative Politics*, Oxford: Oxford University Press.

Gilpin, R. (2001), *Global Political Economy: Understanding the International Economic Order*, Princeton, NJ: Princeton University Press.

Global Business Coalition [GBC] (2019a), 'Global Business Coalition members', accessed 8 March 2019 at http://www.globalbusinesscoalition.org/gbc-members/.

Global Business Coalition [GBC] (2019b), 'Federation of Egyptian Industries (FEI) joins the Global Business Coalition', *Business Federations News*, 16 January, accessed 28 July 2020 at https://globalbusinesscoalition.org/gbc-initiatives/ federation-of-egyptian-industries-fei-joins-the-global-business-coalition/.

Global Business Coalition [GBC] (2019c), 'General Confederation of Moroccan Enterprises (CGEM) joins the Global Business Coalition', *Business Federations News*, 28 January, accessed 28 July 2020 at https://globalbusinesscoalition.org/gbc -initiatives/general-confederation-of-moroccan-enterprises-cgem-joins-the-global -business-coalition/.

Heemskerk, E.M. and F.W. Takes (2016), 'The corporate elite community structure of global capitalism', *New Political Economy*, **21**(1), 90–118.

Hillman, A. and M. Hitt (1999), 'Corporate political strategy formulation', *Academy of Management Review*, **24**(4), 825–42.

Hoekman, B.M. and P.C. Mavroidis (2015), *World Trade Organization (WTO): Law, Economics, and Politics*, London: Routledge.

International Chamber of Commerce [ICC] (2018), 'Joining ICC as a direct member', accessed 1 April 2019 at https://iccwbo.org/become-a-member/joining-icc-direct -member/.

International Chamber of Commerce [ICC] (2019), 'Global network', accessed 15 February 2019 at https://iccwbo.org/about-us/global-network/.

International Organization of Employers [IOE] (2018), 'Become a corporate partner of the IOE', accessed 28 July 2020 at https://www.ioe-emp.org/index.php?eID= dumpFile&t=f&f=132577&token=72a10a303cf9ce89f36bcbdafde5f8d862552052.

International Organization of Employers [IOE] (2019), 'Members and regions', accessed 1 March 2019 at https://www.ioe-emp.org/en/members-regions/.

Jessop, B. and H. Overbeek (eds) (2019), *Transnational Capital and Class Fractions: The Amsterdam School Perspective Reconsidered*, London: Routledge.

Kahler, M. and D.A. Lake (2009), 'Economic integration and global governance: why so little supranationalism?', in W. Mattli and N. Woods (eds), *The Politics of Global Regulation*, Princeton, NJ: Princeton University Press, pp. 242–75.

Lawton, T.C., J.P. Doh and T. Rajwani (2014), *Aligning for Advantage: Competitive Strategies for the Political and Social Arenas*, Oxford: Oxford University Press.

Louis, M. (2016), 'The ILO, social partners and the G20: new prospects for social dialogue at the global level?', *Global Social Policy*, **16**(3), 235–52.

Malope, L. (2018), 'Survé and co booted off BRICs Business Council', 28 October, *News24.com*, accessed 28 October 2018 at https://city-press.news24.com/Business/ surve-and-co-booted-off-brics-business-council-20181027.

Martinelli, A. (ed.) (1991), *International Markets and Global Firms: A Comparative Study of Organized Business in the Chemical Industry*, London: Sage.

May, C. (ed.) (2006), *Global Corporate Power*, Boulder, CO: Lynne Rienner.

McKeen-Edwards, H. and T. Porter (2013), *Transnational Associations and the Governance of Global Finance: Assembling Wealth and Power*, London: Routledge.

Mikler, J. (ed.) (2013), *The Handbook of Global Companies*, Oxford: Wiley-Blackwell.

Mikler, J. (2018), *The Political Power of Global Corporations*, Cambridge, UK: Polity Press.

Mitnick, B.M. (ed.) (1993), *Corporate Political Agency: The Construction of Competition in Public Affairs*, Newbury Park, CA: Sage.

Nölke, A. and C. May (eds) (2018), *Handbook of the International Political Economy of the Corporation*, Cheltenham, UK and Northampton, MA: Edward Elgar Publishing.

Porter, T. and K. Ronit (eds) (2010), *The Challenges of Global Business Authority: Democratic Renewal, Stalemate, or Decay?*, Albany, NY: State University of New York Press.

Putnam, R.D. (1988), 'Diplomacy and domestic politics: the logic of two-level games', *International Organization*, **42**(2), 427–60.

Robinson, W.I. and J. Harris (2000), 'Towards a global ruling class? Globalization and the transnational capitalist class', *Science & Society*, **64**(1), 11–54.

Ronit, K. (2016), 'Global employer and business associations: their relations with members in the development of mutual capacities', *European Review of International Studies*, **3**(1), 53–77.

Ronit, K. (2018), *Global Business Associations*, London: Routledge.

Ronit, K. (2019), 'Organized business and global public policy: administration, participation and regulation', in D. Stone and K. Moloney (eds), *The Oxford Handbook of Global Public Policy and Transnational Administration*, Oxford: Oxford University Press, pp. 565–82.

Ruggie, J.G. (2013), *Just Business: Multinational Corporations and Human Rights*, New York: W.W. Norton & Co.

Scherer, A.G., G. Palazzo and D. Matten (2014), 'The business firm as a political actor: a new theory of the firm for a globalized world', *Business & Society*, **53**(2), 143–56.

Schmitter, P.C. (1991), 'Sectors in modern capitalism: modes of governance and variations in performance', in R. Brunetta and C. Dell'Aringa (eds), *Labor Relations and Economic Performance*, London: Macmillan, pp. 3–39.

Schmitter, P.C. and W. Streeck (1981 [1999]), *The Organization of Business Interests. Studying the Associative Action of Business in Advanced Industrial Societies*, Cologne: MPIfG.

Sell, S. (2003), *Private Power, Public Law: The Globalization of Intellectual Property Rights*, Cambridge, UK: Cambridge University Press.

Strange, S. (1988), *States and Markets*, London: Blackwell.

Trans-Atlantic Business Council [TABC] (2019), 'History & mission', accessed 3 March 2019 at https://transatlanticbusiness.org/about-us/history-mission/.

van der Pijl, K. (1998), *Transnational Classes and International Relations*, London: Routledge.

Vogel, D. (2005), *The Market for Virtue: The Potential and Limits of Corporate Social Responsibility*, Washington, DC: Brookings Institution Press.

Wilks, S. (2013), *The Political Power of the Business Corporation*, Cheltenham, UK and Northampton, MA, USA: Edward Elgar Publishing.

Woll, C. (2016), 'Politics in the interest of capital: a not-so-organized combat', *Politics and Society*, **44**(3), 373–91.

Woods, N. (2007), *The Globalizers: The IMF, the World Bank, and Their Borrowers*, Ithaca, NY: Cornell University Press.

World Business Council for Sustainable Development [WBCSD] (2020a), 'What we do', accessed 28 July 2020 at https://www.wbcsd.org/Overview/Our-approach.

World Business Council for Sustainable Development [WBCSD] (2020b), 'Our members', accessed 28 July 2020 at https://www.wbcsd.org/Overview/Our -members.

World Economic Forum [WEF] (2019a), 'Our mission', accessed 8 April 2019 at https://www.weforum.org/about/world-economic-forum.

World Economic Forum [WEF] (2019b), 'Our members and partners', accessed 8 March 2019 at https://www.weforum.org/about/our-members-and-partners.

Yin, R.K. (2014), *Case Study Research Design and Methods*, 5th edition, Thousand Oaks, CA: Sage.

Yoffie, D.B. (1987), 'Corporate strategies for political action: a rational model', in A.A. Marcus, A.M. Kaufmann and D.R. Beam (eds), *Business Strategy and Public Policy: Perspectives from Industry and Academia*, Westport, CT: Quorum Books, pp. 43–60.

7. The power of mining MNCs: global governance and social conflict[1]

Lian Sinclair

Multinational mining corporations pursue their interests through social and political strategies across political scales. This chapter is concerned with a somewhat surprising phenomenon – that communities affected by mining, their organizations, and allies, including international civil society organizations (CSOs), have been able to reshape the social practice and governance of multinational mining corporations.[2] Indeed, there is a continuous feedback cycle between localized conflicts with people affected by mining, international activism, global governance networks, corporate social responsibility (CSR), and reorganized local conflicts. This observation calls into question the assumption that 'corporations rule the world' (Korten, 1995) and that the creation and effects of private governance are the simple institutionalization of corporate power. While multinational miners consolidate their political influence through pathways of strategic resource allocation, self-governance mechanisms, engaging critics, influencing government policy, and shaping international organizations' agendas, they do so in reaction to challenges to their interests. This chapter contributes to the re-embodiment and re-territorialization of global corporations by considering how multiscalar social and political conflicts construct the strategies, interests, and powers of global mining corporations.

Organized in four sections, the first section briefly locates this chapter within the literature on corporate self-governance and within this book. The first section also introduces social conflict theory and a politics of scale – the theoretical approach used here to analyze the political strategies of multinational mining corporations. The second section provides an account of how the global governance of social dimensions of mining developed since the 1990s in response to crises of legitimacy. At that time, many local activist groups affected by mining 'jumped scales' through alliances with international CSOs. The collective response by multinational corporations (MNCs) involved dual strategies: first was the globalization of self-governance to pre-empt strict(er) regulation by governments and international organizations with a network of self-regulatory standards and organizations. The second strategy was to re-localize and manage conflict through participatory CSR. The third section develops the view of CSR as corporate power and argues that it represents a deeper embedding of corporate interests within social relations. As corporations take on responsibilities for community development programs, environmental sustainability, and human rights, not only are these fields subjected to corporate interests, but corporations must also respond to an ever-expanding set of demands, threats, and opportunities. The point is that these strategies operate together, just as they also influence states' policy and international organizations' agendas.

I then turn to the case of Rio Tinto's ex-Kelian gold mine in Indonesia, which is taken as a typical example of conflicts, with local companies threatening the reputation of the global mining industry. The mine operated from 1985 until 2005, giving insight into how one of the world's largest mining companies evolved its conflict management strategies in response to local conditions and global developments at a time when global standards were taking shape. Indeed, Rio Tinto was a leader in driving new global self-governance arrangements. The Kelian case demonstrates the complex multiscalar feedback cycle of contestation between corporations, business associations, states, people affected by mining, and CSOs. This cycle has and is re-drawing the interests and boundaries of multinational corporations, civil society, and states. Although this argument does not discount the importance of profit maximization as the primary economic interest of MNCs, it draws attention to the multiple ways that corporate interests and strategies to pursue them are constructed through multiscalar conflict with society and CSOs.

CORPORATE POWER, CONFLICT, AND SCALE

In recent years there has been a welcome analysis of corporate self-regulation through networks of global governance mechanisms (Büthe and Mattli, 2011; Eberlein et al., 2014; MacDonald, 2014; Porter and Ronit, 2006). Increasingly, corporations are not seen as mere subjects of regulation, but as actors in the creation of governance regimes (Mikler, 2018), or even as governance institutions (Wilks, 2013). The global nature of corporate self-governance gives rise to debates about the extent to which multinational corporations remain embedded in their home jurisdictions or are forming a disembodied transnational capitalist class (Mikler, 2018; Robinson, 2006). To be sure, global corporations are enmeshed in social and political relations across specific places – across sites of extraction, production, distribution, finance, and regulation. These sites may or may not correspond to national boundaries or existing sites of governance. However, this 'national vs global' debate can obscure other sites and scales of regulation. Indeed, scholars of self-regulation have long acknowledged how the 'decentering' and 'networking' of governance – always a contested process

– have created new sites and spaces of governance (Black, 2001; Crawford, 2006). Establishing private governance mechanisms at new sites or scales is one major pathway of corporate political power.

This book identifies five 'pathways of corporate political influence' – while this chapter touches on each of these, it is the first, fourth and fifth pathways that are most relevant. The first involves how 'MNCs' influence "in their own right" rests on the authority to hire and fire, and the authority to set prices and to invest' (Mikler and Ronit, Chapter 1). Regarding the social impacts of mining, this is most evident in CSR programs that, through providing development goods – including employment – to particular local actors, can create legitimacy and contain conflicts that pose a threat to extractive operations. The fourth, the collective or cooperative organization of corporations through 'cartels, clubs, associations and other networks' that can influence or set standards (Mikler and Ronit, Chapter 1) is most evident in the network of international business associations and associated self-governance standards established by mining corporations and their financiers. The most prominent of these is the International Council on Mining and Metals (ICMM). The fifth, corporate influence 'over and with civil society' (Mikler and Ronit, Chapter 1), is manifest in the ongoing multiscalar contestation between multinational miners and their critics, including national and international environmental, development and human rights CSOs. I add to this that critical voices are not limited to 'civil society' but also include local communities and competing economic interests.

It is central to my argument here, as it is throughout this book, that these pathways are not independent, but are intimately entwined with each other and with the remaining two pathways – influencing government policy and shaping international organizations' agendas. The argument presented here is that multinational mining corporations construct political strategies in relation or reaction to the strategies of other actors. Specifically, in reaction to criticism, conflicts, declining profitability, and the threat of increased regulation, multinational mining corporations construct their legitimacy through networks of self-governance standards and associations. These standards establish frameworks for engaging with local communities and containing conflicts with people affected by mining through community development and CSR.

To analyze these strategies in the context of ongoing contestation over the social impacts of mining, I adopt a social conflict theory approach with an emphasis on the politics of scale. In political economy, social conflict theory understands that development is, 'never merely a public good, but is rather a perpetual process of resource redistribution that is fought over by class-based groups' (Hutchison et al., 2014, p. 79). Political and economic institutions are then conceptualized as both the outcomes of and terrain for political and social conflicts between groups over resources and power (Rodan, Hewison and

Robison, 2006). Institutions (including corporations, governance mechanisms, and consultative committees) embody sets of power relations that shape access to and control over resources (Rodan, 2018, p. 21). Contestation is not limited to material interests but also involves ideology and legitimacy. I use the term 'crisis of legitimacy' in the Gramscian sense, analogous to 'crisis of authority' and 'crisis of hegemony' to signify when a ruling class lost the consensus for their ideological leadership (Filippini, 2017, p. 99). This is applicable to multinational mining corporations as a fraction of the global ruling class – crises threatened their ability to operate with minimal regulation. They then needed to reabsorb control, perhaps through making sacrifices, demagogic promises, modifying their ideological position or face a wider crisis resulting in their displacement (Gramsci, 1971, pp. 210–11).

In political geography, the concept of scale refers to the spatial level (from local, metropolitan, and provincial to national, regional, and global) of social, political, and economic activities (Smith, 2008). The production of scale, along with the issues governed at any particular scale, is never given a priori but is the result of capitalist development, environmental factors, political contestation, and strategic decisions of actors (Allen, 2018; Smith, 2003, pp. 228–30; Swyngedouw and Heynen, 2010).[3] Because different opportunities, allies, and resources are available at any given scale, actors will attempt to contest issues at the scales, or across multiple scales, that are the most beneficial to their interests or detrimental to their rivals (Hameiri and Jones, 2015, p. 56). For example, social movements often attempt to 'jump scales' to the national or international where they can access alliances, resources, media, and public scrutiny (Escobar, 2001; Kirsch, 2014). MNCs and their associations often favor global scales of governance because of their relative power and access to resources.

A politics of scale and social conflict theory is useful for analyzing the political power and strategies of multinational mining companies because it rejects the reification of states, governance institutions and markets. Instead, analysis remains focused on how individuals and groups of actors, including corporations, CSOs, people affected by mining, and their allies construct strategies to use power in contestations over the social impacts of mining. It is indispensable for analyzing how multinational mining companies have sought to resolve social conflicts that began at local scales through the creation of global self-governance arrangements. These self-governance arrangements are *relatively* removed from the influence of local activists and national governments, a favorable configuration for multinational miners. To be sure, the implementation of mechanisms prescribed at international scales is also contested at all scales by groups with conflicting interests.

CRISIS AND EMERGENCE OF GLOBAL GOVERNANCE IN EXTRACTIVE INDUSTRIES

For almost any aspect of the environmental and social dimensions of mining, there is a relevant international standard. They take different forms in terms of the actors involved, the problem they respond to, and the political power of the actors involved. Standards range from the broad in scope (ISO 26000), to the specific (the International Cyanide Management Code); focus on interactions with states (the Extractive Industries Transparency Initiative), and with local communities (the Voluntary Principles on Security and Human Rights). Some are directed at financial institutions (the Equator Principles) or development agencies (the World Bank's Extractive Industries Review), are concerned directly with violent conflict (the Kimberley Process) or with development (the UN Global Compact). Some of these are purely private forms of regulation, and some are partnerships between MNCs and states or international organizations. The most prominent and representative association is the International Council on Mining and Metals (ICMM),[4] the successor to the Global Mining Initiative (GMI) (Filer, Burton and Banks, 2008, p. 164) and the ten principles of its Sustainable Development Framework (ICMM, 2015, p. 3).

In the second half of the twentieth century, as exploration and resource extraction in remote areas increasingly became economically viable, the social and environmental dynamics of mining changed dramatically (Colley, 2001; Dashwood, 2013, p. 459). The extraction of minerals and coal from remote areas, especially in developing countries, meant that small agrarian communities and indigenous people became the principal groups affected by mining (Leifsen et al., 2017). These changes led to new forms of conflict – forced relocations, land grabbing, collusion with corrupt regimes and militaries, environmental pollution and even civil war – which had become chronic by the end of the 1990s (Evans, Goodman and Lansbury, 2001). In turn, significant controversies developed from local campaigns, attracting global media attention. CSOs rallied against the lack of regulation, transparency, and accountability of mining companies in their overseas operations, especially when operating in authoritarian contexts (Bünte, 2018). Especially infamous cases include the 1996 execution of nine environmental activists in Nigeria, where Royal Dutch Shell was implicated (Hanlon, 2008); the international campaign on blood diamonds (Fanthorpe and Gabelle, 2013); and the international CSO and labor movement campaign against Rio Tinto (McSorley and Fowler, 2001). Discourses on sustainability, human rights, corruption, and environmental devastation framed global awareness of conflict, severely damaging the reputation of multinational miners and their financiers, notably including the World Bank (Fox and Brown, 2000; Hatcher, 2014; World Bank, 2003).

Beyond reputational damage, several cases saw multinational miners sued by landowners in their home jurisdiction[5] and civil society campaigns for regulations to hold multinational miners to the standards that apply in their home states (Atkinson and Hudson, 1998; Bünte, 2018; Macdonald, 2004). This was famously demonstrated by the Papua New Guinea OK Tedi traditional owners taking BHP to court in the Victorian Supreme Court in Australia (Filer and Macintyre, 2006), Bougainvillian landowners suing Rio Tinto in the Los Angeles District Court, following a ten-year civil war sparked by the mine (Australian Council for Overseas Aid, 1995; Leith, 2003), and indigenous claimants from West Papua suing Freeport-McMoRan in the New Orleans District Court (see Filer et al., 2008; Kirsch, 2014, pp. 84–126; Regan, 1998 for an extended discussion of these international court cases). There is also a significant material cost to conflict with people affected by mining. Franks et al. (2014, p. 7578) show that 'as a result of conflict, a major, world-class mining project with capital expenditure of between US$3 and US$5 billion was reported to suffer roughly US$20 million per week of delayed production in net present value terms', while cancellation of projects runs into billions of dollars of lost capital. In 2002, the global mining sector was achieving a return on investment of only 4.67 percent (Kellow, 2007, p. 115), and desperately needed to control any further threats to profitability.

These crises of legitimacy threatened mining corporations' authority to operate relatively free of regulation and mine closures (Dashwood, 2013). Multinational miners were apparently worried that recommendations of the United Nations Conference on Environment and Development Earth Summit in Rio de Janeiro 1992, if adopted, could pose a 'significant threat to [metals] markets' (Kellow, 2007, p. 123). Multinational miners responded to crises and pre-empted state regulation by establishing the institutional guidelines and ideological legitimacy to manage the social and environmental impacts of mining. The ICMM and its 'Ten Principles for Sustainable Development Framework' (ICMM, 2015, p. 3) is an important example because most of the largest multinational miners and national mining associations are members, it is influential in creating other standards, covers most areas of environmental and social impacts of mining, and provides a primary reference for how its members design community relations programs.

The GMI was formed in 1998 by CEOs of eight of the largest multinational miners who recognized the industry's 'trust deficit' (Kellow, 2007, p. 124), which could result in being 'legislated out of existence' (Dashwood, 2013, p. 446). In 1999, Sir Robert Wilson, chairperson of Rio Tinto, framed the GMI as a response to crisis: 'Unless the major players in the global mining and minerals industry can present a convincing case that their activities are conducted in line with [sustainable development] principles. . .their long term future is in jeopardy' (Sir Robert Wilson, quoted in Evans et al., 2001, pp. xvi–xvii).

The GMI's two-year Mining, Minerals and Sustainable Development (MMSD) project investigated 'disputes concerning land tenure, environmental management, and relationships to communities' (Kirsch, 2014, p. 168). Overcoming the collective action problem of going it alone: 'The MNCs formed a collective citizenship aiming to operate across multiple nation-states, strategically building political influence and the corporate reputation of mining companies [and] engineered reforms from above, via multi-stakeholder networks around CSR' (Phillips, 2012, p. 172). The *collective* organization of the companies is important, as this allows them to claim that the *industry* is now regulated and hence that state regulation is unnecessary. The MMSD resulted in a recommended four-step program for 'Supporting Sustainable Development in the Minerals Sector' (Danielson, 2002, p. xxv). The four steps are: (1) understanding sustainable development; (2) creating organizational policies and management systems; (3) achieving cooperation among those with similar interests; and (4) building capacity for effective actions at all levels (Danielson, 2002, pp. xxv–xxxiv). Although the final report is devoid of concrete recommendations, it did establish a common language of sustainability and provided a baseline for proceeding initiatives.

Realizing the need to secure ongoing legitimacy and profitability, the GMI prompted the existing International Council on Metals and the Environment to broaden its scope and reform as the ICMM in 2001 (ICMM, 2020). The ICMM requires that members commit to the ten principles of its Sustainable Development Framework, which include requirements to 'contribute to the social, economic and institutional development of host countries and communities' and 'proactively engage key stakeholders on sustainable development challenges and opportunities in an open and transparent manner' (ICMM, 2015, p. 6). Members commit to develop and report on company-wide and project-specific policies and procedures relating to the ten principles. The ICMM also harmonizes the principles with other standards applicable to MNCs:

> To ensure their robustness, the principles have been benchmarked against leading international standards. These include: the Rio Declaration, the Global Reporting Initiative, the Global Compact, OECD Guidelines on Multinational Enterprises, World Bank Operational Guidelines, OECD Convention on Combating Bribery, ILO Conventions 98, 169, 176, and the Voluntary Principles on Security and Human Rights. (ICMM, 2015, p. 3)

The principles both borrow legitimacy from these other organizations and link them together as a network of self-governance arrangements. Individual mining companies use the ICMM and other standards to create internal policy and guidelines, while each project will implement programs based on company policy and in response to local conditions. This may result in the creation of consultative committees, community development funding, complaints mechanisms, cultural programs, and participatory environmental monitoring.

The ICMM principles are voluntary, unenforceable, vague, focused on process, neglect measurable outcomes, and have little independent reporting or monitoring requirements, allowing great flexibility for individual corporations in their implementation. The same criticism has been made of almost all self-governance standards (Singh, 2011; Vogel, 2007, p. 164). Yet, as a collective, multinational mining companies overcame threats to their legitimacy through the fourth pathway of corporate political influence – working collectively to create norms and standards.

CORPORATE SOCIAL RESPONSIBILITY AS CORPORATE POWER

Shifting from an analysis of the governance to the implementation of CSR, I argue that CSR is not merely the expression of an ethical imperative or an act of corporate 'greenwashing' but is a corporate strategy to contain conflict and establish legitimacy. In this view, CSR builds corporate power and influence over social and environmental issues (Elbra, 2014; Horowitz, 2015; Welker, 2014). While CSR programs might aim to build trust and legitimacy with the public, civil society, affected communities and state actors, the asymmetric power relations between them are reinforced. Hanlon makes the point that:

> CSR represents a further embedding of capitalist social relations and a deeper opening up of social life to the dictates of the marketplace . . . it is the result of a shift from a fordist to a post-fordist regime of accumulation at the heart of which is both an expansion and deepening of wage relations. (Hanlon, 2008, p. 157)

This amounts to a reorganization of relationships and roles played by corporations, states, and CSOs, driven by conflict over the extractive process (Hatcher, 2014). Through deploying small fractions of their resources, mining corporations can influence key local actors and government decision-makers. For example, Freeport and Newcrest both provide 1 percent of their operating profit from their Grasberg and Gosowong mines for community development funds to villages surrounding their operations, providing health clinics, education, and employment opportunities (Leith, 2003; Newcrest, 2011).[6] Funds are distributed through local government councils, CSOs or community groups (Leith, 2003). Such community development funds are often accompanied by agreements to guarantee local employment, provide education and training, relocation programs, or to protect biodiversity (Wanvik, 2014).

With corporations becoming more involved in community development programs, environmental monitoring, and stakeholder consultation, incentives are created for people affected by mining to engage with corporate actors. Leifsen et al. (2017, p. 1044) argue that 'new types of conflict arise which are often related to what constitute legitimate forms of information, knowledge, impacts and levels of compensation'. Indeed, the main effect of CSR programs is to change conflict, rather than eliminate it (Li, 2015). In the logic of CSR, the subject of conflict is shifted from the impacts of mining to processes of consultation and development and the patterns of conflict from confrontational to collaborative. This is how corporations deploy resources to manage conflict. This direct deployment of resources corresponds to the first pathway of political influence identified in this book.

However, this process is not unidirectional. People affected by mining do not merely adopt corporate interests in response to patronage. Corporations must also make concessions and invest in community development in ways that are not directly reducible to the profit motive. Marina Welker (2014, p. 1), makes precisely this point about Newmont's community development program at its ex-Batu Hijau mine in Sumbawa: 'Without denying profit as a motivation, in this book I show that people enact corporations in multiple ways, and that these enactments involve struggles over the boundaries, interests and responsibilities of the corporation.' Welker continues to argue that the community relations strategy of Newmont evolved through a series of contestations with people affected by mining and other opportunists who learned how to pressure Newmont to provide 'development goods'. Thus, CSR programs, like their governance, evolve as corporate political strategies in relation to contestation and threat. The case of Rio Tinto's ex-Kelian gold mine demonstrates how both the self-governance of social impacts of mining and the practice of CSR overlap as part of broader strategies to reconstitute their legitimacy as a socially responsible miner and contain risky forms of conflict.

RIO TINTO'S KELIAN GOLD MINE[7]

PT Kelian Equatorial Mining (KEM)[8] produced up to 400 000 ounces of gold per year from the Kelian open-pit mine in West Kutai, East Kalimantan between 1992 and 2005 (Atkinson and Hudson, 1998; Darling, 1995; Kemp et al., 2013).[9] Initial conflict with people affected by mining was repressed through military and police violence. However, during the 1990s, local organization Lembaga Kesejahteraan Masyarakat Tambang dan Lingkungan (LKMTL, Council for Mining Communities' Prosperity and the Environment), forged national and international alliances to escalate the conflict beyond the area surrounding the mine. Following revelations of human rights abuses, Kelian became a crucial case in international campaigns against Rio Tinto (International Longshore and Warehouse Union, 2010). Combined with similar cases from across the globe, the effects on Rio Tinto's international reputation were instrumental in its decision to reform its practices at mine sites and support emerging global governance structures for the extractives sector. Now, Rio Tinto holds up Kelian as an award-winning example of mine rehabilitation and community engagement (Rio Tinto, 2015).

Before the Kelian mine was established, around 4000 people lived in several villages within the concession area (Mangkoedilaga, Widjojo and Nainggolan, 2000). In 1985, PT KEM signed a contract of work (CoW) with the Indonesian government to exploit the primary gold deposit (ibid.). Several researchers and investigators found evidence that from 1982 to 1992, police, military, and company security forces evicted residents, in some cases burning their houses and gardens, arresting or shooting those who did not comply (Atkinson and Hudson, 1998, pp. 26–8; Bachriadi, 1998; Kennedy, 2001; Mangkoedilaga et al., 2000; Nyompe, 2003). From 1991 to 1998, the relationship between evictees and KEM was extremely confrontational. Hundreds of protests, blockades, and occupations were staged. However, given the remote location and authoritarian government, there was little incentive for Rio Tinto to address the concerns of people affected by its practices. In 1996, through contacts with national CSOs including JATAM (the Mining Advocacy Network) and WALHI (Friends of the Earth Indonesia), LKMTL began working with Community Aid Abroad (CAA, now Oxfam Australia) (Atkinson, Brown and Ensor, 2001; Atkinson and Hudson, 1998; Macdonald, 2004; Macdonald and Ross, 2002, 2003).

Meanwhile, Rio Tinto had become the target of a multi-issue international campaign. The Australian Construction, Forestry, Mining and Energy Union (CFMEU), together with the International Federation of Chemical, Energy, Mine and General Workers' Union (ICEM), brought together a loose coalition of unions and indigenous, environmental, and human rights organizations impacted by or struggling against Rio Tinto (McSorley and Fowler, 2001). The network produced the *Tainted Titan* alternative annual report (ICEM, 1997). However, Rio refused to directly respond to the report or the network as a whole and instead singled out particular groups to engage in negotiations (McSorley and Fowler, 2001).

Most important for this case study was the involvement of JATAM and CAA, both working with LKMTL about human rights violations surrounding the Kelian mine. Representatives from the Kelian area were brought to Australia by CAA in 1998. They spoke at union stop-work meetings and met with union officials and other CSO representatives (ibid.). Most significantly, LKMTL representatives demonstrated against and then met with Rio Tinto management in Melbourne, and then again at Rio's London AGM in 1999.

Rio Tinto realized it was facing a crisis of legitimacy as early as 1996 when it commissioned its Community Issues and Priorities Survey (Burton, 2001, p. 115). The results showed that campaigns against Rio Tinto had a substantial effect on its public image. In addition to taking a leading role in forming the GMI, in 1999 Rio Tinto decided to respond to its negative image through a series of partnerships with CSOs, both to improve its public image and to court some of its critics. One such partnership was with Australian Legal Resources International (ALRI) in 2000. Burton (2001, pp. 117–19) reports that Rio staff seconded to ALRI worked with the Australian Embassy in Jakarta providing technical assistance to Indonesian legislators in drafting new legislation on the environment, human rights, and corporations. While it is not clear what, if any, influence this partnership had on the Indonesian legislative process, they occurred at the same time Indonesia's Komnas HAM (National Commission on Human Rights) was investigating allegations of human rights abuses surrounding Kelian (Burton, 2001).

The international pressure convinced Rio Tinto executives in Melbourne and London to order KEM to begin negotiations. A series of meetings between KEM, LKMTL, WALHI and other stakeholders in 1997 and 1998 concluded with KEM agreeing to pay close to AU$1 million (10 million Indonesian rupiah) in compensation to 440 displaced families (Atkinson et al., 2001, p. 15; Phillips, 2001, p. 189). Negotiations with Rio continued and focused on the provision of clean water – after the Kelian River was no longer suitable for human consumption – the sealing of roads and other infrastructure needs in surrounding villages (Phillips, 2001, p. 189). Negotiations and community development work began to divide opposition to the mine after some villages and groups received benefits.

After the fall of the authoritarian New Order regime and the beginning of *reformasi* (reform, or reformation), in 1999 political space opened to campaign within Indonesia. LKMTL began organizing locally again, signing up members and mobilizing them to demand compensation for outstanding issues. Since 1998, LKMTL blocked the access road to the mine more than ten times.[10] In July 1999, LKMTL members blocked the access road between the mine and port for 40 days. KEM declared *force majeure* on their contracts for the delivery of gold. Because gold mines are considered nationally significant infrastructure in Indonesia, this triggered a national security incident. Police and military reinforcements were dispatched to repress the demonstration. Desperately wanting to avoid violence and international publicity, KEM reopened negotiations with LKMTL, which ended the blockade and the need for armed intervention.[11]

Along with creating space for the return of physical protest against KEM, *reformasi* allowed more space for civil society organizations and state institutions to operate. LKTML and WALHI facilitated an investigation by the National Human Rights Commission, Komnas HAM, in 2001. The report found evidence supporting claims that the human rights of people forcibly relocated were violated, including unlawful detentions, deaths in custody, destruction of houses and property, and sexual violence. It recommended further investigation to verify each accusation, followed by negotiation of compensation and prosecution by Indonesian courts (Mangkoedilaga et al., 2000). Rio has since admitted that human rights violations occurred and offered a 'public expression of regret' (Kemp et al., 2013, p. 82). However, no party involved ever faced court. In March 2001, following further negotiations with LKMTL, Rio Tinto announced a 60 billion Indonesian rupiah compensation package (AU$10.5 million) for victims without admitting guilt or liability for any specific case (Macdonald and Ross, 2003, p. 51). Again, Rio's strategy of providing compensation through negotiations partially pacified opposition and averted the threat of litigation, including the possibility of charges being brought against individual senior managers (Mangkoedilaga et al., 2000; Sinclair, 2020).

At the same time, Rio Tinto and KEM were preparing mine closure plans. The World Bank provided technical assistance to Rio Tinto, advising that a 'trilateral process of consultation and problem solving, involving mining companies, governments, and communities, is required for a mine to be closed successfully' (World Bank and International Finance Corporation, 2002, p. v). This proactive approach to avoiding conflict drew on the lessons of the GMI's MMSD. Rio Tinto describes the Mine Closure Steering Committee as representative of 'Kelian Equatorial Mining, Rio Tinto, the surrounding community, and the district, provincial and central governments' and that 'key decisions on all aspects of mine closure were to be made by consensus' (Everingham et al., 2016, p. 136). After KEM concluded mining-related activities, the mine site was rehabilitated and turned into a 6670-hectare protected forest. The Anum Lio Foundation (YAL) was set up with US$2.4 million in funding to continue community development programs and US$11 million to manage the protected forest (Down to Earth, 2005). Its status as a protected forest precludes people returning to the area. This more proactive approach established the legitimacy of Rio Tinto as a responsible operator before further challenges emerged.

This case provided both impetus and a testing ground for evolving global governance standards, which Rio Tinto was instrumental in creating through its leadership in the GMI from 1999 and ICMM from 2001. Negotiations between LKMTL, KEM, and Rio Tinto proceeded in three discrete rounds – first the negotiation of compensation for land and dwellings of evictees, second the negotiations over compensation for human rights abuses, and finally, consultation as part of the mine closure steering committee. The first two rounds were preceded by LKMTL mobilizing threats to Rio Tinto – internationally through the CAA alliance, blockades, and demonstrations, and the Komnas HAM investigation. The final round drew from international experience and collaboration with the World Bank, yet the outcomes of the mine closure planning responded to local conditions. Each round concluded with a limited concession to LKMTL's demands by KEM and a corresponding reprieve of the threat. Although it is impossible to tell how likely further state intervention in the case was, Rio Tinto's compensation, consultation and collaboration showed both Australian and Indonesian state actors that their intervention was not required. This is most evident in the negotiations for the 60 billion Indonesian rupiah compensation package, which was constructed as an alternative to formal litigation. In this case, CSR was both an attempt to change patterns of local conflict from confrontational to collaborative and respond to international campaigns by presenting an image of a good global citizen.

CONCLUSION

This chapter analyzed how multinational mining corporations have pursued strategies to maintain their legitimacy and influence through the five pathways of corporate political influence identified in this book. They have strategically deployed resources at local scales through community development programs to contain conflicts with people affected by mining and create local social relations favorable to mining (the first pathway). Through international business associations, they have created rules that reconstitute their legitimacy as responsible self-governing actors (the fourth pathway) and engaged with critics across civil society and affected communities (the fifth). These pathways of corporate political influence operate together and reinforce each other. The standards established through international business associations both guide and are guided by methods of engaging local communities through community development programs. Both are constructed in relation to critical voices from local communities affected by mining and civil society organizations. While this chapter has not focused as much on pathways of influence involving influencing state policy or international organizations' agendas (the second and third), these too are entangled. The international legitimacy of self-governance and the effectiveness of CSR is designed to influence states and international organizations not to regulate the social impacts of mining.

The case of the Kelian gold mine in Indonesia demonstrates how corporate responsibilities, interests, and power are shaped through series of conflicts with people affected by mining and their allies across political scales, institutional and non-institutional sites. At Kelian, the international campaign supported by CAA and the fall of the authoritarian New Order meant that Rio Tinto could no longer rely solely on the Indonesian military and police to repress critics. Rio Tinto responded to the international challenges with two distinct scalar strategies: first to globalize the issues through the formation of new global governance standards, and second to re-localize the issue by engaging LKMTL directly and cutting out its international allies. The techniques developed by Rio Tinto at Kelian with the assistance of the World Bank have since been adopted as global standards, which in turn inform how other mining corporations engage with people in other localities. A methodological focus on only global governance mechanisms, only localized conflicts or only state–corporate relations would fail to appreciate how conflicts at one scale are affected by and can become entangled with conflicts across other scales.

Kelian was just one of the cases influencing Rio Tinto's strategy and Rio Tinto just one corporation developing collective industrial strategies, one of which was the ICMM. Rio Tinto's local and global strategies were formed in response to pressure from people affected by mining, civil society actors, and associated risk of increased regulation. This shows how the various pathways for corporate political influence entangle together *and* with the strategies of other actors. That is to say, MNCs do not pursue power entirely on their own terms and that their strategies are as much an effect of challenges to their power as a simple expression of it. As international self-governance standards appropriated practices of sustainability and community development through CSR, mining corporations have taken on additional responsibilities in their quest for legitimacy. Criss-crossed by diverse interests and demands, MNCs are mutually constituted with the societies they interact with, not only their home states and international associations.

While the particular strategies discussed here are immediately relevant to the governance and management of the social dimensions of mining, multinational corporations in any industry can follow these pathways to political influence over any issue. The degree of success will depend on the dynamic multiscalar contestations surrounding an issue or industry. Furthermore, all multinational mining companies that are members of the ICMM and other major international standards are headquartered in North America, South America, Europe, South Africa, Australia or Japan. Although it is yet to be seen how multinational corporations from emerging powers – China, India, and Russia – will implement CSR in their overseas operations, we should anticipate similar strategies to be engaged as far as they respond to similar patterns of contestation. Social conflict theory and a politics of scale prove fruitful for examining the interconnected pathways to corporate political influence in any industry and based in any country. The power of this approach is to examine the contestations that shape and determine corporate power and strategies, regardless of institutional context. Although profitability remains the primary interest of corporations, and although controlling the risk of conflict is undeniably important for profitability, corporate interests and strategies are not entirely reducible to measurable or predictable effects on profitability. The way that corporations decide to manage relations with people affected by their operations and the way these techniques are enshrined in global standards is the outcome of ongoing historical conflicts that traverse multiple political scales. They are worked out in contestation, negotiation, and response to threats, not (only) by the rational calculation of accountants and economists.

NOTES

1. I would like to thank all research participants who agreed to be interviewed for this project, colleagues at the 2018 International Political Science Association World Congress for their feedback and Jane Hutchison, Garry Rodan, Shahar Hameiri and John Mikler for comments on earlier versions of this chapter. Fieldwork in Indonesia was made possible by a 2017 *Endeavour Postgraduate Scholarship for Long-term Fieldwork*, and being hosted by the Centre for Security and Peace Studies, Gadjah Mada University.
2. This chapter addresses the social dimensions of mining, which intersect with environmental impacts. Dynamics around the economic governance of mining companies, including conflict over 'resource nationalism' are significantly different and outside the scope of this chapter. For example, see the work of Eve Warburton (2014, 2016, 2017) on 'resource nationalism', multinational corporations (MNCs) and the Indonesian national state.
3. For example, in this chapter, I define 'local' scales as the areas immediately surrounding a mine and extractive operations. The precise area varies from case to case as is it often determined by environmental impacts, identities of 'local' people, state and corporate policies. Who counts as 'local' is frequently hotly contested, because it can carry implications for resource distribution.
4. As of 2018, ICMM has 27 mining corporations as members, 15 of which are ranked in the top 40 mining companies by market capitalization (ICMM, 2018; PWC, 2018). ICMM members have headquarters across most major origins of mining capital – North America, South America, Europe, South Africa, Australia and Japan, conspicuous in their absence are Chinese-, Russian- and Indian-based mining companies, which together account for 14 of the 40 largest mining companies (PWC, 2018).
5. As opposed to the operating jurisdiction.
6. In the case of Newcrest's Gosowong mine, the '1 percent' fund grew to AU$22.5 million by 2011.
7. For a more comprehensive account of the Kelian case, see Sinclair (2020).
8. Until 1995, KEM was 90 percent owned by Conzinc Riotinto of Australia (CRA) and 10 percent by Indonesian company PT Harita Jayaraya. In 1995, CRA merged with its parent company, UK-based Rio Tinto – Zinc Corporation (RTZ) to form the dual-listed Rio Tinto Group, known as Rio Tinto Limited in Australia and Rio Tinto Plc in the UK. For simplicity, I refer to all these related companies as Rio Tinto unless a distinction is necessary.
9. Mining ceased in 2003 and ore processing ceased in 2005.
10. Community relations manager, KEM, interview with author, 8 August 2017.
11. KEM consultant, interview with author, 7 August 2017.

REFERENCES

Allen, M.G. (2018), *Resource Extraction and Contentious States: Mining and the Politics of Scale in the Pacific Islands*, Singapore: Palgrave Macmillan.

Atkinson, J., A. Brown and J. Ensor (2001), *Mining Ombudsman Annual Report 2000–2001*, Melbourne: Oxfam Community Aid Abroad Australia.

Atkinson, J. and D. Hudson (1998), *Undermined: The Impact of Australian Mining Companies in Developing Countries*, Melbourne: Community Aid Abroad.

Australian Council for Overseas Aid [ACFOA] (1995), *Trouble at Freeport: Eyewitness Accounts of West Papuan Resistance to the Freeport-McMoRan Mine in Irian Jaya, Indonesia and Indonesian Military Repression: June 1994–February 1995*, Canberra: ACFOA [Human Rights Office].

Bachriadi, D. (1998), *Merana Di Tengah Kelimpahan, Pelanggaran-pelanggaran HAM Pada Industri Pertambangan di Indonesia* [Languishing Amongst Abundance, Human Rights Violations in the Indonesian Mining Industry], Jakarta: ELSAM.

Black, J. (2001), 'Decentring regulation: understanding the role of regulation and self-regulation in a "post-regulatory" world', *Current Legal Problems*, **54**(1), 103–46.

Bünte, M. (2018), 'Building governance from scratch: Myanmar and the Extractive Industry Transparency Initiative', *Journal of Contemporary Asia*, **48**(2), 230–51.

Burton, B. (2001), 'When corporations want to cuddle', in G. Evans, J. Goodman and N. Lansbury (eds), *Moving Mountains: Communities Confront Mining and Globalization*, Otford, NSW: Mineral Policy Institute and Otford Press, pp. 109–24.

Büthe, T. and W. Mattli (2011), *The New Global Rulers: The Privatization of Regulation in the World Economy*, Princeton, NJ: Princeton University Press.

Colley, P. (2001), 'Political economy of mining', in G. Evans, J. Goodman and N. Lansbury (eds), *Moving Mountains: Communities Confront Mining and Globalization*, Otford, NSW: Mineral Policy Institute and Otford Press, pp. 19–36.

Crawford, A. (2006), 'Networked governance and the post-regulatory state? Steering, rowing and anchoring the provision of policing and security', *Theoretical Criminology*, **10**(4), 449–79.

Danielson, L. (2002), *Breaking New Ground: Mining, Minerals, and Sustainable Development: The Report of the MMSD Project*, London: Earthscan, accessed 29 July 2020 at https://pubs.iied.org/pdfs/9084IIED.pdf.

Darling, P. (1995), 'Kelian – Indonesia's largest gold operation', *Engineering and Mining Journal*, **196**(10), 28–30.

Dashwood, H.S. (2013), 'Global private governance: explaining initiatives in the global mining sector', in J. Mikler (ed.), *The Handbook of Global Companies*, Oxford: Wiley-Blackwell, pp. 456–72.

Down to Earth (2005), 'Rio Tinto closes Kelian mine – history of human rights abuses', accessed 26 July 2016 at http://www.downtoearth-indonesia.org/node/636.

Eberlein, B., K.W. Abbott and J. Black et al. (2014), 'Transnational business governance interactions: conceptualization and framework for analysis', *Regulation and Governance*, **8**(1), 1–21.

Elbra, A. (2014), 'Interests need not be pursued if they can be created: private governance in African gold mining', *Business and Politics*, **16**(2), 247–66.

Escobar, A. (2001), 'Culture sits in places: reflections on globalism and subaltern strategies of localization', *Political Geography*, **20**(2), 139–74.

Evans, G., J. Goodman and N. Lansbury (2001), 'Introduction', in G. Evans, J. Goodman and N. Lansbury (eds), *Moving Mountains: Communities Confront Mining and Globalization*, Otford, NSW: Mineral Policy Institute and Otford Press.

Everingham, J.-A., D. Kemp and S. Ali et al. (2016), *Why Agreements Matter: A Resource Guide for Integrating Agreements into Communities and Social Performance Work at Rio Tinto*, Melbourne: Rio Tinto in partnership with the

Centre for Social Responsibility in Mining, University of Queensland, accessed 29 July 2020 at https://www.commdev.org/pdf/publications/P_Rio_Tinto_Why_Agreements_Matter.pdf.

Fanthorpe, R. and C. Gabelle (2013), *Political Economy of Extractives Governance in Sierra Leone*, accessed 8 April 2015 at https://openknowledge.worldbank.org/handle/10986/16726.

Filer, C., J. Burton and G. Banks (2008), 'The fragmentation of responsibilities in the Melanesian mining sector', in C. O'Faircheallaigh and S. Ali (eds), *Earth Matters: Indigenous Peoples, the Extractive Industries and Corporate Social Responsibility*, Sheffield: Greenleaf Publishing Ltd, pp. 163–79.

Filer, C. and M. Macintyre (2006), 'Grass roots and deep holes: community responses to mining in Melanesia', *Contemporary Pacific*, **18**(2), 215–32.

Filippini, M. (2017), *Using Gramsci: A New Approach*, London: Pluto Press.

Fox, J.A. and L.D. Brown (2000), *The Struggle for Accountability: The World Bank, NGOs, and Grassroots Movements*, 2nd edition, Cambridge, MA: MIT Press.

Franks, D.M., R. Davis and A.J. Bebbington et al. (2014), 'Conflict translates environmental and social risk into business costs', *Proceedings of the National Academy of Sciences of the United States of America*, **111**(21), 7576–81.

Gramsci, A. (1971), *Selections from the Prison Notebooks of Antonio Gramsci*, edited and translated by Q. Hoare and G. Nowell-Smith, New York: International Publishers.

Hameiri, S. and L. Jones (2015), *Governing Borderless Threats: Non-Traditional Security and the Politics of State Transformation*, Cambridge, UK: Cambridge University Press.

Hanlon, G. (2008), 'Rethinking corporate social responsibility and the role of the firm – on the denial of politics', in A. Crane, A. McWilliams and D. Matten et al. (eds), *The Oxford Handbook of Corporate Social Responsibility*, Oxford: Oxford University Press, pp. 156–72.

Hatcher, P. (2014), *Regimes of Risk: The World Bank and the Transformation of Mining in Asia*, New York: Palgrave Macmillan.

Horowitz, L.S. (2015), 'Culturally articulated neoliberalisation: corporate social responsibility and the capture of indigenous legitimacy in New Caledonia', *Transactions of the Institute of British Geographers*, **40**(1), 88–101.

Hutchison, J., W. Hout, C. Hughes and R. Robison (2014), *Political Economy and the Aid Industry in Asia*, Basingstoke: Palgrave Macmillan.

International Council on Mining and Metals [ICMM] (2015), *Sustainable Development Framework: ICMM Principles*, London: ICMM, accessed 29 July 2020 at http://icmm.uat.byng.uk.net/website/publications/pdfs/commitments/revised-2015_icmm-principles.pdf.

International Council on Mining and Metals [ICMM] (2018), 'Member companies', accessed 27 June 2018 at http://www.icmm.com/en-gb/members/member-companies.

International Council on Mining and Metals [ICMM] (2020), 'Our history', accessed 30 May 2020 at https://www.icmm.com/en-gb/about-us/our-organisation/annual-reviews/our-history.

International Federation of Chemical, Energy, Mine and General Workers' Union [ICEM] (1997), *Rio Tinto Tainted Titan: The Stakeholders' Report*, Brussels: ICEM.

International Longshore and Warehouse Union (2010), 'Rio Tinto: a shameful history of human and labour rights abuses and environmental degradation around the globe', accessed 20 November 2015 at http://londonminingnetwork.org/2010/04/

rio-tinto-a-shameful-history-of-human-and-labour-rights-abuses-and-environmental
-degradation-around-the-globe/.

Kellow, A. (2007), 'Privilege and underprivilege: countervailing groups, policy and
mining industry at the global level', in K. Ronit (ed.), *Global Public Policy: Business
and the Countervailing Powers of Civil Society*, Abingdon: Routledge, pp. 110–31.

Kemp, D., J. Gronow and V. Zimmerman et al. (2013), *Why Human Rights Matter*,
London: Rio Tinto, accessed 29 July 2020 at https://mc-56397411-4872-452d
-b48e-428890-cdn-endpoint.azureedge.net/-/media/Content/Documents/
Sustainability/Corporate-policies/RT-Why-human-rights-matter-EN.pdf?rev=
ff7b1377899441a9b4deadaaac6a48f3.

Kennedy, D. (2001), 'Rio Tinto: Global Compact violator', *CorpWatch.org*, 13 July,
accessed 20 November 2015 at http://www.corpwatch.org/article.php?id=622.

Kirsch, S. (2014), *Mining Capitalism: The Relationship Between Corporations and
Their Critics*, Oakland, CA: University of California Press.

Korten, D.C. (1995), *When Corporations Rule the World*, London: Earthscan
Publications.

Leifsen, E., M.-T. Gustafsson, M.A. Guzmán-Gallegos and A. Schilling-Vacaflor
(2017), 'New mechanisms of participation in extractive governance: between
technologies of governance and resistance work', *Third World Quarterly*, **38**(5),
1043–57.

Leith, D. (2003), *The Politics of Power: Freeport in Suharto's Indonesia*, Honolulu:
University of Hawaii Press.

Li, F. (2015), *Unearthing Conflict: Corporate Mining, Activism, and Expertise in Peru*,
Durham, NC: Duke University Press.

Macdonald, I. (2004), *Mining Ombudsman Annual Report 2004*, Melbourne: Oxfam
Community Aid Abroad Australia.

Macdonald, I. and B. Ross (2002), *Mining Ombudsman Annual Report 2001–2002*,
Melbourne: Oxfam Community Aid Abroad Australia.

Macdonald, I. and B. Ross (2003), *Mining Ombudsman Annual Report 2003*,
Melbourne: Oxfam Community Aid Abroad Australia.

Macdonald, K. (2014), *The Politics of Global Supply Chains*, Oxford: Wiley-Blackwell.

Mangkoedilaga, B., M.S. Widjojo and A.T. Nainggolan (2000), *Laporan Hasil
Investigasi Masalah Hak Asasi Manusia di Sekitar Wilayah Pertambangan PT
Kelian Equatorial Mining, Kabupaten Kutai Barat, Kalimantan Timur, Indonesia*,
[Report of Results of the Investigation into Problems with Fundamental Human
Rights in the Mining Area of PT Kelian Equatorial Mining, West Kutai Regency,
East Kalimantan, Indonesia], Jakarta: Komnas HAM [National Commission on
Fundamental Human Rights].

McSorley, J. and R. Fowler (2001), 'Mineworkers on the offensive', in G. Evans,
J. Goodman and N. Lansbury (eds), *Moving Mountains: Communities Confront
Mining and Globalization*, Otford, NSW: Mineral Policy Institute and Otford Press,
pp. 165–80.

Mikler, J. (2018), *The Political Power of Global Corporations*, Cambridge, UK: Polity
Press.

Newcrest (2011), *Newcrest Sustainability Report 2011*, Melbourne: Newcrest Mining
Limited, accessed 25 July 2016 at http://www.newcrest.com.au/media/sustainability
_reports/Sustainability_Report_2010.pdf.

Nyompe, P.E. (2003), 'The closure of the Kelian gold mine and the role of the Business
Partnership for Development/World Bank', paper presented at the EIR's Eminent
Person Meeting on Indigenous Peoples, Extractive Industries and the World Bank,

Oxford, 15 April, accessed 26 July 2016 at http://www.forestpeoples.org/sites/fpp/files/publication/2010/08/eirinternatwshopindonesiacaseengapr03.pdf.

Phillips, R. (2001), 'Engagement or confrontation?', in G. Evans, J. Goodman and N. Lansbury (eds), *Moving Mountains: Communities Confront Mining and Globalization*, Otford, NSW: Mineral Policy Institute and Otford Press, pp. 181–94.

Phillips, R. (2012), 'Non-government organisations in a sustainable relationship for sustainable mining? The Australian NGO perspective on what happened after the MMSD initiative', *Third Sector Review*, **18**(1), 171–93.

Porter, T. and K. Ronit (2006), 'Self-regulation as policy process: the multiple and criss-crossing stages of private rule-making', *Policy Sciences*, **39**(1), 41–72.

PWC (2018), *Mine 2018: Tempting Times*, accessed 29 July 2020 at https://www.pwc.com/id/mine-2018.

Regan, A.J. (1998), 'Causes and course of the Bougainville conflict', *The Journal of Pacific History*, **33**(3), 269–85.

Rio Tinto (2015), *Working for Mutual Benefit: Sustainable Development 2015*, accessed 29 July 2020 at https://mc-56397411-4872-452d-b48e-428890-cdn-endpoint.azureedge.net/-/media/Content/Documents/Invest/Reports/Sustainable-development-reports/RT-Sustainable-development-2015.pdf?rev=4b256b056e5c43dc97228ca9456b27cb.

Robinson, W.I. (2006), 'Gramsci and globalisation: from nation-state to transnational hegemony', in A. Bieler and A.D. Morton (eds), *Images of Gramsci: Connections and Contentions in Political Theory and International Relations*, New York: Routledge, pp. 165–80.

Rodan, G. (2018), *Participation Without Democracy: Containing Conflict in Southeast Asia*, Ithaca, NY: Cornell University Press.

Rodan, G., K. Hewison and R. Robison (2006), *The Political Economy of South-East Asia: Markets, Power and Contestation*, 3rd edition, Melbourne: Oxford University Press.

Sinclair, L. (2020), 'Undermining conflict: multinational miners, conflict and participation in Indonesia', PhD thesis, Murdoch University, Perth, Australia.

Singh, K. (2011), 'Corporate accountability: is self-regulation the answer?', in G. Teeple and S. McBride (eds), *Relations of Global Power: Neoliberal Order and Disorder*, Toronto: University of Toronto Press, pp. 60–72.

Smith, N. (2003), 'Remaking scale: competition and cooperation in pre-national and post-national Europe', in N. Brenner, B. Jessop, M. Jones and M. Gordon (eds), *State/Space: A Reader*, Malden, MA: Blackwell Publishing, pp. 227–38.

Smith, N. (2008), *Uneven Development: Nature, Capital, and the Production of Space*, 3rd edition, Athens, GA: University of Georgia Press.

Swyngedouw, E. and N.C. Heynen (2010), 'Urban political ecology, justice and the politics of scale', *Antipode*, **35**(5), 898–918.

Vogel, D. (2007), *The Market for Virtue: The Potential and Limits of Corporate Social Responsibility*, Washington, DC: Brookings Institution Press.

Wanvik, T.I. (2014), 'Encountering a multidimensional assemblage: the case of Norwegian corporate social responsibility activities in Indonesia', *Norsk Geografisk Tidsskrift – Norwegian Journal of Geography*, **68**(5), 282–90.

Warburton, E. (2014), 'In whose interest? Debating resource nationalism in Indonesia', *Kyoto Review of Southeast Asia*, No. 15, accessed 9 September 2015 at http://kyotoreview.org/yav/in-whose-interest-debating-resource-nationalism-in-indonesia/.

Warburton, E. (2016), 'Jokowi and the new developmentalism', *Bulletin of Indonesian Economic Studies*, **52**(3), 297–320.

Warburton, E. (2017), 'Resource nationalism in post-boom Indonesia: the new normal?', *LowyInstitute.org*, 27 April, accessed 11 May 2017 at https://www .lowyinstitute.org/publications/resource-nationalism-post-boom-indonesia-new -normal.

Welker, M. (2014), *Enacting the Corporation: An American Mining Firm in Post-Authoritarian Indonesia*, Berkeley, CA: University of California Press.

Wilks, S. (2013), *The Political Power of the Business Corporation*, Cheltenham, UK and Northampton, MA, USA: Edward Elgar Publishing.

World Bank (2003), *Striking a Better Balance: Volume 1. The World Bank Group and Extractive Industries*, Washington, DC: World Bank, accessed 12 May 2015 at https://openknowledge.worldbank.org/handle/10986/17705.

World Bank and International Finance Corporation (2002), *It's Not Over When It's Over: Mine Closure Around the World*, Washington, DC: World Bank, accessed 28 July 2016 at http://siteresources.worldbank.org/INTOGMC/Resources/ notoverwhenover.pdf.

8. Knowledge and power: the role of the Big Four in the competitive disharmonization of global corporate tax avoidance regulations[1]

Ainsley Elbra, John Mikler and Hannah Murphy-Gregory

In 2015, the Big Four professional services firms – PwC, Deloitte, KPMG and EY – appeared before the Australian Senate Economic References Committee Inquiry into Corporate Tax Avoidance (hereafter the Senate Committee). Unlike the other firms called before the Senate Committee, these firms were not required to answer questions about their own tax practices, but instead were asked to respond to questions regarding their role as tax advisors to large multinational corporations (MNCs). The Big Four are at the heart of the multinational tax avoidance regime. They are MNCs themselves, but they also serve as facilitators of other MNCs' tax avoidance strategies and shapers of national and global regulations in respect of the problem. Without their expertise, MNCs would be unable to implement the complex structures required to shift profits out of 'high tax' jurisdictions, into low tax jurisdictions. Without their cooperation, states will be unable to address the problem. Therefore, they sit critically at the crossroads of global corporate tax avoidance: between the facilitation of the problem, and proposed solutions to it. As explained in Chapter 1, they therefore also occupy crucial positions in three of the pathways in which MNCs exercise political influence: in their own right, in respect of business community in general, and in respect of states.

MNC tax avoidance denies governments around the world US$240–650 billion per annum, of which the revenue losses to governments from tax avoidance by US-based MNCs alone have been estimated at US$100 billion (Crivelli, De Mooij and Keen, 2015; Gravelle, 2015; Organisation for Economic Co-operation and Development [OECD], 2015). Yet, it should be stressed that the tax avoidance strategies and structures developed by the Big Four, and utilized by their MNC clients, are not illegal. Instead, they have been argued to be highly immoral, largely because they shift the tax burden to individual citizens and domestic firms. How then, did the representatives of the Big Four who appeared at the Senate Committee characterize the problem and solutions to it? Their testimonies were strikingly similar, and closely followed what the Big Four said when they appeared before parliamentary committees in the UK, Canada and the US (Latulippe, 2018). All focused on the norms of profitability, economic growth and competition. Moreover, they all suggested that Australian tax reform should move only in line with that of other nation states. In advocating for a harmonized tax system achieved through multilateral reform, the representatives of the Big Four placed a heavy emphasis on OECD-led action. Several representatives suggested that Australia should remain part of the 'pack'. Furthermore, all emphasized that unilateral tax reform would place Australia at a disadvantage. Some of the representatives went as far as to label unilateral action taken by the Australian and UK governments as undesirable due to it being the result of 'political' rather than economic motivations.

This seems counter-intuitive at first glance, because if the business model of the Big Four is the exploitation of differences in national tax jurisdictions to minimize the taxation obligations of their clients, then the harmonization of the laws in these jurisdictions surely reduces the opportunities for doing so. This chapter therefore seeks to unpack the logic behind the Big Four making such arguments. It does so by locating their operations, and explanation of the rationales for them, in debates about addressing global corporate tax avoidance, and the insights provided by the literature on the role of reputational intermediaries in respect of the political power of MNCs. First, the operation of the global taxation system, and the problem of global corporate tax avoidance as facilitated by it, is explained. The OECD's efforts at reforming this system are considered in the context of this problem. Second, the role played by the Big Four in theory and in practice as reputational intermediaries is explained. Third, the nature of the problem and the role played by the Big Four are brought together in the context of the testimony their representatives gave to the Senate Committee.

We conclude that while it could appear as though representatives of the Big Four were uniformly promoting global tax reform, this is not the case. In reality, they share what amounts to a strategic vision for dealing with global corporate tax avoidance, which we find is actually also a vision for (re-) enabling it. As the transcripts of the Senate Committee reveal, their representatives were more accurately advocating not global taxation reform, but reform sought specifically through the *OECD* process, which is not an encompassing global project. This is quite different from a truly global response. What they were advocating in practice was harmonization across OECD member country tax law, while leaving non-OECD states as distinct and differentiated from the OECD regime that would be established. As such, we argue that the Big

Four were essentially making a case for competitive disharmonization in the (perhaps unlikely) event that global governance is successful: an 'us versus them' scenario in which the Big Four could still utilize their deep tax expertise to take advantage of the arbitrage opportunities facilitated by a harmonized tax system for OECD countries, where most major MNCs are headquartered, and those of non-OECD states whose tax systems still offer a range of tax avoidance possibilities.

THE GLOBAL TAXATION SYSTEM AND THE HARMONIZING ROLE OF THE OECD

The global taxation system suffers from serious flaws, dating back to the development of legal mechanisms to avoid double taxation in the 1920s. Most of these flaws stem from the fact that the international tax system was developed prior to MNCs rising to prominence (Eccleston, 2018). These flaws have been utilized as loopholes to allow MNCs to shift profits from high tax jurisdictions to low tax jurisdictions, or what are known as 'tax havens'. MNCs take advantage of these loopholes through accounting methods that allow profits to be moved artificially, in order to minimize taxable profits. The OECD refers to much of this behavior as base erosion and profit shifting (BEPS), because it erodes the tax bases of states where economic activity occurs to other locations where profits are reported. Instead of preventing double taxation, these antiquated, multilayer regulations now provide plenty of opportunity for what Pascal Saint-Amans, Director of the Center for Tax Policy and Administration at the OECD, labels 'double non-taxation' (Australian Senate, 2015).

This type of behavior has been a concern of civil society groups since the 1970s but it was not until the 1990s that it appeared on the political agenda. In 1998, the OECD published its report *Harmful Tax Competition: An Emerging Global Issue*, which was the first attempt by an inter-governmental agency to name and shame tax havens (Sharman, 2006). This was an unprecedented step, in that it not only acknowledged the harm aggressive tax avoidance caused, but also shifted some of the blame from corporations onto the states that harbored and promoted these practices. Encouraged by the OECD's report, Oxfam, a non-governmental organization (NGO) that had been working on this issue intermittently throughout the 1990s, released its seminal report *Tax Havens: Releasing the Hidden Billions for Poverty Eradication* in 2000 (Oxfam, 2000). This report highlighted the injustice of MNC tax avoidance and the harm that aggressive tax regimes caused developing states in particular. Oxfam was working alongside other civil society actors such as Action Aid, Attac and War on Want to draw attention to the impacts of MNC tax avoidance on developing states (Elbra, 2018). By the early 2000s, the G7 finance ministers had publicly committed to addressing the issue of MNC tax avoidance, and it appeared as though the campaign may have gained traction in order to produce agreement on a harmonized approach to tax avoidance.

This progress was short-lived. International cooperation on the issue, let alone some degree of regulatory harmonization, remained elusive. The attitude of George W. Bush's administration in the US was in fact actively anti-reform, as it worked to undermine OECD efforts to reduce the opportunities for tax avoidance. The justification for this position revolved around a pro-business ideology coupled with arguments regarding sovereignty (Palan, Murphy and Chavagneux, 2013, p. 217). Ultimately, US Treasury Secretary at the time, Paul O'Neill, stated that the US 'does not support efforts to dictate to any country what its own tax rates or tax system should be, and will not participate in any initiative to harmonize world tax systems' (O'Neill, 2001). In 2001, the US was the home base for 41 percent of the world's 500 largest MNCs listed in the Forbes Global 500, which ranks them on the basis of a composition of sales, profits, assets and market value (Forbes, 2002). In essence, this position meant that the world's most economically powerful state, where most of the world's major tax avoidance culprits are headquartered (or at the very least potential culprits on the basis of the multinationality of their operations), was unwilling to curtail their abilities to engage in tax avoidance strategies. At the same time, Oxfam abandoned its campaign in recognition that the political environment made it too intractable. This was due to a mixture of US intransigence and the inability to attract attention to the plight of developing states (Palan et al., 2013, p. 227; Seabrooke and Wigan, 2013).

The result was that the issue remained on the fringes of political debate for almost another decade until the onset of the Global Financial Crisis (GFC) in 2008. This, coupled with the economic, social and political fallout resulting from it over the subsequent decade due to the austerity measures taken to address the costs of dealing with its impact, changed the political landscape dramatically. The Bank of International Settlements finds that 'governments became crucial during the crisis, as traditional sources of funding for financial institutions dried up' (Panetta et al., 2009, p. 1), to the point that they spent trillions of dollars on various bailout and stimulus packages. For those states most severely affected, the outlays of public funds were truly staggering. For example, the UK's was 44 percent of its GDP (Langley, 2015; Panetta et al., 2009). Suddenly, the issue of MNC tax avoidance was not something that only affected developing states, the angle on which Oxfam had earlier attempted to campaign. The new tax justice campaign was centered around the shifting tax burden produced by government bailouts, and the manner in which the 'bill' for these was effectively sent to individuals and society at large, rather than the institutions that had benefited from states' fiscal largesse. As MNCs avoided their taxation obligations, and developed states suffered from budgetary constraints, it was increasingly plain that the tax burden was being shouldered by ordinary citizens in these states who were not responsible for the GFC, through cuts to social services (Elbra, 2018).

Civil society organizations such as Occupy and UK Uncut harnessed growing resentment of inequality, unemployment, and in some cases capitalism itself, to highlight the uneven nature of the global tax system in this context. These movements led to a greater demand for political action, by moving the issue of tax avoidance into the forefront of political discourse (Fitzgerald, 2015). They were more successful than previous efforts in this, because the political salience of global corporate tax avoidance in developed states in the aftermath of the GFC prompted action. Indeed, the political response to the issue of corporate tax avoidance has largely tracked public sentiment in these states. Prior to the GFC there was very little action, either at the multilateral or unilateral level against egregious tax planning. After the onset of the GFC, and the realization that government revenues could be enhanced through greater collection of corporate taxes, developed countries' governments have moved both multilaterally and unilaterally to force MNCs to 'pay a fair share'. The timing of the GFC also matched the OECD's tax transparency agenda, and this represented a window of opportunity to embrace global tax reform at the highest levels (Eccleston, Kellow and Carroll, 2015). By 2012, the OECD had moved from promoting bilateral information exchange agreements to a more serious overhaul of the global tax system, to the point where Palan and Wigan (2014, p. 334) identified the emergence of 'a genuine consensus for the need for multilateral efforts to tackle tax abuse'. As a result, the OECD initiated the base erosion and profit shifting action plan in 2013, which was agreed upon by OECD members in September 2013, and quickly endorsed by the G20. Over the following two years, the BEPS final reports were prepared, and these included recommendations, standards and guidelines for signatory states (European Parliament Think Tank, 2016). The final reports were released in November 2015 and have been described as 'designed to be flexible as a consequence of its adoption by consensus', rather than binding commitments (ibid.).

So, the goal of a degree of harmonization among OECD member states, at least in their response to the problem, seemed within reach. In November 2016, negotiations were concluded on the OECD's Multilateral Convention to Implement Tax Treaty Related Measures to Prevent BEPS (hereafter 'BEPS'), the goal of which is to 'flexibly amend bilateral treaties and combat profit-shifting activity by requiring companies to pay tax in the jurisdictions in which the economic activity actually occurs' (OECD, 2013, p. 11). By 2019, BEPS had 87 signatories. These countries and jurisdictions have agreed to collaborate on the domestic and international tax rules being developed as part of the BEPS process; however, this rhetoric masks some serious concerns about implementation at the technical level. While all participants have agreed to the broad ideal of creating a more transparent and 'fair' corporate tax system, Christiansen (2017) argues that effectiveness and success require the resolution of a number of debates around how much tax data is made public, which firms are exempt from providing this and how much data is provided. Reports by signatory countries indicate caution towards full implementation of BEPS. This stems from a lack of participation in the design process, lack of expected benefit from the proposed reforms, a desire to wait for other states to implement first, or a combination of these factors (Christians and Shay, 2017). Furthermore, reporting from non-OECD members that could be described as tax havens, such as Liechtenstein, Mauritius and Singapore, notes a strong emphasis on preserving a 'level playing field' as an impediment to full implementation (ibid.). Overall, success in achieving the BEPS outcomes would require unprecedented levels of international cooperation. One indication that this may be problematic is the OECD's development of the BEPS Inclusive Framework. This forum is designed to broaden the scope of BEPS to include more developing states by limiting the number of actions to four. The BEPS Inclusive Framework currently has 127 signatories. While this may suggest widespread support for BEPS more broadly, the ultimate test for BEPS is whether each of these signatories proceeds to implementation at the domestic level, and this is in no way clear cut.

Further complicating the OECD's attempts to harmonize the global tax system is the role played by the Big Four in advising MNCs on, and therefore effectively implementing in practice, the measures agreed on as part of BEPS. This may include circumventing the intent of them, if one accepts that this may be in the interests of their clients. After all, the Big Four are the designers of tax structures for MNCs such as the infamous 'double Irish Dutch sandwich', which reduces taxable income by sending profits through Irish subsidiaries and the Netherlands, before this income finally 'resides' in Caribbean tax havens (Duhigg and Kocieniewski, 2012). This chapter does not go into details of the complex accounting structures utilized by MNCs such as this, although these can be understood through an examination of the accounting literature. However, our focus is on the Big Four as enablers of, and advisers to, the MNCs that are so often targeted for their immoral behavior in the realm of corporate taxation. There is surely scope to shift at least some of this attention to the designers of their complex corporate tax structures, whose historical ascent to power is outlined in the next section.

UNDERSTANDING THE POWER OF THE BIG FOUR

The accounting sector was not always dominated by the Big Four. As recently as 1988 there were eight large global players in the accounting, auditing and advisory industry, themselves a result of a series of mergers. In 1989, the first of the mergers that led to the current concentration in the industry occurred, between Touche Ross and Deloitte Haskins & Sells (Deloitte, 2019). Following further mergers, the Big Five became the Big Four in 2001 after the collapse of Enron and its auditor, Arthur Andersen, then the world's largest auditing firm (Shore and Wright, 2018). Over a period of 13 years the accounting and auditing sector consolidated dramatically, but this was not the only change to take place during this time. Over the same period as their market consolidation, the culture of privatization and managerialism ushered in by the Thatcher administration in the UK, and exported elsewhere over the 1980s, was bearing fruit in the drastically expanded remit of what had been auditing-focused accountancy firms (ibid., p. 308). The result was that they transformed into 'professional services firms' performing strategic governance as well as technical accountancy functions.

Of course, the role played by the Big Four was never *purely* technical. It is not just a matter of expertise, and advice given to clients on the basis of it. This they possess as well, but politically they have always been engaged in an *ideas game*. Through this they help to define what technical expertise is, prior to giving advice to their clients and influencing governments, thereby consolidating political as well as technical power. To understand this, a three faces of power approach to global business, as outlined by Doris Fuchs (2007) and discussed in Chapter 1, is useful. Her point is that all business actors are political as well as economic actors. They are not just competitive economic entities operating in markets. They are politically as well as economically motivated to satisfy their interests, and therefore employ instrumental, structural and discursive power relationally with other actors. They do so especially with respect to states.

As noted in Chapter 1, instrumental power is the most basic form of power MNCs wield. It entails them directly influencing the policy process through staffing governments with industry supporters, and influencing government decision-makers through campaign contributions and lobbying (Hacker and Pierson, 2002; Lukes, 1974). The lobbying efforts and connections established mean that corporations, including those comprising the Big Four, are in a position to 'capture' the regulatory agencies of states on behalf of corporate interests (e.g., Carpenter and Moss, 2014; Weidenbaum, 2004). Yet, it should also be recognized that this type of power is relatively weak due to its high visibility if exercised publicly, or because of the personal relations needed for it to be exercised covertly (e.g., see Culpepper, 2010). MNCs like the Big Four also possess considerable structural power due to their size, geographical reach and dominance of the market for their services. For MNCs in general, it has long been noted that one manifestation of this face of power is their ability to punish or reward countries for the provision of favorable investment conditions, not just by explicitly but also implicitly threatening to relocate their operations (e.g., see Cox, 1987; Frank, 1978). In the case of the Big Four, their very nomenclature indicates the structural power they have to define what these conditions should be. However, they seek to provide advice on these conditions not just as inevitable due to the size of the MNCs whose interests they represent, their positions of market dominance in respect of the provision of advice and services, or their links with elites in business and government. They also seek to do so on the basis that it is *right* as a result of their knowledge, their expertise as a result of the role they play, and therefore their claims on 'truth'. In this respect, discursive power, and the perceived legitimacy to which it potentially gives rise, is the political 'prize' the Big Four, and the MNCs they represent, seek because it facilitates the creation of a world in the image of their interests.

If the central question for all political scholars is 'who governs?', then the political power of MNCs is not just a question of whether they have political influence. It is obvious that they do. But the extent to which they do so, and how they do so, is also related to the question of whether they are seen – in the true sense of the word, highly visibly by the public and other political actors – as possessing the *discursive legitimacy* to set agendas and maybe even govern in their own right. This is also why their responses to the Senate Committee are enlightening, as we shall explain in the following section. Before studying their testimony though, the point is that they are coordination services firms whose *raison d'être* is the promotion, sanctioning and regularization of the behavior and practices of other firms. They do this in respect of governments too. The result is that, as Amoore (2006) sees it, they engage in concerted efforts to make states in their 'image', with this also being the image they promote for other MNCs and the governments that support or regulate them. They create, embody and enact the informal as well as formal industry norms and practices that are accepted by MNCs, industry associations, and states. It might even be said that, ultimately, this means that they regulate the operation of the global economy.

In doing so, they are similar in their functions to the three major credit rating agencies: Standard & Poor's, Moody's, and Fitch Ratings.

These three firms are responsible for 96 percent of all credit ratings issued worldwide (Council on Foreign Relations, 2015; US Securities and Exchange Commission, 2018). They make what verge on being official pronouncements of the creditworthiness of both corporations and governments. Therefore, they act as 'reputational intermediaries' (Gourevitch and Shinn, 2005, p. 114). So do the Big Four. Together they audit the vast majority of publicly listed MNCs, in addition to offering a variety of advisory and business consulting services – for example, PwC provides services to 85 percent of those listed in the Fortune Global 500 (Christodoulou, 2011; PwC, 2020). Ramirez (2012, p. 49) argues that their 'shared expertise, common interests and jointly run projects are enough to define the Big Firms [Big Four] as a community' in a way that differs from the rest of the accounting community. As with the credit rating agencies, they dominate the global market for their services. Therefore, rather than simply being competitive market actors, they possess great structural power. This enhances the instrumental power they can exercise with policy-makers and others in influential positions as they operate vast networks of firms owned and managed independently, but sharing a common brand and offering standardized services. In coordinating these networks from their headquarters in the US and UK (which is where they are based), they do not neutrally or simply technically ensure accounting best practice. Instead, as they justify MNCs' actions and interests, and advocate to governments how these may be made to serve the national interest, they are actually not just involved but create 'an ideological debate about how the corporate system enhances public benefits and the public interest' (Wilks, 2013, p. 79).

The result is that the function they serve is not just quasi-regulatory. They are agents of constructing and enhancing the legitimacy and discursive power of MNCs worldwide in a liberal institutional context. This is also the case in respect of corporate tax. As they represent their interests, the interests of business in general, and provide advice to governments, they are active in three political pathways. But here, we consider their influence on the Australian government in particular as it considered addressing global corporate tax avoidance.

THE AUSTRALIAN SENATE ECONOMIC REFERENCES COMMITTEE INQUIRY INTO CORPORATE TAX AVOIDANCE

Between April 2015 and April 2016, the Senate Committee held public hearings as part of its inquiry into corporate tax avoidance. Appearing at its hearings, amongst other industry leaders, were representatives of the Big Four. In doing so, they were exercising all three faces of their firms' power. The Big Four characterize themselves as experts in the global tax system, and insert themselves into any discussion of reform. Before analyzing their representatives' discourse as indicative of their firms' discursive power though – that is, studying their discourse – it is therefore also important to recognize the structural and instrumental power they possess prior to doing so. They have this not only as advisers to MNCs, but also to governments. Between 2016 and 2019, the Big Four have received more than A$2.1 billion in revenue from selling advisory and consulting services to the Australian federal government alone. They have done so over a period that included their representatives' appearing at the Senate Committee to answer questions of suspect corporate tax dealings (Dingwall and Mannheim, 2019). As such, their 'privileged position' to offer advice and 'revolving door' access in the provision of it come before, and contemporaneously with, their contribution to the tax reform debate in Australia. The following analysis is based on the transcripts from these appearances. We have chosen to rely on the oral evidence given by these representatives at the time of the inquiry, rather than the companies' written statements. This is because the written statements are the result of several drafts, passed through the firms' legal and public relations departments. However, we are interested in how representatives of these firms responded to questions without notice. And how they engaged in dynamic discussions about the behavior of their firms in respect of tax advice and tax reform. The transcripts were analyzed for statements regarding tax reform at the national and global level. The representatives' comments were coded for whether or not they expressed 'support for unilateral corporate tax reform' (i.e., whether they expressed a preference for Australia taking unilateral action on tax avoidance) and whether or not they expressed 'support for multilateral tax reform' (i.e., the OECD BEPS program). A summary of the coding results is given in Table 8.1. The statements they made in this regard were then also qualitatively analyzed. The table shows the number of statements made during inquiry hearings either in support, or against, multilateral and unilateral reform.

Table 8.1   *Support for multilateral and unilateral corporate tax reform*

	Multilateral Reform		Unilateral Reform	
Big Four Firms	Yes	No	Yes	No
KPMG	13	0	5	4
EY	7	0	5	7
PwC	14	2	6	5
Deloitte	16	0	9	6

Overall, all four firms' representatives expressed a relatively neutral position on unilateral reform, with responses split almost evenly across support/non-support for Australia taking action alone. Three of the four firms' representatives – those of KPMG, EY and Deloitte – were asked specifically about their roles in advising the government on potential changes to tax exemptions under the Income Tax Assessment Act. This question arose as the 2014–15 Mid-Year Economic and Fiscal Outlook raised the potential removal of Sections 25–90 of the Act, which provide MNCs with the ability to obtain interest deductions on certain foreign income. Such a measure would be highly unpalatable to MNCs and deprive the Big Four of one method by which taxable income could be reduced. When Partner in Charge of the KPMG Tax Centre, Mr. Grant Wardell-Johnson, was asked about whether his company lobbied the federal government against removing Sections 25–90, he said 'people who advise on 25–90 basically said: "Repeal this and you will not get the income that you expect to get, and it is a poor set of rules with capricious results"'. He supported this statement by suggesting that he thought it 'was a widespread view within the tax community'. Mr. Wardell-Johnson was careful to imply that these views were held widely in the tax professional community, lending further legitimacy to his claims as well as the very idea that the Big Four present uniform truths about the impacts of tax reform.

Mr. Glenn Williams, Partner at EY, was also asked about the proposal to remove Sections 25–90. He responded by suggesting that 'it is important that anyone making a decision to either create or repeal a section understands what all the consequences would be. So one of our duties is to ensure that those making decisions are fully informed about what the consequences would be of repealing a section or indeed introducing a new section.' Mr. Williams demonstrates the discursive power held by the Big Four by explaining to the committee that the expert knowledge around the implications of this proposed change lay substantially with tax professionals employed by his firm, while those responsible for making changes in governments and the bureaucracy are less aware of the situation. His choice of words also suggests that it is the role of tax professionals to inform government of the potential negative outcomes from their actions – that is, there is a threat implied in raising the potential for 'consequences'.

This was also present in the response made by Mr. David Watkins, Partner/ Leader of Tax Insight and Policy at Deloitte, who was also asked about his firm's role in lobbying against the repeal of Sections 25–90. He was more circumspect than his peers, suggesting 'we were not asked for, and we did not make, a recommendation to government' on the matter of potential repeal. However, again, he did demonstrate Deloitte's expertise on the issue of interest exemptions on foreign income by reminding the Senate Committee, 'in the course of those discussions, [we] made it known that there were consequences, and perhaps in some cases unintended consequences, associated with the government's proposal'. From his testimony, it seems his firm was attempting to leverage its power in reminding the government of negative economic outcomes associated with changes to the tax code. However, it is also framing itself as more knowledgeable on the issue than the government's own tax department! As such, while a negative economic threat could be implied in raising the potential for 'consequences', the use of the term '*unintentional consequences*' (our emphasis) suggests that while the government thinks it is acting in the national interest, Deloitte has a clearer understanding of the implications of reforming the tax code.

All firms' representatives were also asked about their views on tax reform at the global level. Their responses to questions about multilateral reform were overwhelmingly supportive. All agreed it was imperative that reform be undertaken through the OECD. Ms. Rosheen Garnon, National Managing Partner of Tax at KPMG, was highly supportive of reform, noting 'every time we have the opportunity to shine a light on the tax system in my view is a good thing'. Many of Ms. Garnon's peers were also happy to suggest that reform at the OECD level was preferable to domestic regulation. For example, Mr. Wardell-Johnson said that Australia needed to 'stay in the pack' along with other countries. There was a clear preference for Australia to move *with* the OECD, rather than before it, to avoid risking becoming economically uncompetitive.

After noting the role of national parliaments in making laws, Mr. Rob McLeod, Tax Partner at EY, emphasized that international tax requires a multilateral response due to the number of jurisdictions involved. However, he very quickly reminded the Senate Committee 'that taxes act like tariffs on cross-border capital and labor. A trade analogy in that regard is a useful way to think about the economic effect of taxes in the international arena. Countries cannot take an unlimited approach to imposing those taxes without economically damaging the welfare of the country concerned.' In doing so, Mr. McLeod reminded the Senate Committee of the benefits of the status quo – in other words, a system supported and used by the Big Four. Mr. McLeod also cautioned against Australia moving ahead of the OECD, even on issues where it was assumed the OECD would eventually implement a similar ruling. He argued: 'In principle, there is nothing stopping that. However, one has to think about the cost of reform and whether two changes are better than one, or vice versa.' In other words, once again a threat was implied to Australia's national interest. But Mr. McLeod then went further to argue that many of the issues the OECD is addressing simply *cannot* be solved by unilateral measures. He said that the BEPS measures do not lend themselves to domestic action as 'finding a joint solution to a joint problem does not really lend itself to unilateral action'. In his concluding remarks, Mr. McLeod stressed that the OECD process 'remains vibrant' and that Australian has 'no choice but to ride that process and to keep the pressure on [the OECD]'. Here, again, Mr. McLeod assumed that OECD reform is forthcoming and that any pre-emptive movement by an Australian government hoping to increase revenue in the meantime would be damaging to business and, by extension, the Australian economy.

The interplay between structural 'realities' for Australia's interests and the discursive legitimacy lent by the expertise of the Big Four were also evident in the arguments made by Mr. Thomas Seymour, Managing Partner, Tax and Legal, at PwC. He too argued strongly for OECD reform, noting that 'on the topic of international tax reform, we support the OECD's approach to multilateral consensus-based international tax reform'. He added that PwC sees participation in this process as the best way to meet Australia's interests. Mr.

Seymour added that if cooperation between states fell away, 'to be frank, that would be great for our business, but it's not good for the country'. Another PwC representative, Mr. Peter Collins, National Leader, International Tax Services, later reaffirmed this point by suggesting that Australia should be patient for OECD reform, rhetorically posing the question 'shouldn't we wait until that work is finished before we go and run off with unilateral action?'

Mr. Watkins from Deloitte provided yet another statement supporting OECD reform, and cautioning against the damage likely to be done by unilateral reform. He noted, 'the danger of alternative unilateral solutions is to risk a series of uncoordinated unilateral actions that could result in dispute, in double taxation and in greater uncertainty, none of which are conducive to encouraging business activity'. Again, Deloitte's representative raised the structural power of his firm and MNCs – that is, an implied threat that if the Australian government takes unilateral action it risks economic damage against the national interest. But Mr. Watkins went further, describing OECD reform as *global* reform. When discussing waiting for OECD reform, he said 'we [Australia] do not want to find ourselves an outrider compared to the future global consensus'. It is unclear in this statement what global consensus Mr. Watkins is referring to. The BEPS initiative has widespread support as a way to promote fairness in taxation; however, as the representatives of the Big Four would be aware, reform of the global corporate tax system requires the BEPS initiatives to be implemented not just by OECD member states, and the likelihood of this is debatable. It is questionable, for example, whether Singapore, although a current BEPS signatory, will relinquish its place as a leading tax haven in the Asia-Pacific region for the goal of working towards a 'fairer' international tax system. When asked if base erosion and profit shifting were a threat to the Australian tax base, it is therefore telling that Mr. Watkins shifted the discussion back to the global level. He replied, 'base erosion and profit shifting is a threat to the *global* tax base' (our emphasis). He added that Deloitte was not in front of the Senate Committee to defend the current global tax rules, and was instead calling for global tax reform.

Representatives not only enthusiastically supported OECD efforts, but also went as far as suggesting how the government should implement these. Ms. Garnon, of KPMG, emphasized her company's private authority, effectively dictating how the Australian government should respond to OECD progress. She suggested, 'a lot of work will be coming out of the OECD program of work. Both Treasury and the Australian Taxation Office will need additional resources if we want to act promptly. That is something I cannot reiterate enough – to work through it in the way that the OECD has, to have a defined timetable, to hit the benchmarks and the times, it is really important that we are seen to act quickly.' Here, Ms. Garnon refers to herself, as a representative of KPMG, and the Treasury and Australian Taxation Office. The use of the pronoun 'we' in this instance may not suggest a literal meaning but it certainly implies a closeness between the tax professional community and government agencies responsible for legislating corporate tax. Additionally, this comment can be understood as an attempt to reiterate her experience with multinational tax reform, her understanding of business processes, and ultimately an attempt to paint KPMG as highly informed and experienced in matters of tax reform. This position of authority was supported by Mr. McCleod from EY, who noted that firms see consulting to governments as 'a social obligation' and that they are 'quite public-spirited in coming to those assignments and giving their input'. Mr. David Linke, National Managing Partner, Tax and Legal at KPMG, noted that his firm had made more than 60 recommendations to a government white paper on tax reform. Additionally, KPMG were central to the National Reform Summit. This is hardly surprising when one considers the results of their input and lobbying.

The excerpts above demonstrate the power of the Big Four at all levels, and in all three faces. Moreover, they suggest a certain sense of entitlement that stems from this power – an entitlement to wield it in their pathways of influence. They see themselves as best placed not only to evaluate potential regulation, but also to promote their own models for reform. This is captured in a statement by KPMG's Ms. Garnon who refers to her firm as a *rule-maker* when she says: 'The reason why is that as we develop the laws, we are trying to make sure that. Sorry – let me rephrase that. As Treasury.' While Ms. Garnon apologizes for mis-speaking, suggesting she intended to say that Treasury makes the laws, it is evident through the analysis presented above that the Big Four possess significant power. They see themselves as central to reforming the rules that govern them, and the products they on-sell to MNCs that assist in minimizing corporate tax.

CONCLUSION

The Big Four are continually given a seat at the policy-making table to give advice. They are paid to be there and do so. They second staff into government tax offices, lobby for/against a range of reforms, and in the case of global corporate tax avoidance argue loudly and consistently that unilateral tax reform will have negative effects on economies. However, they are in a privileged position to influence the reform agenda not just because of the revolving door access to government this grants them, but also because of the concentration of their industry and the structural power of the MNCs, which are their clients. Their instrumental and structural power are then further enhanced by their discursive power. The discursive legitimacy of their advice is mutually reinforcing with regard to their other two faces of power, and they have an interest in ensuring that perceptions of their expertise remain in place both in general, as well as specifically in the case of multilateral reforms for reducing corporate tax avoidance.

It is therefore likely that the Big Four will continue to willingly provide their input to corporate tax legislation and reform, whether it is proactively sought or not. Obviously, our contention is that, due to their discursive legitimacy, it is rather more likely that the former rather than the latter will remain the case. As the transcripts demonstrate, these firms portray themselves as the holders of expertise or knowledge in terms of global taxation, continually reminding the committee and legislators of the 'unintended consequences' of tightening tax laws. By suggesting that changes to taxation laws will not lead to the increased revenue the government expects, we can again see how the Big Four present themselves as more knowledgeable than those making the laws, or those implementing them through the Treasury and Australian Taxation Office. What they recommend instead are multilateral reforms through the OECD.

The Australian case has an important global dimension, in that it offers an insight into the multi-pronged approach of the Big Four in regard to corporate tax reform in different policy arenas. The consistent emphasis of the Big Four's representatives on OECD reforms, often described as global reform, should be seen in the broader context of the political power they possess and seek to wield. The OECD-led reform is anything but global, despite efforts to portray it as such. Not all countries will be bound by changes to OECD tax policy, which is likely to be incremental and non-binding (Eccleston, 2018). Those states that do not fully implement the suite of reforms will be best placed to participate in a 'race to the bottom', allowing the Big Four to create complex tax regimes that utilize their disharmony with the OECD countries. This may not be the best outcome for the Big Four's clients, and it may not be better for the Big Four's business model compared to the status quo of varying tax treatments and tax competition between all states. They may indeed be hoping that it does not eventuate, as indeed it may not. Yet, arguing against global governance is discursively less tenable than arguing for it, and arguing for this particular form of global governance is a better outcome for the Big Four than having to deal with the possibility of a truly globally harmonized system for addressing corporate tax avoidance. None of their representatives advocated this. Nor did they advocate a 'race to the top' through unilateral reforms, which representatives constantly reminded the committee would damage Australia's economic prosperity.

What the Big Four are recommending then is essentially the competitive disharmonization of global tax avoidance regulations that maintains those aspects of the existing status quo that facilitate global corporate tax avoidance. It may even make this easier, as they would deal with a bloc of developed countries with harmonized regulations, yet still different taxation rates and systems, versus a handful of those that remain tax havens. The OECD BEPS framework may have 127 signatories, but harmonization of tax rules between these states requires unprecedented international cooperation, as the OECD itself recognizes (OECD, 2019). If the Big Four understand the low likelihood of this occurring, with the chances of limited multilateralism being more likely, then it would seem that they are willing to 'bet the house' on continued disharmony in the global tax system.

NOTE

1. We acknowledge support provided for the research conducted for this chapter by the Australian Research Council under grant number DP180100167 for the project Catching Capital: Understanding and Influencing Corporate Tax Strategy. We would also like to thank Dr Delphine Rabet for her research assistance, and for their advice on earlier drafts we thank Richard Eccleston, Lachlan Johnson, Rick Krever, Jason Ward, Kerrie Zadiq, Bronwyn McCredie, Heidi Zummo and Peter Mellor.

REFERENCES

Amoore, L. (2006), 'Making the modern multinational', in C. May (ed.), *Global Corporate Power*, Boulder, CO: Lynne Rienner Publishers, pp. 32–54.
Australian Senate (2015), *Australian Senate Economic References Committee Hearing into Corporate Tax Avoidance*, accessed 10 October 2018 at https://parlinfo.aph .gov.au/parlInfo/search/display/display.w3p;query=Id:%22committees/commsen/ aa68d895-38dc-4165-bce7-2082c796519b/0000%22.
Carpenter, D. and D.A. Moss (eds) (2014), *Preventing Regulatory Capture: Special Interest Influence and How to Limit It*, Cambridge, UK: Cambridge University Press.
Christensen, R. (2017), 'Professional competition in global tax reform: transparency in global wealth chains', *SocArXiv Papers*, https://doi.org/10.31235/osf.io/gu63m.
Christians, A. and S.E. Shay (2017), 'General report', *102A Cahiers de Droit Fiscal International: Assessing BEPS: Origins, Standards, and Responses 17 (Int'l Fiscal Ass'n 2017)*, accessed 19 March 2020 at https://ssrn.com/abstract=2997548.
Christodoulou, M. (2011), 'UK auditors criticized on bank crisis', *The Wall Street Journal*, 30 March, accessed 31 January 2019 at https://www.wsj.com/articles/ SB10001424052748703806304576232231353594682.
Council on Foreign Relations (2015), 'The credit rating controversy', 19 February, accessed 31 January 2019 at https://www.cfr.org/backgrounder/credit-rating -controversy.
Cox, R.W. (1987), *Production, Power and World Order: Social Forces in the Making of History*, New York: Columbia University Press.
Crivelli, E., R. De Mooij and M. Keen (2015), 'Base erosion, profit shifting and developing countries', *IMF Working Papers*, No. 15/118, accessed 19 March 2020 at https://www.imf.org/en/Publications/WP/Issues/2016/12/31/Base-Erosion-Profit -Shifting-and-Developing-Countries-42973.
Culpepper, P.D. (2010), *Quiet Politics and Business Power: Corporate Control in Europe and Japan*, Cambridge, UK: Cambridge University Press.

Deloitte (2019), 'About us: a timeline of our history', accessed 31 January 2019 at https://www2.deloitte.com/us/en/pages/about-deloitte/articles/about-deloitte-history -timeline.html#.

Dingwall, D. and M. Mannheim (2019), 'Govt nearly triples spend on big four consultancies as donations rise', 20 March, *Sydney Morning Herald*, accessed 26 March 2019 at https://www.smh.com.au/politics/federal/govt-nearly-triples-spend-on-big -four-consultancies-as-donations-rise-20190220-p50z22.html.

Duhigg, C. and D. Kocieniewski (2012), 'How Apple sidesteps billions in taxes', 28 April, *The New York Times*, accessed 8 February 2019 at https://www.nytimes.com/ 2012/04/29/business/apples-tax-strategy-aims-at-low-tax-states-and-nations.html.

Eccleston, R. (2018), 'BEPS and the new politics of corporate tax justice', in R. Eccleston and A. Elbra (eds), *Business, Civil Society and the 'New' Politics of Corporate Tax Justice: Paying a Fair Share?*, Cheltenham, UK and Northampton, MA, USA: Edward Elgar Publishing, pp. 40–67.

Eccleston, R., A. Kellow and P. Carroll (2015), 'G20 endorsement in post crisis global governance: more than a toothless talking shop?', *The British Journal of Politics and International Relations*, **17**(2), 298–317.

Elbra, A. (2018), 'Activism and the "new" politics of tax justice', in R. Eccleston and A. Elbra (eds), *Business, Civil Society and the 'New' Politics of Corporate Tax Justice: Paying a Fair Share?*, Cheltenham, UK and Northampton, MA, USA: Edward Elgar Publishing, pp. 68–89.

European Parliament Think Tank (2016), 'Understanding the OECD tax plan to address "base erosion and profit shifting" – BEPS', 14 April, accessed 8 February 2019 at http://www.europarl.europa.eu/thinktank/en/document.html?reference=EPRS_BRI %282016%29580911.

Fitzgerald, S.T. (2015), 'Is equality the goal? Challenging economic inequality in the US and UK', in E. Avril and J.N. Neem (eds), *Democracy, Participation and Contestation: Civil Society, Governance and the Future of Liberal Democracy*, Abingdon: Routledge, pp. 51–66.

Forbes (2002), 'The Global 500', accessed 8 February 2019 at https://www.forbes.com/ global/2002/0722/global.html#6044586d47f6.

Frank, A.G. (1978), *Dependent Accumulation and Underdevelopment*, London: Macmillan.

Fuchs, D. (2007), *Business Power in Global Governance*, Boulder, CO: Lynne Rienner Publishers.

Gourevitch, P.A. and J. Shinn (2005), *Political Power and Corporate Control: The New Global Politics of Corporate Governance*, Princeton, NJ: Princeton University Press.

Gravelle, J.G. (2015), *Tax Havens: International Tax Avoidance and Evasion*, Washington, DC: Congressional Research Service.

Hacker, J.S. and P. Pierson (2002), 'Business power and social policy: employers and the formation of the American welfare state', *Politics and Society*, **30**(2), 277–325.

Langley, P. (2015), *Liquidity Lost: The Governance of the Global Financial Crisis*, Oxford: Oxford University Press.

Latulippe, L. (2018), 'Large accounting firms and tax planning in a "fair tax" era', in R. Eccleston and A. Elbra (eds), *Business, Civil Society and the 'New' Politics of Corporate Tax Justice: Paying a Fair Share?*, Cheltenham, UK and Northampton, MA, USA: Edward Elgar Publishing, pp. 128–54.

Lukes, S. (1974), *Power: A Radical View*, London: Palgrave Macmillan.

O'Neill, P. (2001), 'Treasury Secretary O'Neill statement on OECD tax havens', US Department of the Treasury, 10 May [press release], accessed 15 January 2019 at http://www.treasury.gov/press-center/press-releases/Pages/po366.aspx.

Organisation for Economic Co-operation and Development [OECD] (1998), *Harmful Tax Competition: An Emerging Global Issue*, Paris: OECD Publishing.

Organisation for Economic Co-operation and Development [OECD] (2013), *Action Plan on Base Erosion and Profit Shifting*, Paris: OECD Publishing, accessed 18 March 2020 at https://www.oecd.org/ctp/BEPSActionPlan.pdf.

Organisation for Economic Co-operation and Development [OECD] (2015), *OECD Secretary-General Report to G20 Finance Ministers*, accessed 18 March 2020 at http://www.oecd.org/g20/topics/international-taxation/oecd-secretary-general -report-to-g20-finance-ministers-april-2015.pdf.

Organisation for Economic Co-operation and Development [OECD] (2019), 'Members of the OECD/G20 Inclusive Framework on BEPS', accessed 31 January 2019 at http://www.oecd.org/tax/beps/inclusive-framework-on-beps-composition.pdf.

Oxfam (2000), *Tax Havens: Releasing the Hidden Billions for Poverty Eradication*, accessed 19 March 2020 at http://iffoadatabase.trustafrica.org/iff/bp-tax-havens -010600-en.pdf.

Palan, R., R. Murphy and C. Chavagneux (2013), *Tax Havens: How Globalization Really Works*, Ithaca, NY: Cornell University Press.

Palan, R. and D. Wigan (2014), 'Herding cats and taming tax havens: the US strategy of "not in my backyard"', *Global Policy*, **5**(3), 334–43.

Panetta, F., T. Faeh and G. Grande et al. (2009), 'An assessment of financial sector rescue programmes', *BIS Papers*, No. 48, Basel: Bank for International Settlements, accessed 3 November 2016 at http://www.bis.org/publ/bppdf/bispap48.pdf.

PwC (2020), 'Clients: 2019 global annual review', accessed 7 August 2020 at https:// www.pwc.com/gx/en/about/global-annual-review-2019/clients.html.

Ramirez, C. (2012), 'How Big Four audit firms control standard-setting in accounting and auditing', in I. Huault and C. Richard (eds), *Finance: The Discreet Regulator*, Basingstoke: Palgrave Macmillan, pp. 40–58.

Seabrooke, L. and D. Wigan (2013), *Emergent Entrepreneurs in Transnational Advocacy Networks: Professional Mobilization in the Fight for Global Tax Justice*, GR:EEN Working Paper No. 41, Centre for the Study of Globalisation and Regionalisation, University of Warwick.

Sharman, J.C. (2006), *Havens in a Storm: The Struggle for Global Tax Regulation*, Ithaca, NY: Cornell University Press.

Shore, C. and S. Wright (2018), 'How the Big 4 got big: audit culture and the metamorphosis of international accountancy firms', *Critique of Anthropology*, **38**(3), 303–24.

US Securities and Exchange Commission (2018), *Annual Report on Nationally Recognized Statistical Ratings Organizations*, accessed 31 January 2019 at https:// www.sec.gov/2018-annual-report-on-nrsros.pdf.

Weidenbaum, M. (2004), *Business and Government in the Global Marketplace*, 7th edition, Upper Saddle River, NJ: Prentice Hall.

Wilks, S. (2013), *The Political Power of the Business Corporation*, Cheltenham, UK and Northampton, MA, USA: Edward Elgar Publishing.

9. Conclusion: combining pathways of MNCs' influence in global politics

John Mikler and Karsten Ronit

The contributors to this book have analyzed the different pathways of influence that multinational corporations (MNCs) have in global politics. Although it is in no way possible to analyze the pattern of pathways among MNCs in general, at all times and in all places, they have nevertheless considered the individual pathways in particular cases, as well as how they are linked in these cases. In this concluding chapter, we draw some further links in MNCs' pathways of influence in order to pave the way for further investigations into the role played by MNCs in global politics.

Before doing so, some qualifications are in order. The key goal of drawing together the contributions in this collection has not been to discover where MNCs are actually influential versus where influence is not achieved. Nor, what it takes for MNCs to become more influential. No scale or measurement of influence was intended. Instead, the goal has been to explain and shed more light on the different mechanisms that MNCs employ. Indeed, the ultimate influence of MNCs cannot be properly examined if we do not recognize that influence has many sources and is expressed in many different ways. Thus, it is important to consider the influence of MNCs holistically. Their influence is much more multifaceted than an impact on public policy through the targeted efforts of a particular corporation desiring a particular outcome, through one particular pathway or another. The pathways need to be mapped, but more importantly their connections need to be understood.

Following such a holistic perspective, we also recognize that MNCs must be active in many contexts. As such, a variety of economic, social and political factors enable and constrain their behavior. Although MNCs are powerful players, they do not find themselves in situations where they can freely choose one strategy or another, so any kind of strategy-building must take into account the institutional environments in which they find themselves embedded. Of course, these conditions vary from case to case, as is shown in each of the chapters where both certain pathways and environments, and the links between them, are explored. Therefore, multiple pathways of influence characterize MNCs' engagement in global politics.

There are also limits, or contingencies, to consider in respect of their influence. Traditional market activities have important political implications, as a strong market position can be politically enabling, but may not always be sufficient to convince regulators and other interested parties to deliver desired outcomes. In addition, as their activities and interests cross borders, the pathways unfold at multiple levels, from the local to national and global. MNCs may have strong and often tacit support from government in their home country, yet they also must be present on the international stage and often act in a coordinated manner. They may be competitors in the market, but great concentration in industries, coupled with the desire for coordinated action, tends to alleviate political conflict, and sometimes promotes cooperation. Finally, MNCs are challenged by organized civil society at national and global levels, and this opens up many avenues for both conflict and cooperation. In all cases, actions in one pathway of influence usually 'spill over' and influence how the other pathways are used, and thus the arrangement of relations within one pathway complement the analysis of the others.

In this concluding chapter, we therefore present some of the key findings of contributors to the book by focusing on each of the pathways in order to draw lessons as to how these experiences contribute to our understanding of *combinations* of pathways and the overall role of MNCs in global politics.

MNCS' INFLUENCE IN THEIR OWN RIGHT

Because MNCs tend to control their industries, in the sense that they control the markets for their products and services, they are in a position to exert influence in their own right. They do not always need to compete in aggressive ways, although they may do so with a handful of others in their industry. But if they do, this is to some extent a choice rather than a necessity. Considerably freed from the necessity of aggressive market competition, they are in a position to exercise power in all its faces: instrumentally, structurally and discursively. Seeing them as atomistic actors in competitive markets is such a limited view of them as to be inaccurate. Seeing them as political actors that act at multiple levels – national, regional and global – is more accurate. So is seeing them as embedded in networks at these levels, including the global supply (in the case of manufacturers) and value (in the case of service providers) chains they strategically coordinate.

This is clearly demonstrated in Chapter 4, where Hendriksen notes that shipping MNCs are able to influence and set global environmental standards, as by controlling markets they are integral to global trade and the structural integrity of the global economy. Likewise, in Chapters 5 and 7, Macdonald and Sinclair show that MNCs are able to exert influence in their own right across spaces and places that do not simply conform to debates about what is national versus global, but which are defined by their operations, interests and contexts where and when these play out. They focus on MNCs' corporate social responsibility (CSR) programs as a form of private governance, along with self-regulatory standards, whether employed individually or collectively through business associations (as noted below), to show that the level at which they bring their influence to bear is a matter of the extent to which they can successfully influence outcomes at particular sites, on various issues and in multiple scales. Macdonald considers sustainability in corporate supply chains, while Sinclair considers the mining industry in Indonesia, but in both cases they show that it is not a simple matter of MNCs extending and wielding power in their own right. This is a possible outcome, in the sense that their influence in their own right may be enhanced, yet it may also be channeled and modified by other actors.

Therefore, it is problematic to speak of MNCs' influence in their own right without considering what this entails in relation to other actors that are being influenced. In Chapter 8, Elbra, Mikler and Murphy-Gregory consider similar strategies and effects to Sinclair and Macdonald, by focusing on the role of the Big Four professional services firms. These are MNCs themselves that advise and provide services to other MNCs. As they dominate the provision of this advice, the strategies they promote and guidelines that they give to their clients are not simply technical, or in some sense neutral, but proactively shape and construct private rules and norms of global economic governance. They illustrate this with the case of global governance in corporate taxation. The Big Four may be regarded as being at the heart of a global tax minimization regime, as they facilitate other MNCs' tax minimization strategies through legally exploiting loopholes in the global tax system. They have therefore come to occupy a pivotal role in the space between private practice and public regulation.

What is true in the specific cases of shipping, mining and global corporate tax avoidance is part of a broader pattern of influence that may be discerned in respect of MNCs more generally. This is true not just for issues like sustainability, but also in relation to state power. In this respect, in Chapter 3, Weiss and Thurbon explore the impact of US MNCs' structural power at the global level on the infrastructural power of the US state domestically. They demonstrate that as US MNCs have grown in economic power abroad, they have been able to translate their economic influence into political and social influence at the domestic level. Where they once benefited from, and served, the interests of the US state, they now have the ability to act more unfettered in their own right. For example, as their profits have surged, the taxes they pay in the US have not. And while they enjoy intellectual property protection underpinned by the actions of the US government, they have become less innovative. The US government, in turn, has had to 'pick up the check' in the form of debt, while its MNCs enjoy the benefits of its support and protections. Where once they were more institutionally enmeshed with the US state, they have become more de-linked from it while benefitting from its policies

In these cases, and chapters, it is always not so much a question of whether MNCs have 'go-it-alone' power, but whether they do so in relation to other actors, or the extent to which they work with them. Of course, among these other actors, states are among the most important.

MNCS' INFLUENCE AND STATES

Clearly, MNCs are not just one of a range of contending actors that impact on, and seek to influence, states. They are in a 'privileged position' as a result of their structural power in the global economy, their importance to national economies, and as a result of their ability to exert influence in their own right. While it may seem that they can dispense with and act independently of states, this is actually not necessarily accurate in all cases or respects. They need the support provided by states to operate, they need the laws made by governments, and they need the agreements in intergovernmental organizations (IGOs) to go about satisfying their business interests. Therefore, it is not just a matter of them getting what they want. It is about them influencing, and maybe even transforming, states in achieving this outcome.

In Chapter 5, Macdonald shows that MNCs are certainly in a position to dominate many decision-making processes that might normally be seen as more the prerogative of states, as they have access to resources and control processes to an extent that other contending actors do not. What is true in general is shown specifically in Chapter 8, where Elbra, Mikler and Murphy-Gregory demonstrate that there are implications of the role played by the Big Four professional services firms that goes beyond the advice they give to other MNCs. As noted in the previous section, the pivotal position they occupy in global governance to address corporate tax avoidance comes not just from the advice they provide their clients, and the private norms and rules constructed in the process, but also the professional knowledge not possessed by governments. However, their influence is more subtle than just the advice they give, and the position they occupy as experts on the matter. It is also about the indirect influence they have on governments' ability to fund the great variety of programs – whether in health, education, basic infrastructure, transportation and so on – due to the tax revenues foregone. The politics of austerity following the Great Recession illustrates the impact this can have in a crisis, but at other times we may surmise that the burden of taxation falls increasingly on society rather than on MNCs, or that MNCs are in a position to 'call the shots' regarding the taxes they are willing to pay and the programs they are willing to support.

Weiss and Thurbon suggest a similarly negative impact on state sovereignty in Chapter 3. The dominant position of many US MNCs at the global level allows them to be a 'vector' for the penetration of the global economy by the US state, and for it to set the rules of global economic governance. However, this was true historically more than is the case today, as the growth of MNCs' power has created a pathway of influence back towards the US state, and from the external (or global) to internal (or domestic) levels. This influence is negative in the sense that it is a form of 'blowback', as the successes of the past are reflected in the weakened infrastructural power of the US state today. Due to the strength of US MNCs abroad, the US government is less able to transform its economy, implement social programs, and generally act in a manner other than that which suits its creditors, while its MNCs are far less constrained.

While Weiss and Thurbon demonstrate that the economic power of US MNCs is no longer a proxy for the power of the US state, and instead constrains it, May shows in Chapter 2 that it is possible for this influence to flow rather more in both directions, *between* MNCs and states rather than from one to the other. Focusing on Brazil and India as case studies, he shows how MNCs from emerging economies have a special relationship with their governments, this being a characteristic of contemporary state capitalism. Discussions of markets recede into the background in the understanding of this relationship, while long-standing relationships between office holders in both the state and MNCs are to the fore. The result is that it is not that the state is 'captured' by private interests, nor that the state gives 'orders' to its national business champions, but that a symbiotic relationship exists.

A similar, though differentiated, relationship is explored by Hendriksen in Chapter 4. As noted in the following section, he considers the way in which shipping MNCs participate directly in the International Maritime Organization (IMO), but before this he also notes that their perceived legitimacy to do so is a product of the instrumental, structural and discursive power they have in respect of the home states' governments. In fact, in some cases, the dividing line between states and MNCs, presuming one can be imagined, is so tenuous that it is effectively non-existent. The result is that the identity of delegations to the IMO is neither public nor private, state nor MNC, but 'fuses into one'.

There are links between the national and global levels, and just as it is can be hard to separate what is public from private at one level, so it is at the other. MNCs influence states, and through states they influence IGOs. Indeed, in Chapter 6, Ronit shows that MNCs has a strong tradition of leveraging states through national and global associations. However, they also influence IGOs in their own right, as well as through their business associations. Therefore, it is possible to conceive of MNCs influencing states and the IGOs to which they belong simultaneously. The extent of one versus the other is more a matter of degree than alternatives.

MNCS' INFLUENCE AND INTERGOVERNMENTAL ORGANIZATIONS

MNCs engage with IGOs in multiple ways. Through the relationships MNCs have with the governments of particular states, especially their home states, they are usually seen as influencers of IGOs. However, they may be most influential when they have backing from the governments of several states. Either way, states that are members of IGOs are a potential vector for the interests of 'their' MNCs, and vice versa. As noted above, this is essentially the point made in Chapter 3 by Weiss and Thurbon, who see US MNCs as initially serving American national interests, but now rather more have their interests served by the US state. Yet, sometimes, and perhaps especially in the case of many more successfully emerging economies, it is not so much the case that IGOs are the 'field' on which the game of state versus corporate interests is played out. As May shows in Chapter 2, there is a symbiotic relationship between states and MNCs in emerging economies, and this affects and transforms the position taken by their home states' governments in multilateral negotiations. The influence of MNCs at home is thus projected abroad in foreign economic policy. The results produced are different from that of developed states like the US, because where MNCs from developed countries might push their governments for trade and investment liberalization in intergovernmental organizations, those from emerging economies instead press for a more conservative and defensive approach to their interests. In doing so, it is not that they seek protection *per se*. Nor that they are getting their home states merely to serve their interests. Instead, it is the mutual interests of their states and the MNCs that are served as a result of close, supportive relations in the political sphere at home.

An even more direct expression of combined MNC and state interests is demonstrated by Hendriksen in Chapter 4. He shows that MNCs are involved in IMO negotiations through participation in state delegations, yet their influence is more than just the relations they have with their home states' governments. In addition, they formally participate through a variety of national and global business associations. Their contributions to institutionalized deliberations at the international level are seen as legitimate. They are invited to help write international agreements, their views are taken into account, and they are part of the regulatory process at the global level. They are 'fused' with states, yet they also participate to some extent as if they were states through the business associations to which they belong.

In fact, as analyzed by Ronit in Chapter 6, interest representation through relevant business associations in IGOs is common. Some business associations are tasked with the representation of general business interests in interactions with IGOs that have a range of economic issues on their agendas. For example, the International Organization of Employers is the recognized voice of business in exchanges with the International Labour Organization. Indeed, these IGOs have a general preference for exchanging with representative bodies in the business community rather than with individual MNCs. Associations are considered more legitimate and can speak for business in broader terms. As a key pathway of influence, MNCs use their membership of national associations to leverage global associations that participate in these forums, and global associations can therefore represent the interests of MNCs in addition to the coordinated interests of business. Furthermore, in some global business associations, MNCs can be members in their own right. The result is that today many MNCs see an advantage in direct membership of global business associations as a means to reach IGOs.

MNCS' INFLUENCE AND THE BUSINESS COMMUNITY

MNCs are central constituents of the global business community. As noted in the previous section, formal cooperation through business associations has become a pathway of MNC influence in and across industries. MNCs are able to coordinate their interests through a range of different business associations, in the process integrating their various positions. But while this enhances their positions and pathways of influence with states, civil society organizations (CSOs) and IGOs, it also does so in their own *collective* right. MNCs comprise and develop a range of private institutions to coordinate business behavior through various norms and rules. In some cases, these norms and rules are defined and disseminated by particular corporations or industries first, and then gain authority within the wider business community. This is, for instance, shown in Chapter 8 in which Elbra, Mikler and Murphy-Gregory discuss the role of the Big Four professional service firms that act effectively as rule intermediaries embodying and enacting informal industry practices. But in other cases, it is done through more formal cooperation and organization.

In Chapter 6, Ronit distinguishes between global associations that admit national associations as members versus associations that offer direct membership to MNCs. MNCs are in most cases members via various national business associations, but there also exist some opportunities for stronger and direct MNC participation, and in organizations, such as the World Economic Forum, direct membership is the key principle of affiliation. Participation in these forums is important to influence certain norms and rules in the business community, but associations also represent business in many contexts, and especially in exchanges with intergovernmental agencies. This allows particular peak associations to speak authoritatively for business.

Associations are also important for MNCs in specific industries. In Chapter 4, Hendriksen demonstrates how well-organized the maritime industry is at national and global levels. Like many others, the maritime industry is characterized by a high degree of market concentration, and this affords the opportunity for a small group of MNCs to thrive and have a dominant voice. As the industry plays an important part in the economy of many countries, and has a symbiotic relationship with regulatory bodies, it therefore also enjoys a strong position at the global level where it is integrated into many aspects of policy-making of the IMO. At both levels, the industry disposes of significant resources to set agendas and influence regulation.

Another example of MNC influence through associations is found in the mining industry, as shown in Chapter 7 by Sinclair. In this industry, there are a number of MNCs that are directly affiliated with the global industry body, the International Council on Mining and Metals (ICMM), which is tasked with the coordination of different aspects of corporate behavior in the global mining community. However, the association is relatively weaker and, unlike shipping, is not rooted in strong organizational traditions to the same degree. At least, that is true in the case considered. Interestingly, the activities of the global association are not targeted at a particular IGO, as there is no single organization that is responsible for the regulation of the industry. Rather, the ICMM works with multiple IGOs and counters CSO criticism in order to legitimize self-regulation. Therefore, we need to understand this pathway in global politics in a somewhat broader context.

Business communities constitute an important pathway of MNC influence. MNCs are active in many forms of coordination and use these as vehicles to win influence in as well as beyond the business community. Indeed, there are many forms of collaboration, but associations express a quite formal kind of cooperation and exist at both national and global levels. Much research on MNCs tend to portray these as agents of individual rather than collective action, but a huge challenge for MNCs is to find the proper *balance* between individual and collective action. The nature of this balance can vary from country to country, and from industry to industry. Indeed, we should not underestimate collective action both between MNCs and between MNCs and other firms, in order to create a broader basis for addressing problems of mutual concern and for establishing norms and rules. To be considered legitimate in exchanges with public authority and civil society, they further need to coordinate interests and present a unified business position.

MNCS' INFLUENCE AND CIVIL SOCIETY

MNCs must address a rich variety of concerns, but not only in relation to state and market governance. Exchanges with civil society are also important. In recent years, more light has been shed on this challenge and MNCs must act carefully and systematically in how they present themselves to society, but more than this, how they are located *in* society. This means that their interactions with CSOs are an important factor and a potential pathway of influence that complements the picture of the many pathways of influence available to MNCs.

In many cases, civil society is still relatively poorly organized as an active countervailing power that can effectively challenge business interests. From Chapters 2 and 3 by May on Brazil and India, and Weiss and Thurbon on the US, we learn that strong MNCs in the Global North as well as in the Global South use the support of their home states in various ways to strengthen their positions in both global markets and global politics. If there is a lack of strong CSOs to confront or moderate the power of MNCs, then it seems that this scene is very much open for MNC influence. However, it is of course possible for civil society to leverage governments – for instance, through elections or agenda-setting – and in this way moderate the power of MNCs. In such cases, the pathways of MNC influence are not really activated in direct relations with CSOs.

Some of the chapters, however, deliver stronger examples of how MNCs interact with an organized civil society. In Sinclair's study of the mining industry's operations in Indonesia in Chapter 7, the different ways in which MNCs connect with civil society are considered. In this case, they meet a relatively fragmented civil society in Indonesia, but strong efforts have been launched to forge broader alliances spanning local and global CSOs. This is an important factor in empowering countervailing groups from civil society. In turn, this has prompted MNCs themselves to significantly improve the coordination of industry interests at the global level, in recognition that individual action by single MNCs is often problematic in global politics, as noted in the above section on MNC influence in the business community. It is therefore interesting to see how relations with civil society tend to spill over into the organization of the business community, and, in a broader perspective, this coordination influences possible exchanges with governments and IGOs.

There are many historical examples of firms and industries defining and managing their own rules of self-regulation but, in recent years, new initiatives have given us more insight into these initiatives. In Chapter 5 on social and environmental sustainability initiatives in the food and forestry industries, Macdonald shows that MNCs have engineered many new schemes, some of them involving civil society but all of them in one way or another responding to concerns expressed by civil society, especially at the global level. However, the adoption of such schemes is also a strategy to forestall traditional top-down public regulation and weaken the pressures of civil society. Indeed, we must understand these organizations and voluntary schemes from the perspective of market power and the ambitions of MNCs to control standards, as they tend to dominate the industries and global supply chains in which the schemes are adopted, and thus different pathways of influence are combined.

Relations with civil society are one of the many pathways that can be used by MNCs in their struggle for influence in global politics, and civil society can be an important factor in building legitimacy around business. However, as the role of civil society is often expressed through the activity of specific organizations, it is often highly varied. In some cases, there are no powerful CSOs to confront business, whether they be MNCs or other firms. In other cases, we find highly active CSOs with an ambition to set agendas and influence regulation. They can assume a range of different roles from protest to participation, with patterns of action that need to be better conceptualized in research. Although MNCs must carefully consider how to approach CSOs at national and global levels, the shaping of these relations is not determined exclusively by the strategies of MNCs. As shown particularly by Sinclair and Macdonald, there is much ingenuity in civil society that MNCs must respond to, and MNCs have different interests and adopt different strategies depending on their position in the market and on the benefits from private schemes, while avoiding imposed regulatory responses. Indeed, it seems easier to develop civil society action in relation to very concrete issues in specific industries rather than in relation to broader concerns in politics. These patterns of civil society activity can condition the behavior of MNCs and make connections with CSOs more or less relevant in finding the appropriate pathways of influence.

FINAL THOUGHTS

The above discussion, like the contributions in this collection, demonstrate that it is not so much one pathway or another that is used for influence by MNCs, nor is it a simple matter of them picking and choosing between pathways. While our summary of the findings is admittedly over-simplified for the sake of brevity, it is also not a matter of simple models whereby we may say that an MNC employing one pathway or another in a certain way will deliver certain, specific outcomes. Things are rather more complex than this. What has been shown is that these pathways overlap and that MNCs potentially use all of them in myriad ways to achieve the outcomes they desire. Sometimes the results benefit them over states and their societies, sometimes the opposite is the case, and it is also possible that the results are mutually beneficial. In all cases though, seeing MNCs as simply global market actors driven by market forces is insufficient for comprehending them as political and social, in addition to economic, actors.

It makes as much sense to see MNCs as following purely economic interests as it does to see states as purely political or society as purely social. MNCs' interests and influence go beyond the economic, just as other contending actors are complexly constructed as well. It may be that there is a desire on the part of anyone analyzing MNCs' pathways of influence that they be separate and independent from states and societies as much as possible, and somehow 'confined' to markets – for example, a liberal or pluralist perspective. Or that their activities should serve the national interest – for example, a more neo-mercantilist perspective. Or, from a more radical perspective, that there should be some rupture between state and corporate interests in order to end the global capitalist relations that bind elites in both together and give MNCs their current 'special' relationship with states. These, and many other perspectives, can be brought to bear on the framework that animates the contributions in our book. They can be brought to bear in a critical as well as supportive fashion to the analysis of the contributors. It is not a matter of the analysis being 'right' or 'wrong', so much as that our, and their, intention has been to show that MNCs pathways of influence should be analyzed holistically, and in the process demonstrate that MNCs are key influencers, and indeed makers, of global politics.

Index

194MNCs in global politics

Trans-Atlantic Business Council (TABC)
135
transformative capacity
as cornerstone of state's ability to
project power 67
dependency factors 53
explanation of 51, 53
and IPRs 61–2
as second face of infrastructural
power 49, 51
under stress 53–4
transnational corporations (TNCs) 3

United States (US)
corporate profits vs corporate tax 55
corporate versus state power 52–3,
61, 70–71
federal debt 60
federal deficit 61
global profits by firms in most
IP-intensive industries 55
labor force participation 59
non-residential fixed investment 58
offshoring trend 63–4, 70–71
percentage share in world high-tech
manufacturing value added
65

power paradox 21–2, 48–9, 70–71,
179–80
trade balance in goods with
advanced technology 64
understanding of structural power in
context of 47–9

Walmart 6, 101–2
World Business Council for Sustainable
Development (WBCSD)
fulfilling multiple criteria 123
functions and nature of 129
membership model 134
membership profiles 132–3
World Chambers Federation (WCF) 135
World Economic Forum (WEF)
fulfilling multiple criteria 123
functions and nature of 127–8
having MNCs as members on direct
basis 15
membership model 134
membership profiles 132–3
World Shipping Council (WSC) 86, 87,
92
World Trade Organization (WTO) 12,
52, 71